The Place Of Dragons
A Mystery

by
William Le Queux

The Place Of Dragons
A Mystery
by William Le Queux

Copyright © 2023

All Rights reserved.

No part of this publication may be reproduced, stored in a retrieval system, or transmitted in any form or by any means, electronic, mechanical, photocopying or Otherwise, without the written permission of the publisher.
The author/editor asserts the moral right to be identified as the author/editor of this work.

ISBN: 978-93-60468-06-4

Published by

DOUBLE 9 BOOKS

2/13-B, Ansari Road
Daryaganj, New Delhi – 110002
info@double9books.com
www.double9books.com
Tel. 011-40042856

This book is under public domain

ABOUT THE AUTHOR

Anglo-French journalist and author William Tufnell Le Queux was born on July 2, 1864, and died on October 13, 1927. He was also a diplomat (honorary consul for San Marino), a traveler (in Europe, the Balkans, and North Africa), a fan of flying (he presided over the first British air meeting at Doncaster in 1909), and a wireless pioneer who played music on his own station long before radio was widely available. However, he often exaggerated his own skills and accomplishments. The Great War in England in 1897 (1894), a fantasy about an invasion by France and Russia, and The Invasion of 1910 (1906), a fantasy about an invasion by Germany, are his best-known works. Le Queux was born in the city. The man who raised him was English, and his father was French. He went to school in Europe and learned art in Paris from Ignazio (or Ignace) Spiridon. As a young man, he walked across Europe and then made a living by writing for French newspapers. He moved back to London in the late 1880s and managed the magazines Gossip and Piccadilly. In 1891, he became a parliamentary reporter for The Globe. He stopped working as a reporter in 1893 to focus on writing and traveling.

CONTENTS

CHAPTER I
    PRESENTS A PROBLEM 9

CHAPTER II
    IS MAINLY ASTONISHING 15

CHAPTER III
    SHOWS LIGHTS FROM THE MIST 23

CHAPTER IV
    OPENS SEVERAL QUESTIONS 30

CHAPTER V
    IN WHICH THE SHADOW FALLS 36

CHAPTER VI
    MYSTERY INEXPLICABLE 42

CHAPTER VII
    TELLS OF TWO MEN 48

CHAPTER VIII
    REMAINS AN ENIGMA 54

CHAPTER IX
    DESCRIBES A NIGHT-VIGIL 60

CHAPTER X
    CONTAINS A CLUE 65

CHAPTER XI
    THE AFFAIR ON THE SEVENTEENTH 72

CHAPTER XII
    LOLA 77

CHAPTER XIII
    RELATES A STRANGE STORY 84

CHAPTER XIV
    WHEREIN CONFESSION IS MADE 91
CHAPTER XV
    CONFIRMS CERTAIN SUSPICIONS 97
CHAPTER XVI
    "WHERE THE TWO C'S MEET" 104
CHAPTER XVII
    REVEALS ANOTHER PLOT 110
CHAPTER XVIII
    DONE IN THE NIGHT 115
CHAPTER XIX
    RECORDS FURTHER FACTS 122
CHAPTER XX
    ANOTHER DISCOVERY IS MADE 128
CHAPTER XXI
    EXPLAINS LOLA'S FEARS 134
CHAPTER XXII
    THE ROAD OF RICHES 140
CHAPTER XXIII
    FOLLOWS THE ELUSIVE JULES 146
CHAPTER XXIV
    MAKES A STARTLING DISCLOSURE 151
CHAPTER XXV
    IS MORE MYSTERIOUS 158
CHAPTER XXVI
    HOT-FOOT ACROSS EUROPE 165
CHAPTER XXVII
    OPENS A DEATH-TRAP 172
CHAPTER XXVIII - DESCRIBES A CHASE 178
CHAPTER XXIX
    THE HOUSE IN HAMPSTEAD 185

CHAPTER XXX
 NARRATES A STARTLING AFFAIR 191

CHAPTER XXXI
 "SHEEP OF THY PASTURE" 197

CHAPTER XXXII
 THE TENTS OF UNGODLINESS 204

CHAPTER XXXIII
 DISCLOSES A STRANGE TRUTH 209

CHAPTER XXXIV
 CONCERNS TO-DAY 216

CHAPTER I
PRESENTS A PROBLEM

"Curious affair, isn't it?"

"Very."

"Now, you're a bit of a mystery-monger, Vidal. What's your theory—eh?"

"I haven't one," I replied with a smile.

"I knew the old boy quite well by sight. Didn't you?" asked my friend, Major Keppell, as we stood gossiping together in the doorway of the *Hôtel de Paris*, high up on the cliff opposite the pier at Cromer.

"Perfectly. His habit was to go down the slope yonder, to the pier each morning at ten, and to remain there till eleven," I said. "I used to watch him every morning. He went as regularly as the clock, wet or fine."

"A bit eccentric, I thought," remarked the Major, standing astride in his rough golfing clothes, and puffing at his briar pipe. "Quite a character for a novel—eh?" and he laughed. "You'll do a book about this strange affair—what?"

I shrugged my shoulders and smiled, as I replied: "Not very likely, I think. Yet the circumstances are, to say the least, extremely curious."

"They are, from all I hear," said my friend. Then, glancing at his wristlet watch, he exclaimed: "By Jove!—nearly seven! I must get in and dress for dinner. See you later."

With this he passed through the swing-doors of the hotel, leaving me standing upon the short sweep of gravel gazing out upon the summer sea, golden in the glorious June sunset.

The Major had spoken the truth. A discovery had been made in Cromer that morning which possessed many remarkable features, and to me, an investigator of crime, it presented an extremely interesting problem—one such as I, Herbert Vidal, had never before heard of.

Briefly related, the facts were as follows. Early in February—four months before—there had arrived in Cromer a queer, wizened, little old man named Vernon Gregory. He was accompanied by his nephew, a rather dandified, overdressed young fellow of twenty-three, named Edward Craig.

Strangers are very few in Cromer in winter, and therefore Mrs. Dean, landlady of Beacon House, on the West Cliff, a few doors west of the *Hôtel de Paris*, where the asphalted footpath runs along the top of the cliff, was very glad to let the new-comers the first-floor front sitting-room with two bedrooms above.

In winter and spring, Cromer, high and bleak, and swept by the wild, howling winds from the grey North Sea, its beach white with the spume of storm, is practically deserted. The hotels, with the exception of the *Paris*, are closed, the boarding-houses are mostly shut, and the landladies who let apartments wait weeks and weeks in vain for the arrival of a chance visitor. In August, however, the place overflows with visitors, all of the best class, and for six weeks each year Cromer becomes one of the gayest little towns on the breezy East Coast.

So, all through the spring, with its grey, wet days, when the spindrift swept in a haze across the promenade, old Mr. Gregory was a familiar figure taking his daily walk, no matter how inclement the weather.

In appearance he was unusual, and seedy. His bony face was long, thin, and grey; a countenance that was broad at the brow and narrowed to a pointed chin. He had a longish white beard, yet his deep-set eyes with their big bushy brows were so dark and piercing that the fire of youth seemed still to burn within them. He was of medium height, rather round-shouldered, and walked with a decided limp, aided by a stout ash stick. Invariably he wore an old, dark grey, mackintosh cape, very greasy at the collar; black trousers, old and baggy; boots very down at heel; and on his mass of long white hair a broad-brimmed felt hat, which gave him the appearance of a musician, or an artist.

Sometimes, on rare occasions, his well-dressed nephew walked with him—but very seldom were they together.

Craig was a tall, well-set-up young fellow, who generally wore a drab golf-suit, smoked cigarettes eternally, and frequently played billiards at the *Red Lion*. He was also a golfer and well known on the links for the excellence of his play.

Between uncle and nephew there was nothing in common. Craig had dropped a hint that he was down there with his relative "just to look after the old boy." He undoubtedly preferred London life, and it was stated that a few years before he had succeeded to a large estate somewhere on the Welsh border.

The residents of Cromer are as inquisitive as those of most small towns. Therefore, it was not very long after the arrival of this curious couple, that everybody knew that old Mr. Gregory was concealing the fact that he was head of the famous Sheffield armour-plate making firm, Messrs. Gregory and Thorpe, though he now took but little part in the active work of the world-famed house that rolled plates for Britain's mighty "Dreadnoughts."

Cromer, on learning his identity, at once regarded old Gregory's queer figure with due reverence. His parsimonious ways, the clockwork regularity with which he took his morning walk, bought his daily paper at Munday's Library, and took his afternoon stroll up past the coast-guard station, or towards the links, or along the Overstrand or Sheringham roads, were looked upon as the eccentricities of an immensely wealthy man.

In rich men the public tolerate idiosyncrasies, that in poorer persons are declared to betoken either lunacy, or that vague excuse for the contravention of the conventionalities known as "the artistic temperament." Many men have actually earned reputations, and even popularity, by the sheer force of cultivated eccentricities. With professional men eccentricity is one of the pegs on which their astute press-agents can always hang a paragraph.

In the case of Mr. Vernon Gregory, as he limped by, the good shop-keeping public of Cromer looked after him with benevolent glances. He was the great steel magnate who ate frugally, who grumbled loudly at Mrs. Dean if his weekly bill exceeded that of the City clerk and his wife who had occupied the same rooms for a fortnight in the previous July. He was pointed at with admiration as the man of millions who eked out every scuttleful of coal as though it were gold.

Undoubtedly Mr. Gregory was a person of many eccentricities. From his secretary in Sheffield he daily received a bulky package of correspondence, and this, each morning, was attended to by his nephew. Yet the old man always made a point of posting all the letters with his own hand, putting them into the box at the post-office opposite the church.

Sometimes, but only at rare intervals—because, as he declared, "it was so very costly"—Mr. Gregory hired an open motor-car from Miller's garage. On such occasions, Craig, who was a practised motorist, would drive, and the pair would go on long day excursions towards Yarmouth, or Hunstanton, or inland to Holt or Norwich. At such times the old man would don many wraps, and a big blue muffler, and wear an unsightly pair of goggles.

Again, the old fellow preferred to do much of his shopping himself, and it was no uncommon sight to see him in the street carrying home two-pennyworth of cream in a little jug. Hence the good people of Cromer grew to regard their out-of-season visitor as a harmless, but philanthropic old buffer, for his hand was in his pocket for every local charity. His amusements were as frugal as his housekeeping. During the spring his only recreation was a visit to the cinema at the Town Hall twice a week. When, however, the orchestral concerts commenced on the pier, he became a constant attendant at them.

So small is Cromer, with its narrow streets near the sea, that in the off-season strangers are constantly running into each other. Hence, I frequently met old Gregory, and on such occasions we chatted about the weather, or upon local topics. His voice was strangely high-pitched, thin, but not unmusical. Indeed, he was a great lover of music, as was afterwards shown by his constant attendance at the pier concerts.

His nephew, Craig, was what the people of Cromer, in vulgar parlance, dubbed a "nut." He was always immaculately dressed, wore loud socks, seemed to possess a dozen styles of hats, and was never seen without perfectly clean wash-leather gloves. He laughed loudly, talked loudly, displayed money freely and put on patronizing airs which filled those who met him with an instinctive dislike.

I first made his acquaintance in April in the cosy bar of the *Albion*, where, after a long walk one morning, I went to quench my thirst. Craig was laughing with the barmaid and gingerly lighting a cigarette. Having passed me by many times, he now addressed a casual remark to me, to which I politely responded, and we got into conversation. But, somehow, his speech jarred upon me, and, like his personal appearance, struck an unpleasant note, for his white shoes and pale blue socks, his light green Tyrolese hat, and his suit of check tweeds distinctly marked him as being more of a cad than a gentleman.

I remarked that I had walked to Overstrand, whereupon he asked—

"Did you chance to meet my uncle? He's gone out that way, somewhere."

I replied in the negative.

"Wonderful old boy, you know," he went on. "Walks me clean right out! But oh! such a dreadful old bore! Always talking about what he did in the seventies, and how much better life was then than now. I don't believe it. Do you?"

"I hardly know," was my reply. "I wasn't old enough then to appreciate life."

"Neither was I," he responded. "But really, these eccentric old people ought all to be put in an asylum. You don't know what I have to put up with. I tell you, it's a terrible self-sacrifice to be down in this confounded hole, instead of being on the Riviera in decent sunny weather, and in decent society."

"Your uncle is always extremely pleasant to me when I meet him," I said.

"Ah, yes, but you don't know him, my dear sir," said his nephew. "He's the very Old Nick himself sometimes, and his eccentricities border upon insanity. Why, only last night, before he went to bed, he put on his bed-gown, cut two wings out of brown paper, pinned them on his back, and fancied himself the Archangel Gabriel. Last week he didn't speak to me for two days because I bought a box of sardines. He declares they are luxuries and he can't afford them—he, with an income of forty thousand a year!"

"Rich men are often rather niggardly," I remarked.

"Oh, yes. But with Uncle Vernon it's become a craze. He shivers with cold at night but won't have a fire in his bedroom because, he says, coals are so dear."

I confess I did not like this young fellow. Why should he reveal all his private grievances to me, a perfect stranger?

"Why did your uncle come to Cromer?" I asked. "This place is hardly a winter resort, except for a few golfers."

"Oh, because when he was in Egypt last winter, some fool of a woman he met at the *Savoy* in Cairo, told him that Cromer was so horribly healthy in the winter, and that if he spent six months each year in this God-forgotten place, he'd live to be a hundred. Bad luck to her and her words! I've had to come here with the old boy, and am their victim." Then he added warmly: "My dear sir, just put yourself in my place. I've nobody to talk to except the provincial Norfolk tradespeople, who think they can play a good game at billiards. I've got the absolute hump, I tell you frankly!"

Well, afterwards I met the loud-socked young man more frequently, but somehow I had taken a violent and unaccountable dislike to him. Why, I cannot tell, except perhaps that he had disgusted me by the way he unbosomed himself to a stranger and aired his grievances against his eccentric uncle.

To descend that asphalted slope which led, on the face of the cliff, from the roadway in front of the *Hôtel de Paris*, away to the Promenade, old Gregory had to pass beneath my window. Hence I saw him several times daily, and noted how the brown-bloused fishermen who lounged there hour after hour, gazing idly seaward, leaning upon the railings and gossiping, respectfully touched their caps to the limping, eccentric old gentleman who in his slouch hat and cape looked more like a poet than a steel magnate, and who so regularly took the fresh, bracing air on that breezy promenade.

On that morning—the morning of the twelfth of June—a startling rumour had spread through the town. It at once reached me through Charles, the head-waiter of the hotel, who told me the whole place was agog. The strange story was that old Mr. Gregory had at three o'clock that morning been found by a coast-guard lying near a seat on the top of the east cliff at a point near the links, from which a delightful view could be obtained westward over the town towards Rimton and Sheringham.

The coast-guard had at once summoned a doctor by telephone, and on arrival the medical man had pronounced the mysterious old gentleman dead, and, moreover, that he had been dead several hours.

More than that, nobody knew, except that the dead man's nephew could not be found.

That fact in itself was certainly extraordinary, but it was not half so curious, or startling, as certain other features of the amazing affair, which were now being carefully withheld from the public by the police—facts, which when viewed as a whole, formed one of the most inexplicable criminal problems ever presented for solution.

CHAPTER II
IS MAINLY ASTONISHING

In virtue of the facts that I was well known in Cromer, on friendly terms with the local superintendent of police, and what was more to the purpose, known to be a close friend of the Chief Constable at Norwich—also that I was a recognized writer of some authority upon problems of crime—Inspector Treeton, of the Norfolk Constabulary, greeted me affably when, after a very hasty breakfast, I called at the police station.

Treeton was a thin, grey-haired man, usually very quiet and thoughtful in manner, but this staggering affair had quite upset his normal coolness.

"I expect the detectives over from Norwich in half an hour," he said, with a distinct trace of excitement in his tones, as we stood in his bare little office discussing the morning's discovery. "You being such a close friend of the Chief Constable, I don't suppose there'll be any objection whatever to your being present during our investigations."

All the same, his tone was somewhat dubious as he added cautiously, "You won't, of course, give anything to the Press?"

"Certainly not," I replied. "You can rely upon my discretion. This isn't the first mystery I have assisted the police to investigate. This sort of thing is, so to speak, part of my profession."

"Yes," said Treeton, still with some hesitation, "so I understand, Mr. Vidal. But our people are terribly particular, as you know, about admitting unofficial persons into police work. No offence. But we are bound to be very careful."

"If you like, I'll 'phone to the Chief Constable," I suggested.

"No, sir. No need for that," he said hastily. "When the plain-clothes men arrive, I don't think any difficulty will be made as to your accompanying them." Then he added, as if to give the conversation a turn, "It's a very queer business, very. But I mustn't talk about it at present. No doubt you'll soon see for yourself what a strange affair it is."

"What is the curious feature, then?" I inquired anxiously.

"No," said Treeton, with a deprecatory gesture. "No. Mr. Vidal. Don't ask me. You must wait till the officers come from Norwich. They'll have a surprise, I can assure you they will. That's all I can say. I've taken care to have everything kept as it was found so as not to interfere with any clues, finger-prints, or things of that sort."

"Ah," I said. "Then you suspect foul play, eh?"

Treeton flushed slightly, as if annoyed with himself at having let slip the words that prompted my query.

Then he said slowly: "Well, at present we can't tell. But there's certainly something very mysterious about the whole business."

"Where is the body?"

"They've put it in the life-boat house."

"And that young fellow, Craig? I hear he's missing."

The Inspector looked at me with a strange expression on his face.

"Ah," he said briefly, "that isn't the only remarkable feature of this affair by any manner of means." Then impatiently: "I wish they'd come. I 'phoned to Norwich at six o'clock this morning, and now it's nearly ten. They might have come over in a car, instead of waiting for the train."

"Yes," I responded. "That is how so many inquiries are bungled. Red tape and delay. In the meantime a criminal often gets away hours ahead of the sleuths of the law and eventually may escape altogether. I've known a dozen cases where, because of the delay in making expert investigation, the culprit has never been caught."

As I spoke the telephone bell tinkled and Treeton answered the call. The Superintendent at Holt was asking for information, but my companion could give him but very little.

"I am watching the railway-station, sir," said Treeton over the 'phone, "and I've sent word to all the fishermen in my district not to take out any strangers. I've also warned all the garages to let me know if any stranger hires a car. The party we fancy may be wanted won't be able to get away if he's still in the district."

"Which is not very likely," I murmured in a low voice so that my words should not be heard over the wire.

When the conversation over the phone was ended, I sat chatting with Treeton, until, some twenty minutes later, three men, bearing unmistakably the cut of police-officers in plain clothes, entered the station.

Two of them were tall, dark-haired young fellows, dressed in neat navy-blue serge and wearing bowler hats. The third man, Inspector Frayne, as I learnt afterwards, was in dark grey, with a soft grey felt hat with the brim turned down in front.

"Well Treeton," said the Inspector briskly, "what's all the fuss about down here?"

"A case—a very funny case. That's all," replied the local inspector. "I told you over the 'phone all I know about it."

Then followed a brief, low-pitched conversation between the two officers. I saw Frayne look over at me inquisitively, and caught a few snatches of Treeton's words to him. "Great personal friend of the Chief Constable.... Yes, quite all right.... Writes about crime.... No, no, nothing to do with newspapers ... amateur, of course ... decent sort."

I gathered from this that there was going to be no difficulty about my joining the party of police investigators. I was right. In a few moments Treeton brought Inspector Frayne over to me and we were introduced. Then, after a few friendly words, we started for the scene of the startling discovery of the morning.

We slipped out of the station in pairs, so as to avoid attracting attention, which might have led to our being followed and hampered in our movements by a crowd of idle and curious inhabitants.

Proceeding by way of the path which wound round the back of the high-up coast-guard station and so up over the cliff, we soon came to the seat where the body of old Mr. Gregory had been found.

The seat, a green-painted one with a curved back, that had more than once afforded me a comfortable resting-place, was the first out of the town towards the links. It was situate a little way from the footpath amid the rough grass of the cliff-top. Around it the herbage never grew on account of the constant tread from the feet of many daily visitors, so that clear about it was a small patch of bare sand.

On the right, upon the next point of the cliff, was another similar seat, while on the left the path leading back to the town was railed off because it was dangerous to approach too near the crumbling edge.

At the seat stood a very tall, thin, fair-haired young constable who had, since the discovery of old Gregory's body, remained on duty at the spot to prevent any one approaching it. This was done by Treeton's orders, who hoped, and very logically, that if the sand about the seat was not disturbed some tell-tale mark or footprint might be found by the detectives that would give a clue to the person or persons who had visited the seat with old Gregory in the early hours of that fatal morning.

Near the constable were two men with cameras, and at a little distance a small knot of curious idlers, all that remained of the many inquisitive folks who were at first attracted to the spot, but who, finding nothing to satisfy their curiosity, had soon returned to the town.

The morning was bright and calm, the sunlight reflected from a glassy sea, upon the surface of which were a dozen or so fishing-boats lifting their crab-pots, for the crabs of Cromer are far-famed amongst epicures for their excellencies. It was a peaceful, happy scene, that none could have suspected was the setting of a ghastly tragedy.

On arrival, Inspector Frayne, tall, grey-haired, with aquiline, clean-shaven face, assumed an attitude of ubiquitous importance that amused me.

"The body was found lying face downwards six feet beyond the south end of the seat," Treeton explained. "You see this mark in the grass?"

Looking, we all saw distinctly the impression that marked the spot where the unfortunate man had lain.

"No doubt," said the detective inspector, "the old gentleman was sitting on the seat when he was attacked from behind by somebody who sneaked quietly across the footpath, and he fell sideways from the seat. Have you looked for footprints?"

"There are a number of them, as you see," was Treeton's reply. "Nothing has been disturbed. I left all to you."

Gazing around, I saw that there were many prints of soles and heels in the soft sand about the seat. Many people had evidently sat there on the previous day. In the sand, too, some one had traced with a stick, in sprawly capitals, the word "Alice."

Frayne and his two provincial assistants bent and closely examined the prints in question.

"Women's mostly, I should say," remarked the detective inspector after a pause. "That's plain from the French heels, flat golf-shoe soles, and narrow rubber-pads, that have left their marks behind them. Better take some casts of these, Phelps," he said, addressing the elder of his subordinates.

"Forgive me for making a remark," I ventured. "I'm not a detective, but it strikes me that if anybody did creep across the grass from the path, as the Inspector rightly suggested, to attack the old man, he, or she, may have left some prints in the rear there. In the front here the footprints we have been examining are obviously those of people who had been sitting upon the seat long prior to the arrival of the victim."

"I quite agree, Mr. Vidal," exclaimed Treeton, and at this I thought the expert from Norwich seemed somewhat annoyed. "Yes," continued the local inspector, "it's quite possible, as Mr. Frayne said, that somebody did creep across the grass behind the old man. But unfortunately, there have been dozens of people over that very same spot this morning."

"Hopeless then!" grunted Frayne. "Why on earth, Treeton, did you let them swarm over there?" he queried testily. "Their doing so has rendered our inquiry a hundred per cent. more difficult. In all such cases the public ought to be rigorously kept from the immediate neighbourhood of the crime."

"At least we can make a search," I suggested.

"My dear Mr. Vidal, what is the use if half Cromer has been up here prying about?" asked the detective impatiently. "No, those feminine footprints in front of the seat are much more likely to help us. There's bound to be a woman in such a case as this. My motto in regard to crime mysteries is, first find the woman, and the rest is easy. In every great problem the 'eternal feminine,' as you writers put it, is ever present. She is in this one somewhere, you may depend upon it."

I did not answer him, judging that he merely emitted these sentiments in order to impress his listening subordinates with a due sense of his superior knowledge. But the search went on.

From the footpath across the grass to the seat was about thirty feet, and over the whole area all of us made diligent investigation. In one of the patches where the sand was bare of herbage I found the print of a woman's shoe—a smart little shoe—size 3, I judged it to be. The sole was well shaped and pointed, the heel was of the latest fashionable model—rather American than French.

I at once pointed it out to Frayne, but though he had so strongly expressed the opinion that there was a woman in the case, he dismissed it with a glance.

"Some woman came here yesterday evening with her sweetheart, I suppose," he said with a laugh.

But to me that footprint was distinctly instructive, for among the many impressed on the sand before the seat, I had not detected one that bore any resemblance to it. The owner of that American shoe had walked from the path to the back of the seat, but had certainly not sat down there.

I carefully marked the spot, and telling an old fisherman of my acquaintance, who stood by, to allow no one to obliterate it, continued my investigations.

Three feet behind the seat, in the midst of the trodden grass, I came upon two hairpins lying close together. Picking them up, I found they were rather thick, crinkled in the middle, and both of the same pale bronze shade.

Was it possible there had been a struggle there—a struggle with the woman who wore those American shoes—who was, moreover, a fair woman, if those pins had fallen from her hair in the encounter?

I showed the hairpins to Frayne who was busy taking a measurement of the distance from the seat to where the body had been found.

To my surprise, he seemed impatient and annoyed.

"My dear Mr. Vidal," he exclaimed, "you novelists are, I fear, far too imaginative. I dare say there are hundreds of hairpins about here in the grass if we choose to search for them. This seat is a popular resort for visitors by day and a trysting place for lovers after sundown. In the vicinity of any such seat you will always find hairpins, cigarette ends, wrappings from chocolates, and tinfoil. Look around you and see."

"But these pins have not been here more than a day," I expostulated. "They are bright and were lying lightly on the grass. Besides, are we not looking for a woman?"

"I'll admit that they may perhaps have belonged to somebody who was here last evening," he said. "But I can assure you they are no good to us." With this he turned away with rather a contemptuous smile.

I began to suspect that I had in some way antagonized Frayne, who at that moment seemed more intent upon working up formal evidence to give before the coroner, rather than in pushing forward the investigation of the crime, and so finding a clue to the culprit.

I could see that he regarded the minute investigations I was making with undisguised and contemptuous amusement. Of course, he was polite to me, for was I not the friend of the Chief Constable? But, all the same, I was an amateur investigator, therefore, in his eyes, a blunderer. He, of course, did not know at how many investigations of crime I had assisted in Paris, in Brussels, and in Rome—investigations conducted by the greatest detectives in Europe.

It was not to be expected that an officer of the Norfolk Constabulary, more used to petty larceny than to murder, would be so alert or so thorough in his methods as an officer from Scotland Yard, or of the *Sûreté* in Paris.

Arguing thus, I felt that I could cheerfully disregard the covert sneers and glances of my companions; and plunged with renewed interest into the work I had undertaken.

In the sand before the seat, I saw two long, wide marks which told me that old Mr. Gregory must have slipped from his position in a totally helpless condition. That being so, how was it that his body was found several feet away?

Had it been dragged to that spot in the grass? Or, had he crawled there in his death agony?

In the little knot of people who had gathered I noticed a young fisherman in his brown blouse—a tall youth, with fair curly hair, whom I knew well and could trust. Calling him over, I despatched him to the town for a couple of pounds of plaster of Paris, a bucket, some water, and a trowel.

Then I went on methodically with my investigations.

Presently the coast-guard, George Simmonds, a middle-aged, dark-haired man, who was a well-known figure in Cromer, came up and was introduced to Frayne as the man who, returning from duty as night patrol along the cliffs, early that morning, had discovered the body.

I stood by listening as he described the incident to the detective inspector.

"You see, sir," he said saluting, "I'd been along the cuffs to Trimingham, and was on my way back about a quarter past three, when I noticed a man lying yonder on the grass. It was a fine morning, quite light, and at first I thought it was a tramp, for they often sleep on the cliffs in the warm weather. But on going nearer I saw, to my surprise, that the man was old Mr. Gregory. I thought he was asleep, and bent down and shook him, his face being downwards on the grass and his arms stretched out. He didn't wake up, so I turned him over, and the colour of his face fair startled me. I opened his coat, put my hand on his heart, and found he was quite dead. I then ran along to our station and told Mr. Day, the Chief Officer, and he sent me off sharp to the police."

"You saw nobody about?" Frayne asked sharply. "Nobody passed you?"

"I didn't see a soul all the way from Trimingham."

"Constable Baxter was along there somewhere keeping a point," remarked Treeton. "Didn't you meet him?"

"Going out I met him, just beyond Overstrand, at about one o'clock, and wished him good morning," was the coast-guard's reply.

"But where is Craig, the young nephew of the dead man?" I asked Treeton. "Surely he may know something! He must have missed his uncle, who, apparently, was out all night."

"Ah! That's just the mystery, Mr. Vidal," replied the Inspector. "Let us go down to the life-boat house," he added, addressing the detective.

As they were moving away, and I was about to follow, the tall fisher-youth arrived with the plaster of Paris and a pail of water.

Promising to be with them quickly, I remained behind, mixed the plaster into a paste and within a few minutes had secured casts of the imprint of the woman's American shoe, and those of several other footmarks, which, with his superior knowledge, the expert from Norwich had considered beneath his notice.

Then, placing my casts carefully in the empty pail, I sent them along to the *Hôtel de Paris* by the same fisher-youth. Afterwards, I walked along the path, passed behind the lawn of the coast-guard station, where the White Ensign was flying on the flagstaff, and then descending, at last entered the life-boat house, where the officers and three doctors had assembled.

One of the doctors, named Sladen, a grey-headed practitioner who had been many years in Cromer, recognized me as I entered.

"Hulloa, Mr. Vidal! This is a very curious case, isn't it? Interests you, of course. All mysteries do, no doubt. But this case is astounding. In making our examination, do you know we've discovered a most amazing fact?" and he pointed to the plank whereon lay the body, covered with one of the brown sails from the life-boat.

"No. What?" I asked eagerly.

"Well—though we all at first, naturally, took the body to be that of old Vernon Gregory, it isn't his at all!"

"Not Gregory's?" I gasped.

"No. He has white hair and a beard, and he is wearing old Gregory's cape and hat, but it certainly is not Gregory's body."

"Who, then, is the dead man?" I gasped.

"His nephew, Edward Craig!"

CHAPTER III
SHOWS LIGHTS FROM THE MIST

"But Edward Craig is a young man—while Gregory must be nearly seventy!" I exclaimed, staring at Dr. Sladen in blank amazement.

"Exactly. I attended Mr. Gregory a month ago for influenza. But I tell you the body lying yonder is that of young Craig!" declared my friend. Then he added: "There is something very extraordinary about the whole affair, for Craig was made up to exactly resemble his uncle."

"And because of it was apparently done to death, eh?"

"That is certainly my theory."

"Amazing," I exclaimed. "This increases the mystery very considerably." Then, gazing around, I saw that the two doctors, who had assisted Sladen in his examination, were talking aside eagerly with the detective, while Mr. Day, a short thick-set man, with his white-covered cap removed in the presence of the dead, had joined the party.

Cromer is a "war-station," and Mr. Day was a well-known figure in the place, a fine active type of the British sailor, who had seen many years afloat, and now, with his "sea-time" put in, was an expert signal-man ashore. He noticed me and saluted.

"Look," exclaimed Dr. Sladen, taking me across to a bench against the side of the life-boat shed. "What do you think of these?" and he took up a white wig and a long white beard.

I examined them. Then slowly replied, "There is much, very much more, in this affair than any of us can at present see."

"Certainly. Why should the young man go forth at night, under cover of darkness, made up to exactly resemble the old one?"

"To meet somebody in secret, no doubt; and that somebody killed him," I said.

"Did they—ah, that's just the point," said the doctor. "As far as we can find there's no apparent cause of death, no wound whatever. The superficial examination we have made only reveals a slight abrasion on the left wrist, which might have been caused when he fell from the seat to the ground. The wrist is much swollen—from a recent sprain, I think. But beyond that we can find nothing."

"Won't you prosecute your examination further?" I asked.

"Certainly. This afternoon we shall make a post-mortem—after I get the order from the coroner."

"Ah. Then we shall know something definite?"

"I hope so."

"Gentlemen," exclaimed Inspector Frayne, addressing us all, "this latest discovery, of the identity of the victim, is a very extraordinary and startling one. I trust that you will all regard the matter as one of the greatest secrecy—at least till after the inquest. Publicity now may defeat the ends of justice. Do you all promise?"

With one accord we promised. Then, crossing to where the body lay, I lifted the heavy brown sail that covered it, and in the dim light gazed upon the white, dead countenance.

Yes. It was the face of Edward Craig.

Frayne at that moment came up, and after two men had taken the covering from the body, commenced to search the dead man's pockets. In the old mackintosh cape was a pouch, from which the detective drew a small wallet of crocodile leather, much worn, together with two letters. The latter were carried to the light and at once examined.

One proved to be a bill from a well-known hatter in Piccadilly. The superscription on the other envelope, of pale blue-grey paper, was undoubtedly in the hand of an educated woman.

Frayne drew from this envelope a sheet of notepaper, which bore neither address nor date, merely the words—

"At Ealing, at 10 p.m., on the twenty-ninth of August, where the two C's meet."

"Ah, an appointment," remarked Frayne. Then, looking at the post-mark, he added: "It was posted the day before yesterday at Bridlington. I wonder what it means?"

"I see it is addressed to Mr. Gregory!" I pointed out, "not to the dead man."

"Then the old man had an appointment on the twenty-ninth of August somewhere in Ealing—where the two C's meet. I wonder where that can be?

Some agreed-on spot, I suppose, where two persons, whose initials are C, are in the habit of meeting."

"Probably," was my reply. But I was reflecting deeply.

In the wallet were four five-pound notes; a few of Gregory's cards; a letter from a local charity, thanking him for a contribution of two guineas; and a piece of paper bearing a number of very elaborate calculations, apparently of measured paces.

It seemed as though the writer had been working out some very difficult problem of distances, for the half-sheet of quarto paper was absolutely covered with minute pencilled figures; lengths in metres apparently.

I looked at them, and at a glance saw that old Gregory had either received his education abroad, or had lived for a long time upon the continent when a young man. Why? Because, when he made a figure seven, he drew a short cross-stroke half-way up the downward stroke, in order, as foreigners do, to distinguish it from the figure one.

"I wonder what all these sums can mean?" remarked the detective, as Treeton and I looked over his shoulder.

"Mr. Gregory was a business man," the local police officer said. "These are, no doubt, his things, not his nephew's."

"They seem to be measurements," I said, "not sums of money."

"Perhaps the old man himself will tell us what they are," Frayne remarked. Then again examining the wallet, he drew forth several slips of thin foreign notepaper, which were carefully folded, and had the appearance of having been carried there for a long time. Upon each was written a separate word, together with a number, in carefully-formed handwriting, thus—

"Lavelle 429; Kunzle 191; Geering 289; Souweine 17; Hodrickx 110."

The last one we opened contained the word, "Cromer 900," and I wondered whether they were code words.

"These are rather funny, Mr. Vidal," Frayne remarked, as he slowly replaced them in the wallet. "A little mysterious, eh?"

"No doubt, old Mr. Gregory will explain," I said. "The great puzzle to me is why the nephew should carry the uncle's belongings in his pockets. There was some deep motive in it, without a doubt."

Frayne returned to the body and made further search. There was nothing more in the other pockets save a handkerchief, some loose silver and a pocket-knife.

But, around the dead man's neck, suspended by a fine gold chain, and worn beneath his shirt, was a lady's tiny, round locket, not more than an inch in diameter, and engine-turned like a watch, a thin, neatly-made, old-fashioned little thing.

Frayne carefully unclasped it, and taking it across to the light, opened it, expecting to find a photograph, or, perhaps, a miniature. But there was nothing. It had evidently not been opened for years, for behind the little glass, where once had been a photograph, was only a little grey powder. Something had been preserved there—some relic or other—that had, with age, crumbled into dust.

"This doesn't tell us much," he said. "Yet, men seldom wear such things. Some relic of his sweetheart, eh?" Then he searched once more, and drew from the dead man's hip-pocket a serviceable Browning revolver, the magazine of which was fully loaded.

"He evidently expected trouble, and was prepared for it," Treeton said, as the Norwich detective produced the weapon.

"Well, he certainly had no time to use it," responded Frayne. "Death must have been instantaneous."

"I think not," I ventured. "If so, why was he found several feet away from the seat?"

Again Frayne showed impatience. He disliked any expression of outside opinion.

"Well, Mr. Vidal, we've not yet established that it is a case of murder, have we?" he said. "The young man may have died suddenly—of natural causes."

I smiled.

"Curious," I exclaimed, a moment later, "that he should be made up to so exactly resemble his uncle! No, Inspector Frayne, if I'm not greatly mistaken, you'll find this a case of assassination—a murder by a very subtle and ingenious assassin. It is a case of one master-criminal against another. That is my opinion."

The man from Norwich smiled sarcastically. My opinion was only the opinion of a mere amateur, and, to the professional thief-catcher, the amateur detective is a person upon whom to play practical jokes. The amateur who dares to investigate a crime from a purely independent standpoint is a man to jeer and laugh at—a target for ridicule.

I could follow Frayne's thoughts. I had met many provincial police officers of his type all over Europe, from Paris up to Petersburg. The great detectives of Europe, are, on the contrary, always open to listen to theories or suggestions.

The three doctors were standing aside, discussing the affair—the absence of all outward signs of anything that might have caused death. Until the coroner issued his order they could not, however, put their doubts at rest by making the post-mortem examination. The case puzzled them, and they were all three eager to have the opportunity of deciding how the young man had died.

"The few symptoms offered superficially have some strange points about them," I heard Dr. Sladen say. "Do you notice the clenched hands? and yet the mouth is open. The eyes are open too—and the lips are curiously discoloured. Yes, there is decidedly something very mysterious attaching to the cause of death."

And he being the leading practitioner in Cromer, his two colleagues entirely agreed with him.

After a long conversation, in which many theories—most of them sensational, ridiculous, and baseless—had been advanced, Mr. Day, the Chief Officer of Coast-guard, who had been outside the life-boat house, chatting with some friends, entered and told us the results of some of his own observations regarding the movements of the eccentric Mr. Gregory. Day was a genial, pleasant man and very popular in Cromer. Of course he was in ignorance that the body discovered was not that of the old gentleman.

"I've had a good many opportunities of watching the old man, Mr. Vidal," said the short, keen-eyed naval man, turning to me with his hands in the pockets of his pea-jacket, "and he was a funny 'un. He often went out from Beacon House at one and two in the morning, and took long strolls towards Rimton and Overstrand. But Mrs. Dean never knew as he wasn't indoors, for I gather he used to let himself out very quietly. We often used to meet him a-creepin' about of a night. I can't think what he went out for, but I suppose he was a little bit eccentric, eh? Why," went on the coast-guard officer, "he'd often come into the station early of a mornin', and have a chat with me, and look through the big telescope. He used, sometimes, to stand a-gazin' out at the sea, a-gazin' at nothing, for half an hour on end—lost in thought like. I wonder what he fancied he saw there?"

"Yes," I said. "He was eccentric, like many rich men."

"Well, one night, not long ago," Day went on, "there were some destroyers a-passin' about midnight, and we'd been taking in their signals by flash-light, when, in the middle of it, who should come into the enclosure but old Mr. Gregory. He stood a-watchin' us for ten minutes or so. Then, all at once he says, 'I see they're signalling to the *Hermes* at Harwich.' This remark gave me quite a start, for he'd evidently been a-readin' all we had taken in—and it was a confidential message, too."

"Then he could read the Morse code," I exclaimed.

"Read it? I should rather think he could!" was the coast-guard officer's reply. "And mark you, the *Wolverene* was a-flashin' very quick. It was as much as I could do to pick it up through the haze. After that, I confess I didn't like him hanging about here so much as he did. But after all, I'm sorry—very sorry—that the poor old gent is dead."

"Did you ever see him meet anybody on his nightly rambles?" I asked.

"Yes, once. I saw him about six weeks ago, about three o'clock one dark, and terrible wet, mornin', out on the cliff near Rimton Gap. As I passed by he was a-talkin' to a tall young man in a drab mackintosh. Talkin' excited, he was, and a-wavin' his arms wild-like towards the sea. The young man spotted me first, and said something, whereupon the old gent dropped his argument, and the two of 'em walked on quietly together. I passed them, believing that his companion was only one of them simple-like fools we get about here sometimes in the summer. But I'd never seen him in Cromer. He was a perfect stranger to me."

"That's the only time you've seen him with any companion on these secret night outings?" I asked.

"Yes. I don't remember ever having seen him in the night with anybody else."

"Not even with his nephew?"

"No, not even with Mr. Craig."

"When he dropped in to chat with you at the coastguard station, did he show any inquisitiveness?" I asked.

"Well, he wanted to know all about things, as most of 'em do," laughed Day. "Ours is a war-station, you know, and folk like to look at the inside, and the flash-lamp I invented."

"The old fellow struck you as a bit of a mystery, didn't he?" Frayne asked, in his pleasant Norfolk brogue.

"Well, yes, he did," replied the coast-guard officer. "I remember one night last March—the eleventh, I think it was—when our people at Weybourne detected some mysterious search-lights far out at sea and raised an alarm on the 'phone all along the coast. It was a very dirty night, but the whole lot of us, from Wells right away to Yarmouth, were at once on the look-out. We could see search-lights but could make nothing of the signals. That's what puzzled us so. I went out along the cliff, and up Rimton way, but could see nothing. Yet, on my way back, as I got near the town, I suddenly saw a stream of light—about like a search-light—coming from the sea-front here. It was a-flashin' some signal. I was a couple of miles from the town, and naturally concluded it was one of my men with the flash-lamp. As I passed Beacon House, however, I saw old Mr. Gregory a-leanin' over the railings, looking out to sea. It was then about two o'clock. I supposed he had seen the distant lights, and, passing a word with him, I went along to the station. To my surprise, I found that we'd not been signalling at all. Then I recollected old Mr. Gregory's curious interest in the lights, and I wondered. In fact, I've wondered ever since, whether that answering signal I saw did not come from one of the front windows of Beacon House? Perhaps he was practisin' Morse!"

"Strange, very strange!" Frayne remarked. "Didn't you discover what craft it was making the signals?"

"No, sir. They are a mystery to this day. We reported by wire to the Admiralty, of course, but we've never found out who it was a-signalling. It's a complete mystery—and it gave us a bit of an alarm at the time, I can tell you," he laughed. "There was a big Italian yacht, called the *Carlo Alberta*, reported next day from Hunstanton, and it may, of course, have been her. But I am not inclined to think so."

∴

CHAPTER IV
OPENS SEVERAL QUESTIONS

Our next step in the inquiry was a domiciliary visit to Beacon House.

While the public, including Mr. Day, were expecting to see his nephew, we, of course, were hoping to find old Gregory.

In this we were disappointed. Already Treeton knew that both men were missing from their lodgings. Yet while the police were watching everywhere for the dandified young man from London, the queer, white-haired old Sheffield steel manufacturer had slipped through their fingers and vanished as though the earth had swallowed him up.

Mrs. Dean's house was a typical seaside lodging-house, plainly and comfortably furnished — a double-fronted house painted pale blue, with large airy rooms and bay windows, which, situated high up and on the very edge of the cliff, commanded extensive views up and down the coast.

The sitting-room occupied by uncle and nephew, proved to be a big apartment on the first-floor, to the left of the entrance. The houses in that row had a front door from the asphalt path along the edge of the cliff and also a back entrance abutting upon the narrow street which ran into the centre of the town. Therefore, the hall went from back to front, the staircase ascending in the centre.

The room in which I stood with the detectives, was large, with a cheerful lattice-work wall-paper, and substantial leather-covered furniture. In the window was placed a writing-table, and upon it a telescope mounted on a stand. A comfortable couch was placed against the wall, while before the fire-place were a couple of deep-seated easy chairs, and a large oval table in the centre.

Indeed, the room possessed an air of homely comfort, with an absence of the inartistic seldom found in seaside apartments. The windows were open and the light breeze from the sun-lit sea slowly fanned the lace curtains. On the writing-table lay a quantity of papers, mostly tradesmen's receipts — all of which the old gentleman carefully preserved — some newspapers, a tin of tobacco, and several pipes.

Beside the fire-place lay a pair of Egyptian slippers in crimson morocco, evidently the property of young Craig, while his straw hat and cane lay upon the couch, together with the fawn Burberry coat which had been one of the common objects in Cromer. Everywhere were signs of occupation. Indeed, the cushions in the easy chairs were crumpled just as if the two men had only a little while before arisen from them, while in the grate were a number of ends of those gold-tipped cigarettes without which Craig was never seen.

Upon a peg behind the door hung another old grey mackintosh belonging to old Gregory—an exact replica of which had been worn by the man who had so mysteriously met his death.

But where was old Gregory? Aye, that was the question.

With Mrs. Dean, a homely person with hair brushed tightly back, and her husband looking on, we began a thorough search of the room, as well as of the two bedrooms on the next floor. The sitting-room was investigated first of all, but in the writing-table we found nothing of interest. One of the drawers had been emptied and a mass of tinder in the grate told a significant tale.

Old Mr. Gregory had burned a lot of documents before disappearing.

Why? Were they incriminating?

Why, too, had he so suddenly disappeared? Surely he would not have done so without knowledge of his nephew's tragic death!

For a full half-hour we rummaged that room and all that was in it, but, alas, found nothing.

In the old man's bedroom stood a battered leathern cabin-trunk bearing many labels of Continental hotels. It was unlocked, and we found it filled with clothes, but strangely enough, not the clothes of an old man, but rather the smart attire of a middle-aged person of fashion.

At first Frayne refused to believe that the trunk belonged to old Gregory. But Mrs. Dean was precise upon the point. That was Mr. Gregory's room.

In the bottom of the cabin-trunk we found a number of folded sheets of foolscap, upon which were written many cryptic calculations in feet and metres; "wave-metres," it was written upon one slip. They seemed to be electrical. Upon other sheets were lists of names together with certain figures, all of which conveyed to us no meaning. Frayne, of course, took possession of them for submission to examination later on.

"May I look at them later?" I asked him.

"Certainly, Mr. Vidal. They seem to be a bit of a puzzle, don't they? They have something to do with electricity, I fancy."

In the corner of the room, opposite the window, stood a large wooden sea-chest, similar to those used by naval officers. It was painted black, and bore, in white, the initials "V. G." It had an old and battered appearance, and the many labels upon it told of years of transit by rail and steamer.

I bent to examine it, but found it securely locked and bound round with iron bands.

"That's very heavy, sir," Mrs. Dean remarked. "He always kept it locked, so I don't know what's inside. When the old gentleman came in, he always went straight over to it as though to ascertain whether the lock had been tampered with."

"Ah, then there's something in there he wished to keep away from prying eyes!" said Frayne. "We must see what it is."

I remarked that the lock was a patent one, but he at once ordered a locksmith to be fetched, while we turned our attention to the adjoining room, the one that had been occupied by young Craig.

It was slightly smaller than the other one, and overlooked the narrow street which ran along the back of the houses towards the church.

We searched the drawers carefully, one after another, but found nothing except clothes—a rather extensive wardrobe. Of cravats, Craig had possessed fully a hundred, and of collars, dozens upon dozens.

Upon his dressing-table stood the heavy silver fittings of a travelling-bag, a very handsome set, and, in a little silver box, we found a set of diamond studs, with several valuable scarf-pins. The device of one of these was some intertwined initials, surmounted by a royal crown in diamonds; apparently a present from some exalted personage.

Presently, however, Treeton, who had remained in Gregory's room assisting in the perquisition, entered with an ejaculation of surprise, and we found that on pulling out the small drawer of the washstand, he had discovered beneath it some papers that had been concealed there.

We at once eagerly examined them, and found that there were slips exactly duplicating those discovered in old Gregory's wallet—slips with names and numbers upon them—apparently code numbers.

Together with these were several papers bearing more remarkable calculations, very similar to those we had found at the bottom of the cabin-trunk. The last document we examined was, however, something very different. It was a letter written upon a large sheet of that foreign business paper which is ruled in small squares.

"Hulloa!" Frayne exclaimed, "this is in some foreign language—French or German, I suppose."

"No," I said, glancing over his shoulder. "It's in Italian. I'll read it, shall I?"

"Yes, please, Mr. Vidal," cried the detective, and handed it to me.

It bore no address—only a date—March 17th, and translating it into English, I read as follows:—

"Illustrious Master,—The business we have been so long arranging was most successfully concluded last night. It is in the *Matin* to-day, a copy of which I send you with our greeting. H. left as arranged. J. arrives back in Algiers to-morrow, and the Nightingale still sings on blithely. I leave by Brindisi for Egypt to-night and will wire my safe arrival. Read the *Matin*. Does H. know anything, do you think? Greetings from your most devoted servant, Egisto."

"A very funny letter," remarked Treeton. "I wonder to what it alludes?"

"Mention of the *Matin* newspaper would make it appear that it has been written from Paris," I said. Then, with Frayne's assent, I rapidly scribbled a copy of the letter upon the back of an envelope which I took from my pocket.

A few moments later, the locksmith having arrived, we returned to old Gregory's room, and watched the workman as he used his bunch of skeleton-keys upon the lock of the big sea-chest. For ten minutes or so he worked on unsuccessfully, but presently there was a click, and he lifted the heavy wooden lid, displaying an old brown army blanket, carefully folded, lying within.

This we removed, and then, as our astounded gaze fell upon the contents of the chest, all involuntarily gave vent to loud ejaculations of surprise.

Concealed beneath the rug we saw a quantity of antique ornaments of silver and gold—rare objects of great value—ancient chalices, reliquaries, golden cups studded with precious stones, gold coronets, a great number of fine old watches, and a vast quantity of splendid diamond and ruby jewellery.

The chest was literally crammed with jewels, and gold, and silver—was the storehouse of a magnificent treasure, that must have been worth a fabulous sum.

I assisted Frayne to take out the contents of the chest, until the floor was covered with jewels. In one old brown morocco case that I opened, I found a glorious ruby necklet, with one enormous centre stone of perfect colour—the largest I had ever seen. In another was a wonderful collar of perfectly matched pearls; in a third, a splendid diamond tiara worth several thousand pounds.

"Enough to stock a jeweller's shop," said Frayne in an awed voice. "Why, what's this at the bottom?"

He began to tug at a heavy square wooden box, which, when he had succeeded in dragging it out and we opened it, we found to contain a hand flash-lamp for signalling purposes—one of the most recent and powerful inventions in night-signalling apparatus.

"Ha!" Treeton cried. "That's the lamp which Day suspected had been flashed from these windows on the night of the coast alarm."

"Yes," I remarked reflectively, "I wonder for what purpose that lamp was used?"

"At any rate, the old man has a fine collection of curiosities," said Frayne. "I suppose it was one of his eccentricities to carry them with him? No wonder he was so careful that the lock should not be tampered with!"

I stood looking at that strange collection of valuables. There were pieces of gold and silver plate absolutely unique. I am no connoisseur of antique jewellery, but instinctively I knew that every piece was of enormous value. And it had all been thrown pell-mell into the box, together with some old rags—seemingly once parts of an old damask curtain—in order to prevent the metal rattling. Much of the silver-ware was, of course, blackened, as none of it had been cleaned for years. But the gems sparkled and shone, like liquid drops of parti-coloured fire, as they lay upon the shabby carpet. What could it all mean?

Mrs. Dean, who was standing utterly aghast at this amazing discovery, jumped with nervousness as Frayne suddenly addressed her.

"Did Mr. Gregory have many visitors?"

"Not many, sir," was her reply. "His secretary used to come over from Sheffield sometimes—Mr. Fielder, I think his name was—a tall, thin gentleman, who spoke with an accent as though he were a foreigner. I believe he was a Frenchman, though he had an English name."

"Anybody else?"

"Mr. Clayton, the old schoolmaster from Sheringham, and—oh, yes—a lady came from London one day, a short time ago, to see him—a young French lady," replied Mrs. Dean.

"What was her name?"

"I don't know. It's about a fortnight ago since she came, one morning about eleven, so she must have left London by the newspaper train. She rang, and I answered the bell. She wouldn't let me take her name up to Mr. Gregory, saying: 'She would go up, as she wanted to give him a surprise.' I pointed out his door and she went in. But I don't think the old gentleman exactly welcomed her."

"Why?" I asked.

"Because I heard him raising his voice in anger," replied the landlady.

"Was Mr. Craig there?"

"No. He was out somewhere I think. My own belief is that the young lady was Mr. Gregory's daughter. She stayed about an hour, and once, when I opened the door, I heard her speaking with him very earnestly in French, asking him to do something, it seemed like. But he flatly refused and spoke to her very roughly; and at this she seemed very upset—quite brokenhearted. I watched her leave. Her face was pale, and she looked wretchedly miserable, as though in utter despair. But I forgot," added Mrs. Dean. "Three days later I found her photograph, which the old man, who was very angry, had flung into the waste-paper basket. I kept it, because it was such a pretty face. I'll run down and get it—if you'd like to see it."

"Excellent," exclaimed Frayne, and the good woman descended the stairs.

A few moments later she came back with a cabinet photograph, which she handed to the detective.

I glanced at it over his shoulder.

Then I held my breath, staggered and dumbfounded.

The colour must have left my cheeks, I think, for I was entirely unprepared for such a shock.

But I pulled myself together, bit my lip, and by dint of a great effort managed to remain calm.

Nevertheless, my heart beat quickly as I gazed upon the picture of that pretty face, that most open, innocent countenance, that I knew so well.

Those wide-open, trusting eyes, that sweet smile, those full red lips—ah!

And what was the secret? Aye, what, indeed?

CHAPTER V
IN WHICH THE SHADOW FALLS

"A very charming portrait," Frayne remarked. "I see it was taken in London. We ought to have no great difficulty in discovering the original—eh, Treeton—if we find it necessary?"

I smiled to myself, for well I knew that the police would experience considerable difficulty in ascertaining the identity of the original of that picture.

"Are you quite sure, Mrs. Dean, that it was the same lady who came to visit Mr. Gregory?" I asked the landlady.

"Quite positive, sir. That funny little pendant she is wearing in the photograph, she was wearing when she came to see the old gentleman—a funny little green stone thing—shaped like one of them heathen idols."

I knew to what she referred—the small green figure of Maat, the Goddess of Truth—an ancient amulet I had found, while prying about in the ruins of a temple on the left bank of the Nile, a few miles beyond Wady-Halfa—the gate of the Sudan. I knew that amulet well, knew the hieroglyphic inscription upon its back, for I had given it to her as a souvenir.

Then Lola—the mysterious Lola, whose memory had occupied my thoughts, both night and day, for many and many a month—had reappeared from nowhere, and had visited the eccentric Gregory.

In that room I stood, unconscious of what was going on about me; unconscious of that glittering litter of plate and jewels; of fifteenth century chalices and gem-encrusted cups; of sixteenth century silver, much of it ecclesiastical—probably from churches in France, Italy, and Spain—of those heavy nineteenth century ornaments, that wonderful array of diamonds and other precious stones, in ponderous early-Victorian settings, which lay upon the faded, threadbare carpet at my feet.

I was thinking only of the past—of that strange adventure of mine, which was now almost like some half-forgotten dream—and of Lola, the beautiful and the mysterious—whose photograph I now held in my nerveless fingers, just as the detective had given it to me.

At that moment a constable entered with a note for his inspector, who took it and opened it.

"Ah!" he exclaimed, turning to Frayne. "Here's another surprise for us! I made inquiries this morning of the Sheffield police concerning old Mr. Gregory. Here's their reply. They've been up to Messrs. Gregory and Thorpe's works, but there is no Mr. Gregory. Mr. Vernon Gregory, senior partner in the firm, died, while on a voyage to India, nearly a year ago!"

"What?" shrieked Mrs. Dean in scandalized tones. "Do you mean to say that that there old man, my lodger, wasn't Mr. Gregory?"

"He may have been *a* Mr. Gregory, but he certainly was not Mr. Vernon Gregory, the steel manufacturer," responded Treeton, calmly.

"Well, that beats everything!" she gasped. "Then that old man was a humbugging impostor—eh?"

"So it seems," Frayne replied.

"But it can't be true? I can't believe it! He was a real gentleman. See, here, what he had got put away in that old box of his. Them there Sheffield police is mistook, I'm sure they be. There'll be some good explanation of all this, I'll be bound, if 'tis looked for."

"I sincerely hope so," I remarked. "But at present I certainly don't see any."

Truth to tell, I was utterly staggered and confounded, the more so, by that report from Sheffield. I confess I had all along believed old Gregory to be what he had represented himself as being to the people of Cromer.

Now I realized that I was face to face with a profound and amazing problem—one which those provincial police-officers, patient and well-meaning as they were, could never hope to solve.

Yes, old Vernon Gregory was an impostor. The reply from the Sheffield police proved that beyond a doubt. Therefore, it also followed that the man lying dead was certainly not what he had represented himself to be—nephew of the great steel magnate.

But who was he? That was the present great question that baffled us.

The photograph I held in my hand bore the name: "Callard, Photographer, Shepherd's Bush Road." But I knew that whatever inquiries were made at that address, the result would be negative. The mysterious Lola was an elusive little person, not at all likely to betray her identity to any photographer.

There were reasons for her secrecy—very strong reasons, I knew.

So I smiled, when Frayne announced that he should send the picture up to London, and put through an inquiry.

I picked up some pieces of the jewellery that was lying at my feet. In my hand I held a splendid golden coronet in which were set great emeralds and rubies of enormous value. Even my inexpert eye could see that the workmanship was very ancient, and the stones but roughly cut and polished. I judged it to be a crown which had adorned the head of some famous Madonna in an Italian or Spanish church; a truly regal ornament.

Again stooping, I picked up a small heavy box of blackened repoussé silver of genuine Italian Renaissance work, and opening it, found it filled with rings of all kinds, both ancient and modern. There were signet rings bearing coats of arms; ladies' gem rings; men's plain gold rings; and rings of various fancy devices.

One I picked out was distinctly curious. A man's flat gold ring set with eight finely-coloured turquoises at equal intervals. It looked brighter and newer than the others, and as I fingered it, a small portion of the outer edge opened, revealing a neatly enamelled inscription in French, "Thou art Mine." On further examination I found that each of the spaces in which a turquoise was set, opened, and in each was also a tender love passage, "I love you," "Faithful and True," and so on, executed probably a century ago.

Yes, each piece in that wonderful collection was unique—the treasure of one who was undoubtedly a connoisseur of gems and antiques. Indeed, in no national collection had I ever seen a display more remarkable than that flung out so unceremoniously upon the carpet, around that mysterious flash-lamp.

While one of the detectives, at Frayne's order, began repacking the treasure, I went with the two inspectors to a sitting-room on the ground-floor, where, with the door closed, we discussed the situation.

Outside, upon the path in front of the house, were a knot of curious persons, among them Mr. Day, and his subordinate officer who had made the tragic discovery.

"Well," exclaimed Frayne, slowly rubbing his chin, "it's a very curious case. What will you do now, Treeton?"

"Do?" asked the local officer. "Why, I've done all I can do. I've reported it to the Coroner, and I suppose they'll make the post-mortem to-day, and hold the inquest to-morrow."

"Yes, I know," said the other. "But we must find this old man, Gregory. He seems to have been pretty slick at getting away."

"Frightened, I suppose," said Treeton.

"What. Do you think he killed his nephew?" queried the man from Norwich.

"Looks suspiciously like it," Treeton replied.

"Yes, but why did Craig go out disguised as the old man—that's the question?"

"Yes," I repeated. "That is indeed the question."

"And all that jewellery? The old man is not likely to leave that lot behind—unless he's guilty," said Frayne. "Again, that visit of the young lady. If we could only get track of her, she'd have something to tell us without a doubt."

"Of course," said Treeton. "Send the photograph to London, and find out who she is. What a bit of luck, wasn't it, that Mrs. Dean kept the picture she found in the waste-paper basket?"

I remained silent. Yes, if we could only discover the original of that photograph we should, no doubt, learn much that would be startling. But I felt assured that we should never find trace of her. The police could follow in her direction if they chose. I intended to proceed upon an entirely different path.

What I had learned in that brief hour, had staggered me. I could scarcely realize that once again I was face to face with the mystery of Lola—the sweetest, strangest, most shadowy little person I had ever met in all my life. And yet she was so real, so enchanting, so delightful—such a merry, light-hearted little friend.

Lola!

I drew a long breath when I recalled that perfect oval face, with the wonderful blue eyes, the soft little hand—those lips that were made for kisses.

Even as I stood there in the plainly-furnished sitting-room of that seaside lodging-house, I remembered a strangely different scene. A fine, luxurious chamber, rich with heavy gilt furniture, and crimson damask, aglow under shaded electric lights.

I saw her upon her knees before me, her white hands grasping mine, her hair dishevelled upon her shoulders, pleading with me—pleading, ah! I remembered her wild, passionate words, her bitter tears—her terrible confession.

And this provincial detective, whose chief feats had been confined to cases of petty larceny, speed limit, and trivial offences, dealt with by the local Justices of the Peace, actually hoped to unravel a mystery which I instinctively felt to be fraught with a thousand difficulties.

Any swindler, providing he has made sufficient money by his tricks, has bought a place in the country, and has been agreeable to the Deputy-Lieutenant of the County, can become one of His Majesty's Justices of the Peace. Some such are now and then unmasked, and off to penal servitude have gone, men who have been the foremost to inflict fines and imprisonment on the poor for the most trivial offences—men who made the poaching of a rabbit a heinous crime.

I venture to assert that the past of many a J. P. does not bear investigation. But even when glaring injustices are exposed to the Home Secretary, he is often afraid to order an inquiry, for political reasons. It is always "Party" that must be first considered in this poor old England of ours to-day.

What does "Party" mean? Be it Liberal, Unionist, Conservative, Labour, anything, there should at least be honesty, fair dealing, plain speaking and uprightness. But alas, this is an age of sham in England. Journalists, novelists, preachers, playwrights, are afraid to speak the truth frankly, though they know it, and feel it. It is "Party" always. Many a criminal has escaped conviction before our County Benches because of "Party," and for the same reason many innocents have been condemned and suffered.

This case of Mr. Vernon Gregory was a provincial case. The amusing farce of local investigation, and local justice, would no doubt be duly played. The coroner always agrees with the evidence of his own family doctor, or the prominent local medico, and the twelve honest tradesmen forming the jury are almost invariably led by the coroner in the direction of the verdict.

Oh, the farce of it all! I hold no brief for France, Belgium, Germany, or any other continental nation, for England is my native land. But I do feel that methods of inquiry on the continent are just, though minutely searching, that there Justice is merciful though inexorable, that her scales weigh all evidence to the uttermost gramme.

These reflections passed through my mind as I stood in that lodging-house room, while the two police officers discussed as to their further procedure in the amazing case with which they had been called upon to deal. I could not help such thoughts arising, for I was dubious, very dubious, as to the thoroughness of investigation that would be given to the affair by the local authorities. Slackness, undue delay, party or personal interests, any one of these things might imperil the inquiry and frustrate the ends of justice.

I knew we were confronted by one of the greatest criminal problems that had ever been offered for solution, calling for the most prompt, delicate and minute methods of investigation, if it was to be handled successfully. And as I contrasted the heavy, cumbrous, restricted conditions of English criminal procedure with the swift, far-reaching methods in use across the Channel, I felt that something of the latter was needed here if the mystery of Craig's death was ever to be solved.

CHAPTER VI
MYSTERY INEXPLICABLE

The town of Cromer was agog, when, next day, the coroner held his inquiry.

The afternoon was warm, and the little room usually used as the police court was packed to suffocation.

The jury—the foreman of which was a stout local butcher—having viewed the body, the inquest was formally opened, and Mrs. Dean, the first witness, identified the remains as those of her visitor, Mr. Edward Craig.

This, the first intimation to the public that Mr. Gregory was not dead after all, caused the greatest sensation.

In answer to the coroner, Mrs. Dean explained how, with his uncle, old Mr. Gregory, Craig had taken apartments with her. She had always found him a quiet, well-conducted young gentleman.

"Was he quite idle?" asked the grave-faced coroner.

"No. Not exactly, sir," replied the witness, looking round the closely packed room. "He used to do a good deal of writing for his uncle, more especially after the young man, Mr. Gregory's private secretary, had been over from Sheffield."

"How often did he come?"

"At intervals of a week or more. He always carried a small despatch-box, and on those occasions the three would sit together for half the day, doing their business, with the door closed—and," added the landlady vigorously, "Mr. Craig had no end of business sometimes, for he received lots of telegrams. From what I heard him say one day to his Uncle, I believe he was a betting man, and the telegrams were results of races."

"Ah, probably so," remarked the coroner. "I believe you have not seen the elder gentleman since the tragic evening of his nephew's death?"

"No, sir. The last I saw of Mr. Gregory was when he wished me 'good-night,' and went to bed, as was his habit, about half-past ten, on the night previous."

"And, where was the deceased then?"

"My servant Anne had taken up his hot water, and he had already gone to bed."

"And, did you find next day that the beds had been slept in?"

"Mr. Craig's had, but Mr. Gregory's hadn't," was the reply. Whereat the eager, listening crowd buzzed and moved uneasily.

The grave-faced county official holding the inquiry, having finished writing down the replies to his questions upon blue foolscap, looked across to the row of twelve tradesmen, and exclaimed in his sharp, brusque manner— —

"Have the jury any questions to put to this witness?"

"I'd like to ask, sir," said the fat butcher, "whether this Mr. Gregory was not a very eccentric and extraordinary man?"

"He was," replied the good woman with a smile. "He always suspected that people was a-robbin' him. He'd strike out threepence from my weekly bill, and on the very same day, pay six or seven shillings for a pound of fresh strawberries."

"During the night you heard nobody leave your house?"

"No, neither me, nor my husband, heard any sound. Of course, our dog knew both of 'em, and was very friendly, so he'd make no noise."

"I would like to ask you, Mrs. Dean," said another juryman, the thin-faced manager of a boot-shop, "whether Mr. Craig was in the habit of receiving any strangers?"

"No," interrupted the coroner, "we are not here to inquire into that. We are here solely to establish the identity of the deceased and the cause of his death. The other matters must be left to the police."

"Oh! I beg pardon sir," ejaculated the offending juryman, and sat back in his chair with a jerk.

George Simmonds, a picturesque figure in his coast-guard uniform, was called next, and minutely described how he had found deceased, and had, from his dress, believed him to be old Mr. Gregory. Afterwards he was cross-examined by the foreman of the jury as to whom he had met during his patrol that night, and what he knew personally about the dead man.

"I only know that he was a very nice young gentleman," replied the coast-guard. "Both he and his uncle often used to pass the time o' day with us out against the flagstaff, and sometimes they'd have a look through the glass at the passing ships."

The police evidence then followed, and, after that Dr. Sladen, the chief medical man in Cromer, took the oath and made the following statement, in clear, business-like tones, the coroner writing it down rapidly.

"Henry Harden Sladen, Doctor of Medicine, 36, Cliff Avenue, Cromer. I was called to see deceased by the police, at about half-past four on the morning of the twelfth of June. He was lying upon a public seat on the East Cliff, and on examination I found that he had been dead about two hours or more."

"Any signs of violence?" inquired the coroner, looking up sharply at the witness, and readjusting his gold-rimmed glasses.

"None whatever."

"Yes, Dr. Sladen?"

"Yesterday afternoon," continued the witness, "I made a post-mortem examination in conjunction with Dr. Copping, of Cromer, and found the body to be that of a young man about twenty-five years old, of somewhat athletic build. All the organs were quite normal. There was an old wound under the left shoulder, apparently a bullet wound, and two rather curious scars on the right forearm, which, we agreed, had been received while fencing. We, however, could find no trace of disease or injury."

"Then to what do you attribute death?" inquired the coroner.

"Well, I came to the conclusion that the young man had been suddenly asphyxiated, but how, is a perfect mystery," responded the doctor. "It would be difficult to asphyxiate any one in the open air without leaving any mark of strangulation."

"I take it that you discovered no mark?"

"Not the slightest."

"Then you do not think death was due to natural causes?"

"It was due to asphyxiation—a rapid, almost instantaneous death it must have been—but it was not due to natural causes."

"Briefly put, then, you consider that the deceased was the victim of foul play?"

"Yes. The young man was murdered, without a doubt," replied the doctor, slowly. "But so ingeniously was the crime committed, that no trace of the methods by which death was accomplished has been left. The assassin, whoever he was, must have been a perfect artist in crime."

"Why do you think so?" asked the coroner.

"For several reasons," was the reply. "The victim must have been sitting upon the seat when suddenly attacked. He rose to defend himself and, as he did so, he was struck down by a deadly blow which caused him to stagger, reel, and fall lifeless some distance away from the seat. Yet there is no bruise upon him—no sign of any blow having been struck. His respiratory organs suddenly became paralysed, and he expired—a most mysterious and yet instant death."

"But is there no way, that you—as a medical man—can account for such a death, Dr. Sladen?" asked the coroner dryly.

"There are several ways, but none in which death could ensue in such circumstances and with such an utter absence of symptoms. If death had occurred naturally we should have been quickly able to detect the fact."

After one or two pointless questions had been put to the witness by members of the jury, his place was taken by his colleague, Dr. Copping, a pushing young medico who, though he had only been in Cromer a year, had a rapidly-growing practice.

In every particular he corroborated Dr. Sladen's evidence, and gave it as his professional opinion that the young man had met with foul play, but how, was a complete mystery.

"You do not suspect poison, I take it?" asked the coroner, looking up from his writing.

"Poison is entirely out of the question," was Dr. Copping's reply. "The deceased was asphyxiated, and died almost instantly. How it was done, I fail to understand and can formulate no theory."

The public, seated at the back of the court, were so silent that one could have heard the dropping of the proverbial pin. They had expected some remarkable revelations from the medical men, but were somewhat disappointed.

After the evidence of Inspector Treeton had been taken, the coroner, in a few brief words, put the matter before the jury.

It was, he said, a case which presented several very remarkable features, not the least being the fact that the nephew had gone out in the night, dressed in his uncle's clothes and made up to resemble the elder man. That fact made it evident that there was some unusual motive for going out that night on the part of the deceased man—either a humorous one, or one not altogether honest. The latter seemed the most reasonable theory. The young man evidently went out to keep a tryst in the early morning, and while waiting on the seat, was suddenly attacked and murdered.

"Well, gentlemen," he went on, removing his glasses, and polishing them with his handkerchief, "it is for you to return your verdict—to say how this young man met with his death, to-day, or, if you consider it advisable, you can, of course, adjourn this inquiry in order to obtain additional evidence. Personally, I do not see whence any additional evidence can come. We have heard the depositions of all concerned, and if you decide that it is a case of wilful murder, as both Dr. Sladen and Dr. Copping have unhesitatingly stated it to be, the rest must be left to the police, who will no doubt use their utmost endeavours to discover the identity of this 'artist in crime,' as Dr. Sladen put it, who is responsible for this young man's death. So far as I am concerned, and I have acted as coroner for this district for twenty-three years, I have never before held an inquiry into a case which has presented so many puzzling features. Even the method by which the victim was done to death is inexplicable. The whole thing, gentlemen, is inexplicable, and, as far as we can discern, there is no motive for the crime. It is, of course, for you to arrive at a verdict now, or to adjourn for a week. Perhaps you will consult together."

The twelve Norfolk tradesmen, under the leadership of the obese butcher, whispered together for a few moments and were quickly agreed.

The coroner's officer, a tall constable, standing near the door, saw that the foreman wished to speak, and shouted: "Silence!"

"We will return our verdict at once, Mr. Coroner," said the butcher. "We find that deceased was murdered."

"That is your verdict, eh? Then it will read, 'that deceased was wilfully murdered by some person or persons unknown.' Is that what you all agree?" he asked in his quick, business-like manner.

"Yes, sir. That is our verdict," was the response.

"Any dissentients?" asked the official. But there was none.

"Then the rest must be left to the police," said the coroner, resuming his writing.

At those words, the public, disappointed at the lack of gory details, began to file out into the street, while the jury were discharged.

Who was the murderer? That was the question upon every one's tongue.

And where was Vernon Gregory, the quaint, eccentric old fellow who had become such a notable figure in Cromer streets and along the asphalted parade. What had become of him?

The police had, of course, made no mention in their evidence of the search in the rooms occupied by the two men—of the discovery of the splendid treasure of gold and jewels—or of the fact that the real Mr. Vernon Gregory had died while on a voyage to India.

With Frayne, I walked back to the police-station, where we found that no trace had yet been discovered of the old man. He had disappeared swiftly and completely, probably in clothes which in no way resembled those he habitually wore, for, as his pocket-book and other things were found in the cape worn by his nephew, we assumed that they were actually the uncle's. Therefore, it would be but natural that old Gregory would have left the house wearing clothes suitable to a younger man.

The fact that Lola had visited him told me much.

Gregory, whoever he was, was certainly no amateur in the art of disguise. In all probability he now presented the appearance of a man of thirty or so, and in no way resembled the eccentric old gentleman who looked like a poet and whose habits were so regular.

That there was a mystery, a strange, amazing mystery, I knew instinctively. Edward Craig had, I felt confident, fallen the victim of a bitter and terrible vengeance—had been ingeniously done to death by one whose hand was that of a relentless slayer.

So, as I walked past the grey old church of Cromer, back to the *Hôtel de Paris*, I pondered deeply.

My own particular knowledge I kept a fast secret to myself. Among that heterogeneous collection of treasures had been one object which I recognized—an object I had seen and handled once before, in very different circumstances.

How came it in that old sea-chest, and in the possession of the man who was now exposed as an impostor?

Mr. Day, the chief officer of the coast-guard, passed me by and saluted. But I was so preoccupied that I scarcely noticed him.

I had crossed by the path leading through the churchyard, and arrived at the corner of Jetty Street—a narrow, old-fashioned lane which leads along to the cliff-top in front of the *Hôtel de Paris*, and where an inclined slope goes down to the pier.

Suddenly, on raising my eyes at a passer-by, my gaze met that of a tall, thin, pale-faced, rather gentlemanly man in a dark grey suit, and wearing a grey felt hat.

The stranger, without noticing me, went on with unconcern.

But in that second I had recognized him. We had met before, and in that instant I had fixed him as the one man who knew the truth regarding that remarkable secret I had now set out to investigate.

I halted aghast, and half-turned upon my heel to greet him.

CHAPTER VII
TELLS OF TWO MEN

The stranger, whose age was about forty-five, went on in the direction of the post-office in the Church Square.

Should I dash back, overtake him and claim acquaintance? Or should I keep my knowledge to myself, and watch in patience?

A single second had I in which to decide. And I decided.

I turned back upon my heel again as though I had not recognized him.

But what could that man's presence mean in that little East Coast town? Aye, what indeed?

I tried to think, to conjecture, to form some theory—but I was too confused. Lola had been there—and now that man who had just passed!

Along the narrow, old-fashioned Jetty Street I strode for some yards, and then turned and retraced my steps till I saw him across the old churchyard entering the post-office.

Treeton was coming up in my direction, little dreaming how near he was to the one man who knew the truth. I smiled to myself at the ignorance of the local police. And yet my own knowledge was that of a man who had led a strange cosmopolitan life, who had mixed with all classes on the Continent, who had trodden the streets of more than one capital in disguise, and who had assisted the *Sûreté* in half a dozen countries.

I smiled at Treeton as he went by, and he smiled back. That man in the post-office yonder was a remarkable personage. That I well knew. What would any agent in the *brigade mobile* of Paris have given to be in my place at that moment—to be able to enter the Cromer post-office and lay hands upon Jules Jeanjean—the notorious Jules Jeanjean, of all men!

My thoughts were of Lola. Phew! Had ever man such a strange reverie as I had in those moments when I halted, pretending to look into the shop-window of the jeweller at the corner—yet all the time watching in the direction of the door of the post-office!

To go back would betray recognition, so I was compelled to go forward—to the hotel.

I did not, however, allow the grass to grow beneath my feet. That night, instead of dining at the hotel, I ate a sandwich in the bar of the *Albion*, and soon discovered that the man I had seen passing Cromer Church was living in apartments in the Overstrand Road, the aristocratic quarter of Cromer, close to the Doctor's steps.

I had kept careful watch all the evening. First, quite unconcernedly, he had strolled along the East Cliff, past the seat where the man, now dead, had sat early on that fatal morning. I had followed, and had watched.

He paused close by, ostensibly to light a cigarette with a patent lighter, then, after covertly making observations, he went on away to the edge of the links, and up the path near the *Links Hotel*, where he gained the Overstrand Road.

The evening was clear and bright, the sundown across the North Sea a blaze of crimson and gold. There were many promenaders along that well-trodden path, yet it required the exercise of all my cunning to escape the observation of the shrewd and clever man I was following.

At eight o'clock he entered his lodging. Half an hour later, as I lounged past, I saw him seated at dinner between two elderly women, laughing with that easy-going cosmopolitan air—that foreign charm of his, which had carried him through so many strange adventures.

Then I waited—waited until dusk deepened into night. Silent, and without wind, the summer air was fresh and invigorating after the oppressiveness of the day. The street-lamps were lit, yet I still remained watching, and ever on the alert.

The Norfolk constabulary were observing the old, slow, stereotyped, routine methods of police investigation, as I had expected them to do.

I alone had scented the clue to the mystery.

Not a sign had been seen of the cunning old fugitive. Telegrams had been dispatched by the dozen. Scotland Yard had been, of course, "informed," but information from the country is there but lightly considered. Therefore, in all probability, the shrewd old man, who had so cleverly imposed upon the good people of Cromer, was by that time across the Channel.

But, would he leave that splendid treasure of his behind?

All through that evening I waited in patience in the Overstrand Road—waited to see if Jules Jeanjean would come forth again.

At half-past ten, when the moon was shining brightly over the calm sea, I saw him come out, wearing a soft grey felt hat and light drab overcoat. He laughed at the neat maid who opened the door for him, and instinctively put his hand to his hat to raise it, as foreigners so often do.

Instead of walking towards the town, as I had expected, he turned in the direction of Suffield Park, the pretty suburb of Cromer, and actually passed within a few yards of where I was crouching behind the laurel hedge of somebody's front garden.

I allowed him to get some distance ahead, then, treading lightly upon my rubber heels, swiftly followed.

He made in the direction of the great Eastern Railway Station, until he came to the arch where the line crosses the road, when from the shadow there crept silently another figure of a man.

At that hour, and at that point, all was deserted. From where I stood I could see the lights of the great *Links Hotel* high up, dominating the landscape, and nearer were the long, slowly-moving shafts of extreme brilliance, shining from the lighthouse as a warning to mariners on the North Sea.

Jules Jeanjean, the man of a hundred adventures, met the stranger. It was a tryst, most certainly. Under the shadow of a wall I drew back, and watched the pair with eager interest. They whispered, and it was apparent that they were discussing some very serious and weighty matter. Of necessity I was so far away that I could not distinguish the features of the stranger. All I could see was that he was very well dressed, and wore dark clothes, a straw hat, and carried a cane.

Together they walked slowly in the shadow. Jeanjean had linked his arm in that of the stranger, who seemed young and athletic, and was talking very earnestly—perhaps relating what had occurred at the inquest that afternoon, for, though I had not seen him there, I suspected that he might have been present.

I saw Jeanjean give something to his companion, but I could not detect what it was. Something he took very slowly and carefully from his pocket and handed it to the young man, who at first hesitated to accept it, and only did so after Jeanjean's repeated and firm insistence.

It was as though the man I had recognized that afternoon in Cromer was bending the other by his dominant personality—compelling him to act against his will.

And as I stood there I wondered whether after all Jeanjean had actually recognized me when we met in Church Square—or whether he had been struck merely by what he deemed a chance resemblance, and had passed me by without further thought.

Had he recognized me I do not think he would have dared to remain in Cromer a single hour. Hence, I hoped he had not. The fact would render my work of investigation a thousandfold easier.

Presently, after a full quarter of an hour's conversation, the pair strolled together along the moonlit road back towards the town, which at that hour was wrapped in slumber.

By a circuitous route they reached the narrow street at the back of the house where old Mr. Gregory and his nephew had lived, and, after passing and repassing it several times, returned by the way they had come.

Near the railway bridge, where Jeanjean had first met the stranger, both paused and had another earnest conversation. More than once in the lamplight I had caught sight of the man's face, a keen face, with dark moustache, and sharp, dark eyes. He had a quick, agile gait, and I judged him to be about eight-and-twenty.

Presently the two walked out beyond the arch, and I saw the younger man go behind a hedge, from which he wheeled forth a motor-cycle that had been concealed there. They bade each other adieu, and then, starting his engine, the stranger mounted the machine, and next moment was speeding towards Norwich without having lit his lamp, possibly having forgotten to do so in his hurry to get away.

The Frenchman watched his friend depart, then, leisurely lighting a cigarette, turned and went back to the house in Overstrand Road where he had taken up his temporary abode.

It was half-past two when the night-porter at the *Hôtel de Paris* admitted me, and until the sun had risen over the sea, I sat at my open window, smoking, and thinking.

The discovery that Jules Jeanjean was in that little East Coast town was to me utterly amazing. What was his business in Cromer?

A wire to the *Sûreté* in Paris, stating his whereabouts, would, I knew, create no end of commotion, and Inspector Treeton would no doubt receive urgent orders by telegram from London for the arrest of the seemingly inoffensive man with the jaunty, foreign air.

The little town of Cromer, seething with excitement over the mysterious murder of Edward Craig, little dreamed that it now harboured one of the most dangerous criminals of modern times.

Next day, in the hotel, I was asked on every hand my opinion in regard to the East Cliff murder mystery. The evidence at the inquest was given verbatim in the Norwich papers, and every one was reading it. By reason of my writings, I suppose, I had earned a reputation as a seeker-out of mystery. But to all inquirers I now expressed my inability to theorize on the affair, and carefully preserved an attitude of amazed ignorance.

I scarce dared to go forth that day lest I should again meet Jeanjean, and he should become aware of my presence in Cromer. Had he recognized me when we met? I was continually asking myself that question, and always I came to the conclusion that he had not, or he would not have dared to keep his tryst with the mysterious motor-cyclist.

Were either of the pair responsible for Edward Craig's death? That was the great problem that was before me.

And where was Gregory? If he were not implicated in the crime, why had he absconded?

I examined the copy of that curious letter signed by Egisto, but it conveyed nothing very tangible to me.

Frayne and his men were still passing to and fro in Cromer, making all kinds of abortive inquiries, and were, I knew, entirely on the wrong scent. Like myself, they were seeking the motive which caused the sudden disappearance of old Gregory. They were actually looking for him in the county of Norfolk! I knew, too well, that he must be already safely far away, abroad.

Frayne called in to see me after luncheon, and sat up in my room for an hour, smoking cigarettes.

"I'm leaving the rooms that were occupied by Craig and his uncle just as they are," he said to me. "I'm not touching a thing for the present, so that when we find Gregory we can make him give explanations of what we have secured there. I thought first of taking that sea-chest and its contents over to Norwich with me, but I have now decided to seal up the room and leave everything as it is."

"I understand," I replied, smiling to myself at his forlorn hope of ever finding Mr. Vernon Gregory. For, the further my inquiries had gone, the more apparent was it that the old man was a very wily customer.

"We've made one discovery," said the detective as he lit a fresh cigarette.

"Oh, what's that?" I inquired.

"A young fisherman, named Britton, has come forward and told me that on the night of the murder he was going along the road to Gunton, at about midnight, when he met a man on a motor-cycle, with an empty side-car, coming from the direction of Norwich. The man dismounted and asked Britton how far it was to Cromer. The fisherman told him, and the fellow rode off. Britton, who had been to see his brother, returned just before two, and met the same motor-cyclist coming back from Cromer, and travelling at a very high speed. He then had somebody in the side-car with him. In the darkness Britton could not get a very good view of the passenger, but he believes that it was a woman."

"A woman!" I echoed, somewhat surprised.

"Yes, he was sure it was a woman," Frayne said. "One good point is, that Britton is able to give a fairly good description of the motor-cyclist, whose face he saw when the fellow got off his machine to speak to him. He pictures him as a sharp-faced man, with a small black moustache, who spoke broken English."

"A foreigner, then?"

"Evidently." Then Frayne went on to remark, "It was foolish of this fellow Britton not to have come forward before, Mr. Vidal. But you know how slow these Norfolk fishermen are. It was only after he was pressed by his friends, to whom he related the incident, that he consented to come to the police-station and have a chat with me."

"Well—then you suspect the motor-cyclist and the woman?"

"Not without some further proof," replied the detective, with a look of wisdom on his face. "We don't know yet if the passenger in the side-car was a woman. Britton only believes so. The foreigner evidently only came into Cromer to fetch a friend."

"But could not any foreigner come into Cromer to fetch a lady friend?" I queried.

"Yes. That's just why I do not attach much importance to the young fellow's story."

"Does he say he could recognize the cyclist again?"

"He believes so. But, unfortunately, he's not a lad of very high intelligence," laughed Frayne.

To my companions the statement of that young fisherman evidently meant but little.

To me, however, it revealed a very great deal.

CHAPTER VIII
REMAINS AN ENIGMA

Six days had gone by.

The funeral of the unfortunate Edward Craig had taken place, and locally the sensation caused by the tragic discovery had died down.

The weather was beautifully warm, the sea calm, and gradually a few holiday-makers were appearing in the streets; women in summer blouses, knitted golf coats and cotton skirts, with flannel-trousered men. They were of the class who are compelled to take their holidays early, before their employers; with them came delighted children carrying spades and buckets.

Fearing recognition by the notorious Frenchman, I was greatly handicapped, for I was compelled to remain in the hotel all day, and go forth only at night.

Frayne and his men had locked and sealed the rooms which had been occupied by old Gregory and Craig, and had returned to Norwich. In their place had come a plain-clothes man who, as far as I could gather, lounged about the corners of the streets, and chatted idly with the constables in uniform.

The plain-clothes man in our county constabulary system is not an overwhelming success. His only real use seems to be mostly that of a catcher of small boys who go out stealing fruit.

By dint of judicious inquiry, made by my manservant, Rayner, whom I had summoned from London, I had discovered something regarding the foreign gentleman, who had taken apartments in the Overstrand Road.

Rayner could always keep a secret. He was a fair-haired, bullet-headed chap of thirty-two whom I had found, eight years before the date of this story, wandering penniless in the streets of Constantinople. I had taken him into my service, and never once had occasion to regret having done so. He was a model of discretion, and to a man constantly travelling, like myself, a veritable treasure.

Sometimes upon my erratic journeys on the Continent I took him with me, at others he remained at home in my little flat off Berkeley Square. If

I ever called upon him to make inquiries for me, to watch, or to follow a suspected person, he obeyed with an intelligence that would, I believe, have done credit to any member of that remarkable combination of brains—the Council of Seven, of New Scotland Yard.

Living an adventurous life, as he had done, his wits had been sharpened, and his perception had become as keen as that of any detective. Therefore, I had called upon him, under seal of secrecy, to assist me in the investigation of many a mystery.

Knowing his value, I had wired to him to come to Cromer. He arrived when I was out. First, he looked through my traps, folded my trousers and coats, arranged my shirts and ties in order with professional precision, and when I returned, entered my room, saying briefly—

"I'm here, sir."

I threw myself into a chair and told him all that had occurred—of course, under strictest secrecy.

Then I gave him minute instructions as to making inquiries of the servants at the house in the Overstrand Road. A servant can always get useful information from other servants, for there is a freemasonry among all who are employed in domestic capacities.

Therefore, it was with interest that I sat in my room, overlooking the sea, on the following day, and listened to Rayner's report.

In his straw hat, and well-cut grey tweed suit, my man made a very presentable appearance. It was the same suit in which he went out to Richmond with his "young lady" on Sundays.

"Well, sir," he said, standing by the window, "I've managed to get to know something. The gentleman is a Belgian doctor named Paul Arendt. He has the two best rooms in the house and is the only visitor staying there at present. They say he's a bit eccentric; goes out at all hours, but gives lots of money in tips. Seemingly, he's pretty rich."

"Has he had any visitors?" I asked quickly.

"One. Another foreigner. An Italian named Bertini, who rides a motor-cycle."

"Has he been there often?"

"He came last Monday afternoon—three days ago," my man replied.

"Anything else?"

"Well, sir, I managed to make friends with the maidservant, and then, on pretence of wanting apartments myself, got her to show me several rooms in the house in the absence of her mistress. Doctor Arendt was out, too, therefore I took the opportunity of looking around his bedroom. I'd given the girl a sovereign, so she didn't make any objection to my prying about a bit. Arendt is a rather suspicious character, isn't he, sir?" asked Rayner, looking at me curiously.

"That's for you to find out," I replied.

"Well, sir, I have found out," was his quick answer. "In the small top left-hand drawer of the chest of drawers in his room I found a small false moustache and some grease-paint; while in the right-hand drawer was a Browning revolver in a brown leather case, a bottle of strong ammonia, and a small steel tube, about an inch across, with an india-rubber bulb attached to one end."

"Ah!" I said. "I thought as much. You know what the ammonia and rubber ball are for, eh?"

The man grinned.

"Well, sir, I can guess," was his reply. "It's for blinding dogs—eh?"

"Exactly. We must keep a sharp eye upon that Belgian, Rayner."

"Yes, sir. I took the opportunity to have a chat with the maid about the recent affair on the East Cliff, and she told me she believed that the dead man and Doctor Arendt were friends."

"Friends!" I echoed, starting forward at his words.

"Yes, sir. The girl was not quite certain, but believes she saw the Belgian doctor and young Mr. Craig walking together over the golf-links one evening. It was her Sunday out and she was strolling that way just at dusk with her sweetheart."

"She is not quite positive, eh?" I asked.

"No, sir, not quite positive. She only thinks it was young Mr. Craig."

"Did Craig or Gregory ever go to that house while our friend has been there?"

"No, sir. She was quite positive on that point."

"What does the doctor do with himself all day?" I asked.

"Sits reading novels, or the French papers, greater part of the day. Sometimes he writes letters, but very seldom. According to the books I noticed in his room, he delights in stories of mystery and crime."

I smiled. Too well I knew the literary tastes of Jules Jeanjean, the man who was fearless, and being so, was eminently dangerous, and who was passing as a Belgian doctor. He, who had once distinguished himself by holding the whole of the forces of the Paris police at arms' length, and defying them—committing crimes under their very noses out of sheer anarchical bravado—was actually living there as a quiet, studious, steady-going man of literary tastes and refinement—Doctor Paul Arendt, of Liège, Belgium.

Ah! Some further evil was intended without a doubt. Yet so clever were Jeanjean's methods, and so entirely unsuspicious his actions, that I confess I failed to see what piece of chicanery was now in progress.

My next inquiry was in the direction of establishing the identity of the motor-cyclist.

That night Rayner kept watchful vigil instead of myself, for I had been up five nights in succession and required sleep. But though he waited near the house in the Overstrand Road from ten o'clock until four in the morning, nothing occurred. Jeanjean had evidently retired to rest and to sleep.

After that we took it in turns to watch, I having made it right with the night-porter of the hotel, for a pecuniary consideration, to take no notice of our going or coming.

For a whole week the notorious Frenchman did not emerge after he entered the house at dinner-time. I was sorely puzzled regarding the identity of that motor-cyclist. Would he return, or had he left the neighbourhood?

Early one morning Rayner, having taken his turn of watching, returned to say that Bertini, with his motor-cycle, had again met the "foreign gentleman" at the railway bridge—the same spot at which I had seen them meet.

They had remained about half an hour in conversation, after which the stranger had mounted and rode away again on the Norwich road, while Jeanjean had returned to his lodgings.

My mind was then made up. That same morning I took train to Norwich, where I hired a motor-car for a fortnight, and paying down a substantial deposit, drove the car—an open "forty," though a trifle old-fashioned—as far as Aylsham, a distance of ten miles, or half-way between Norwich and Cromer. There I put up at a small hotel, where I spent the rest of the day in idleness, and afterwards dined.

Aylsham is a sleepy little place, with nothing much to attract the visitor save its church and ancient houses. Therefore, I devoted myself to the newspapers until just before the hotel closed for the night.

Then I rang up Rayner on the telephone as I had made arrangement to do.

"That's me, sir," was his answer to my inquiry.

"Well," I asked, "anything fresh?"

"Yes, sir. A lady called to see you at seven o'clock—a young French lady. I saw her and explained that you were away until to-morrow, and——"

"Yes, yes!" I cried eagerly. "A French lady. Did she give her name?"

"No, sir. She only told me to tell you that if I mentioned the word 'nightingale,' you would know."

"The Nightingale!" I gasped, astounded. It was Lola! And she had called upon me!

"When is she coming back?" I demanded eagerly.

"She didn't say, sir—only told me to tell you how sorry she was that you were out. She had travelled a long way to see you."

"But didn't she say she'd call back?" I demanded, full of chagrin that I should have so unfortunately been absent.

"No, sir. She said she might be able to call sometime to-morrow afternoon, but was not at all certain."

I held the receiver in my trembling fingers in reflection. Nothing could be done. I had missed her—missed seeing Lola!

Surely my absence had been a great, and, perhaps, unredeemable misfortune.

"Very well," I said at last. "You know what to do to-night, Rayner?"

"Yes, sir."

"And I will be back in the morning."

"Very good, sir," responded my man, and I shut off. I paid my bill, went outside and lit up the big headlamps of the car. Then I drove slowly out of the yard, and out of the town, in the direction of Cromer.

It had been a close day, and the night, dark and oppressive, was overcast with a threatening storm. The dust swept up before me with every gust of wind as I went slowly along that high road which led towards the sea. I proceeded very leisurely, my thoughts full of my fair visitor.

Lola had called upon me! Why? Surely, after what had occurred, I could never have hoped for another visit from her.

Yes. It must be something of the greatest importance upon which she wished to consult me. Evidently she knew of my presence in Cromer—knew, possibly, of the efforts I was making to unravel the mystery of old Vernon Gregory.

Yet, I could only wait in impatience for the morrow. But would she return? That was the question.

The car was running well, but I had plenty of time. Therefore, after travelling five miles or so, I pulled up, took out my pipe and smoked.

I stopped my engine, and, in the silence of the night, strained my ears to catch the sound of an approaching motor-cycle. But I could hear nothing — only the distant rumble of thunder far northward across the sea.

By my watch I saw that it was nearly midnight. So I restarted my engine and went slowly along until I was within a couple of miles of Cromer, and could see the flashing of the lighthouse, and the lights of the town twinkling below. Then again I stopped and attended to my headlights, which were growing dim.

A mile and a half further on I knew that Rayner, down the dip of the hill, was lurking in the shadow. But my object in stationing myself there was to follow the mysterious cyclist, not when he went to keep his appointment, but when he left.

In order to avert suspicion, I presently turned the car round with its lights towards Norwich, but scarcely had I done so, and stopped the engine again, when I heard, in the darkness afar off, the throb of a motor-cycle approaching at a furious pace.

My lamps lit up the road, while, standing in the shadow bending as though attending to a tyre, my own form could not, I knew, be seen in the darkness.

On came the cyclist. Was it the man for whom I was watching?

He gave a blast on his horn as he rounded the corner, for he could no doubt see the reflection of my lamps from afar.

Then he passed me like a flash, but, in that instant as he came through the zone of light, I recognized his features.

It was Bertini, the mysterious friend of Jules Jeanjean.

I had but to await his return, and by waiting I should learn the truth.

I confess that my heart beat quickly as I watched his small red light disappear along the road.

CHAPTER IX
DESCRIBES A NIGHT-VIGIL

The gusty wind had died down.

In the silence of the night I listened to the receding noise of the motor-cycle as it swept down the hill into Cromer town, where I knew Rayner would be on the alert.

The sound died away, therefore I relit my pipe, and mounting again into the driver's seat, sat back thinking—thinking mostly of Lola, and my ill-luck at having missed her.

Before me, in the white glare of the lamps upon the road, where insects of the night, attracted by the radiance, were dancing to their deaths, there arose before me that sweet, perfect face, the face that had so attracted me. I saw her smile—smile at me, as she did when first we had met. Ah! How strange had been our friendship, stranger than novelist had ever imagined. I had loved her—loved as I had never loved before, and she had loved me, with that bright, intense look in her wonderful eyes, the woman's look that can never lie.

There is but one love-look. A man knows it by his instinct, just as does a woman. A woman knows by intuition that the fool who takes her out to the theatre and supper, and is so profuse in his protestations of undying admiration, is only uttering outpourings of vapid nonsense. Just so, a man meets insincerity with insincerity. The woman gets to know in time how much her vain, shallow admirer is good for, for she knows he will soon pass out of her life, while the man's instinct is exactly the same. In a word, it is life—the life of this, our Twentieth Century.

The man laughed at and derided to-day, is a hero ten years hence.

A few years ago Mr. John Burns carried a banner perspiringly along the Thames Embankment, in a May Day procession, and I assisted him. To-day he is a Cabinet Minister. A few years ago my dear friend, George Griffith, wrote about air-ships in his romance, *The Angel of the Revolution*, and everybody made merry at his expense. To-day airships are declared to be the chief arm of Continental nations.

Ah, yes! The world proceeds apace, and the unknown to-morrow ever brings its amazing surprises and the adoption of the "crank's" ideas of yesterday.

Lola had called to see me. That fact conjured up in my imagination a thousand startling theories.

Why?

Why had she called, after all that had passed between us?

I waited, waited for the coming of that mysterious cyclist, who arose from nowhere, and whose business with Jules Jeanjean was of such vast and secret importance.

The very fact of Jeanjean being in Cromer had staggered me. As I sat there smoking, and listening, I recollected when last I had heard mention of his name. Hamard—the great Hamard—Chief of the *Sûreté* of Paris, had been seated in his private bureau in the offices of the detective police.

He had leaned back in his chair, and blowing a cloud of tobacco-smoke from his lips, had said in French—

"Ah! Mon cher Vidal, we are face to face in this affair with Jules Jeanjean, the most ingenious and most elusive criminal that we have met this century in France. In other walks of life Jeanjean would have been a great man—a millionaire financier, a Minister of the Cabinet, a great general—a leader of men. But in the circumstances this arch-adventurer, who slips through our fingers, no matter what trap we set for him, is a criminal of a type such as Europe has never known within the memory of living man. Personally I admire his pluck, his energy, his inventiveness, his audacity, his iron nerve, and his amazing cunning. Truly, now, cher ami, he is a marvel. There is but one master-criminal, Jules Jeanjean."

That was the character given him by Monsieur Hamard, the greatest French detective since Lecoq.

And now this master-criminal was beneath the railway arch at Cromer meeting in secret a mysterious cyclist!

What evil was now intended?

I waited, my ears strained to catch every sound. But I only heard the distant rumble of the thunder, away across the North Sea, and, somewhere, the dismal howling of a dog.

I waited, and still waited. The sky grew brighter, and I grew perceptibly colder, so that I turned up my coat-collar, and shivered, even though the previous day had been so unusually warm. The car smelt of petrol and oil—a smell that nauseated me—and yet my face was turned to the open country ready to follow and track down the man who had swept past me to keep that mysterious tryst in the darkness.

Looking back, I saw, away to the right, the white shafts of light from the high-up lighthouse, slowly sweeping the horizon, flashing warning to mariners upon that dangerous coast, while, far away in the distance over the sea, I could just discern a flash from the lightship on the Haisboro' Sands.

In the valley, deep below, lay Cromer, the street-lamps reflecting upon the low storm-clouds. At that moment the thunder-storm threatened to burst.

Yet I waited, and waited, watching the rose of dawn slowly spreading in the Eastern sky.

Silence—a complete and impressive silence had fallen—even the dog had now ceased to howl.

And yet I possessed myself in patience, my ears strained for the "pop-pop" of the returning motor-cycle.

A farmer's cart, with fresh vegetables and fruit for the Cromer shops on the morrow, creaked slowly past, and the driver in his broad Norfolk dialect asked me—

"Any trouble, sir?"

I replied in the negative, whereupon he whipped up his horse, bade me a cheery "good morning," and descended the hill. For a long time, as I refilled and relit my pipe, I could hear the receding wheels, but no sound of a motor-cycle could I hear.

Time passed, the flush of dawn crept over the sea, brightened swiftly, and then overcast night gave place to a calm and clear morning. The larks, in the fields on either side, rose to greet the rising sun, and the day broke gloriously. Many a dawn had I witnessed in various parts of the world, from the snows of Spitzbergen to the baking sands of the Sahara, but never a more glorious one than that June morning in Poppyland, for Cromer is one of the few places in England where you can witness the sun both rise from, and set in the sea.

My headlights had burned themselves out long ago. It was now four o'clock. Strange that the nocturnal cyclist did not return!

All my preparations had, it seemed, been in vain.

I knew, however, that I was dealing with Jules Jeanjean, a past-master in crime, a man who, no doubt, was fully aware of the inquiries being made by the plain-clothes officers from Norwich, and who inwardly laughed them to scorn.

The man who had defied the Paris *Sûreté* would hardly entertain any fear of the Norfolk Constabulary.

Many country carts, most of them going towards Cromer, now passed me, and their drivers wished me "Good morning," but I remained at my lonely vigil until five o'clock. Then I decided that Jeanjean's friend must have taken another road out of Cromer, either the Sheringham, the Holt, or the Overstrand, the three other main roads out of the town.

What had Rayner done, I wondered? Where was he?

I sat down upon the grassy bank at the roadside, still pondering. Of all the mysteries of crime I had assisted in investigating, in order to write down the details in my book, this was assuredly the most remarkable.

I knew that I was face to face with some great and startling affair, some adventure which, when the truth became known, would amaze and astound the world. Jules Jeanjean was not the man to attempt small things. He left those to smaller men. In his profession he was the master, and a thousand *escrocs*, all over the Continent, forgers, international thieves, burglars, coiners, *rats d'hotel*—most ingenious of malefactors—regarded the name of Jeanjean with awe.

One of his exploits was well known up and down the Continent—for the *Matin* had published the full story a year ago. Under another name, and in the guise of a wealthy *rentier* of Paris, he made the acquaintance of one of the Inspectors of the Paris detective service. Inviting him to his private sitting-room in the *Hôtel Royale*, on the Promenade des Anglais, he gave him an *aperitif* which in less than three minutes caused the police official to lose consciousness. Thereupon Jeanjean took from the Inspector's pocket his card of authority as a detective—a card signed by the Prefect of Police—and at once left the hotel.

Next night, at the *Café Américain* in Paris, he went up to a wealthy German who was spending a harmless but gay evening at that well-known supper-resort and arrested him for theft, exhibiting his warrant of authority.

In a taxi he conducted him to the Prefecture of Police, but on their way the German asked him if they could come to terms. The pseudo-Inspector hesitated, then told the taxi-driver to go to a small hotel opposite the Gare du Nord. There he and his prisoner discussed terms, it being eventually agreed that the German—a well-known shipowner of Hamburg—should in the morning telegraph to his bank for eighty thousand marks, for which sum he would be allowed to go at liberty.

It was well known, of course, to Jeanjean that his "prisoner" had been guilty of the offence for which he had "arrested" him, and the *coup* was quite easy.

He kept the German in the hotel till ten o'clock next morning, and then the pair went to the Crédit Lyonnais together. At four o'clock—the bogus Inspector still with his "prisoner,"—the money was brought to the obscure hotel, and after Jeanjean had carefully counted through the notes he allowed his prey to go at liberty, advising him to take the next train back to Germany.

At six o'clock, the sun shining out warm and brightly, my patience was exhausted. I had spent the night hours there in vain. Yet I dare not drive the car into Cromer, for I intended to repeat my effort on the following night. Therefore I started the engine, and was soon back in the yard of the small hotel in Aylsham.

There I put up the car, breakfasted, and then taking the first train to North Walsham, arrived in Cromer about half-past nine o'clock.

When I entered my room at the *Hôtel de Paris* the maid came quickly along, saying—

"Will you please go up to see your servant, sir! He's very unwell!"

"Unwell?" I said. "Why, what's the matter?"

"I don't know, sir. The police brought him in about half an hour ago. He's been out all night, they say. And they found him very ill."

I darted upstairs and entered Rayner's room without knocking.

He was lying upon the bed, still dressed, his face pale as death.

"Ah, sir!" he gasped, "I—I'm so glad you've come back! I—I wondered whether anything had happened to you. I—I——"

He stretched out his hand to me, but no other word escaped his lips.

I saw that he had fainted.

CHAPTER X
CONTAINS A CLUE

At once I knew that some startling incident had happened.

Dr. Sladen, called by the police, entered the room a few moments afterwards, whereupon I turned to him, and in order to allay any undue curiosity, said—

"My man has been taken ill, doctor. Exhaustion, I suppose. He's a great walker, and, unknown to me, has apparently been out for a night ramble."

"Ah, yes," answered the quiet, old-fashioned medical man, peering at the invalid through his glasses.

Slowly he took Rayner's pulse, and then said—

"Heart a little weak, I suppose. There's nothing really wrong—eh?"

"I think not. He was talking to me only a few moments ago, and then suddenly fainted. Been on a long ramble, I should think."

"At night, eh?" asked the doctor in some surprise.

"It is a habit of his to walk at night. He does the same thing in London—walks miles and miles."

We dashed cold water into Rayner's face, gave him a smelling-bottle belonging to one of the maids, and very soon he came round again, opening his eyes in wonder at his surroundings.

"Here's Doctor Sladen," I said. "You feel better now, don't you, Rayner?"

"Yes, sir," was his feeble reply.

"Ah, you've been on one of your night rambles again," I said reprovingly. "You over-do it, you know."

Then Sladen asked him a few questions, and finding that he had recovered, shook my hand and left.

The instant the door was closed upon the doctor Rayner sat up, and with a serious expression upon his face said—

"Something has happened, sir. I don't know what. I'll tell you all I know. I went up to the railway arch as you directed, and lay down in the hedge to wait. After a long time the foreigner from the Overstrand Road came along, lit a cigar, and waited. He was wearing an overcoat, and I suppose he must have waited a full half-hour, until, at last, the cyclist came. They had a brief talk. Then the cyclist left his cycle about fifty yards from where I was in hiding, and both men set off towards the town. I, of course, followed at a decent distance, and they didn't hear me because of the rubber soles on my boots."

"Well, what then?" I inquired impatiently.

"They separated just against the *Albion*, and then followed one another past the church, and to the left, behind this hotel, and along to the house where the dead man lived—the house you pointed out to me. Close by they met another man who, in the darkness, I took to be a chauffeur. But I had, then, to draw back into a doorway to watch their movements. The chap I took to be a chauffeur, after a few words with the two foreigners, came along in my direction, and passed within a yard of me, when of a sudden he turned and faced me. 'What are you doing here?' he asked quickly. 'Nothing,' was my reply. 'Then take that for your inquisitiveness,' he said, and in a second I felt something over both my nose and mouth. It was only for a second, but I recollect I smelt a strong smell of almonds; and then I knew no more, nothing until I found myself here."

"That's most extraordinary!" I exclaimed. "Then you don't know what became of the three men?"

"Not in the least, sir," Rayner replied. "I was so thoroughly taken aback, that I must have gone down like a log."

"Then, that's all you know?"

"Yes, sir."

Scarcely had he finished relating his strange adventure than Inspector Treeton entered, and greeting me, explained how Rayner had been found by a constable, lying senseless, about three miles out of the town on the road to Holt.

By that I knew he must have been conveyed there, probably by a motor-car, driven by the chauffeur who had so mysteriously attacked him, apparently at the foreigners' orders. It was Jeanjean's work, no doubt. The Frenchman had seemingly eyes at the back of his head, and had evidently detected that his actions were being spied upon.

To the police inspector I made no mystery of the affair, merely replying, as I had to the doctor, that my manservant was in the habit of taking long walks, long nocturnal rambles, and that he evidently had overdone it.

"Doctor Sladen has already been here and seen him," I added. "He says he's quite right again."

This satisfied the highly-esteemed local inspector, and presently he left us, expressing the hope that Rayner would very soon be himself once more.

"Well," I said to my man when the inspector had gone, "it's evident that while you were unconscious they picked you up, put you in the car, and tipped you out upon the road outside the town. Perhaps they believed you to be dead."

"Like enough, sir," he said, smiling grimly.

"They evidently trapped you, Rayner," I said, laughing. "You were not sharp enough."

"But, who'd have thought that the fellow could have come straight for me, and rendered me insensible in a tick—as he did?" asked my man as he lay, still extended on the bed, a dirty, dishevelled figure. "I know I was caught, sir; those men were cleverer than I was, I admit."

"Yes, Rayner," was my reply. "I don't blame you in the least. I'm only glad that your plight isn't worse. The men had a motor-car, it seems, at their disposal somewhere, and they went in the direction of Holt."

"That appears so, sir."

"Why, I wonder? Bertini probably obtained his machine and followed the car. They must have gone either through Wells and Fakenham, or East Dereham."

"Back to Norwich, perhaps, sir. All roads from here seem to lead to Norwich."

"But you say the incident happened close to Beacon House, where old Gregory lived—eh?"

"Yes, sir."

"Then they objected to you being present. Evidently something was intended and you prevented it."

"No. Perhaps I didn't prevent it. They prevented me instead."

Rayner was a bit of a humorist.

"Quite likely," I answered, smiling. But I was full of chagrin that I had been out all night, waiting on that lonely road, while that mysterious affair had been in progress.

"Well, at any rate, Rayner, you've had a very funny experience," I said, with a laugh.

"And not the first, sir, eh?" he replied, stretching lazily on the bed. "Do you recollect that funny case at Pegli, just outside Genoa? My word, those two assassins nearly did me in that night, sir."

"And three nights later we gave them over to agents of the Department of Public Security," I said. "Yes, Rayner, you had a tough half-hour, I know. But you're an adventurer, like myself. As long as we solve a mystery we don't regret the peril, or the adventure, do we?"

"No, sir. I don't—as long as you give a guiding eye over it. But I tell you straight, sir, I don't like detectives. They're chumps, most of 'em."

"No. Don't condemn them," I said. "Rather condemn the blind and silly police system of England. The man who snares a rabbit gets a conviction recorded against him, while the shark in the city pays toll to the Party and becomes a Baronet. I'm no socialist," I added, "but I believe in honesty in our daily life. Honesty in man, and modesty in woman, are the two ideals we should always retain, even in this age of degeneracy and irreligion."

"I think the local police are blundering the whole of this affair," Rayner went on. "Yet I can't make out by what means I was so suddenly put out of action. That curious, strong smell of almonds puzzles me. It's in my nostrils now."

"Your fancy, I expect," I said.

At that moment came a knock at the door, and the tall young constable entered, the same man who had been on duty when I had gone up to inspect the seat where Craig's body had been found.

"The Inspector has sent me, sir," he exclaimed, saluting, "to say he'd like to see you at once. He's just along the West Cliff—at Beacon House, where Mr. Craig lived in."

"Certainly," I replied. "Tell him I will come at once."

The constable disappeared, and turning to Rayner, I said: "I wonder why Treeton wishes to see me in such a hurry? What has happened now?" Then, promising to return quickly, I went out.

At Beacon House, I found Treeton standing in the front sitting-room, on the ground-floor, talking seriously with the landlady.

"Hulloa! Mr. Vidal," he exclaimed as I entered. "Something more has occurred in this house during the night. The place has been broken into by burglars, who've got clean away with all old Mr. Gregory's collection of jewellery."

"Burglary," I repeated slowly; and then all that Rayner had told me flashed across my mind. I saw the reason for Jeanjean and his mysterious cyclist companion being near the house, and also why Rayner, on being detected, had been rendered senseless.

"Have you found any trace of the thieves?" I asked, having already decided to keep my own information to myself.

"Lots of traces," laughed Treeton. "Come and see for yourself."

We ascended the stairs, followed by the excited landlady and her husband.

"This is really terrible," moaned the woman. "I wish we'd never set eyes upon the poor young man and his uncle. We heard nothing in the night, nothing. In fact, I didn't discover that the room had been opened until an hour ago, when I was sweeping down the stairs. Then I noticed that the seals placed upon it had been broken, and the lock sawn right out. Why we didn't hear them, I can't think!"

"Ah, you don't hear much when the modern burglar is at work," declared Treeton. "They're far too scientific for that."

He showed me the door, from which the lock had been cut away, saying—

"They evidently got in by the window of the room downstairs, where we've just been, for it was found closed but not latched. They came up these stairs, cut out the lock, as you see—and look at that!" he added as we entered the old man's room.

The strong old sea-chest stood in the centre of the room. The lid, which had been nailed down, and sealed by the police, had been wrenched off and the box stood empty!

"Look!" cried Treeton again. "Every scrap gone—and it must have been a pretty bulky lot—a couple, or even three, sacksful at the least."

I went to the two windows which overlooked the narrow street behind, and examining the sills, saw marks where the paint had recently been rubbed away.

"Yes, I see," I remarked, "and they lowered the plunder to confederates outside."

"But who could have known of the existence of the jewellery, here?" asked Treeton. "Only ourselves were aware of it. At the inquest all mention of it was carefully suppressed."

"Somebody, of course, must have talked, perhaps unthinkingly, about it, and the news got round to the thieves," remarked the landlord.

I remained silent. Had I not, from the first, marvelled that old Mr. Gregory should disappear and leave behind him that collection of valuables?

"I've wired to Norwich, to Frayne, to come over at once, and see if he can find any finger-prints," said the local inspector. "We've discovered something here which the burglars left behind. Look at this."

And from a corner of the room he picked up something and handed it to me.

It was a woman's little, patent leather walking-shoe, with two white pearl buttons as fastening. The size I judged to be threes, but, as it was still fastened, it must have been too large for the wearer, who apparently having dropped it, was unable for some reason to regain it, and so left it behind.

"That's very strange!" I said, turning the little shoe over in my hand. It was not much worn, and of very good quality. "A woman has evidently been here!"

"Evidently, Mr. Vidal," replied the officer. "But surely a woman would never have the pluck to do a job of this sort. Nine people slept in this house last night and never heard a sound."

Truth to tell, I did not expect they would have done, now that I knew the robbery had been engineered by Jules Jeanjean.

"Very remarkable—very," I declared. "Probably Frayne, when he takes the finger-prints, will find some clue," I added, laughing inwardly, for I knew that those who had committed that robbery were far too clever to leave behind any traces of their identity. Besides, to actually lower the booty down into a public street showed a daring spirit which one only finds in the most expert criminals.

I could not, however, account for the discovery of that little shoe. Had it really been lost—or had it been placed there in order to mystify and mislead the police?

The latter suggestion had, of course, never entered Treeton's head.

"I wonder," I said to him, "if you would allow me to take this shoe along to the hotel? I want to take the exact measurements."

"Certainly, Mr. Vidal," was his reply. "You'll send it round to me, at the station, afterwards?"

"In an hour you shall have it," I promised him. Then I placed the shoe in my pocket, and made a tour of the room, touching nothing because of Frayne's coming hunt for finger-prints.

Jeanjean always wore gloves, skin-thin, rubber-gloves, which left no trace of his light touch. The curved lines of his thumb and forefinger were far too well known in Paris, in London, in Berlin and Rome, where the bureaux of detective police all possessed enlarged photographs of them.

Back in my room at the *Hôtel de Paris,* I took from a drawer the plaster cast of the woman's footprints I had found near the spot where Craig had been found.

Then, carrying it down to the shore near the pier, I made a print with the cast in the wet sand left hard by the receding tide.

Afterwards, I took the tiny, patent leather shoe from my pocket, and placed it carefully in the print.

It fitted exactly.

CHAPTER XI
THE AFFAIR ON THE SEVENTEENTH

The ingenious theft of old Gregory's treasure created the greatest consternation amongst the police, though the truth was carefully concealed from the public.

Treeton pledged Mr. and Mrs. Dean and their servant to secrecy, therefore all that was known in Cromer was that there had been an attempted burglary at Beacon House.

Cromer is a quiet, law-abiding town, and burglars had not been known there for years. Therefore the inhabitants were naturally alarmed, and now carefully locked and bolted their doors at night.

I returned the shoe to the police-station, but made no mention of the result of my test.

From the first I had guessed that old Gregory would not leave his treasure behind. Yet, if he were not guilty of Craig's murder, why had he fled?

Lola had visited him, and Jeanjean had been in Cromer. Those two facts were, in themselves, sufficient to tell me that Gregory was an impostor and that Craig, whoever he might really have been, had fallen the victim of some deadly vengeance.

Would Lola return to see me?

In the days that followed—bright June days, with the North Sea lying calm and blue below the cliffs—I waited in patience, scarce leaving the hotel all day, in fear lest she might again seek me, and, paying me a visit, find me absent.

Rayner considered me inactive and grumbled in consequence.

He spent his time lolling upon one of the seats on the cliff-top outside the hotel, idly smoking Virginian cigarettes. He had openly expressed his dissatisfaction that I had not made any attempt to follow the mysterious Doctor Arendt and his Italian friend.

Truth to tell, I was utterly confounded.

To follow Jules Jeanjean, now that he had got clean away with Gregory's treasure, would, I felt, be an utterly futile task. He was too clever to leave any trace behind—a past-master in the art of evasion, and a man of a hundred clever disguises.

What would they say at the Prefecture of Police in Paris, when I related to them the strange story of Jeanjean's exploits in England? Was it possible, I wondered, that the master-criminal, finding the Continent of Europe growing a trifle too hot for him, had come to England to follow his nefarious profession. If so, then he would certainly cause a great deal of trouble to the famous Council of Seven at the Criminal Investigation Department in London.

Thus days went on—warm, idle, summer days with holiday visitors daily arriving, houses being repainted, and Cromer putting on her best appearance for the coming "season." Seaside towns always blossom forth into fresh paint in the month of June, window-sashes in white and doors in green. But Cromer, with its golf and high-class music, is essentially a resort of the wealthy, a place where the tripper is unwanted and where there are no importunate long-shoremen suggesting that it is a "Nice day for a bowot, sir!"

Where was Lola? Would she ever return?

I idled about the hotel, impatient and angry with myself. Yes, Rayner was right after all! I ought to have made some effort to follow the three men. But now, it was quite impossible. They were, no doubt, far away, and probably old Gregory's treasure was by that time safe in his own hands.

The evidence of the shoe puzzled me. The wearer of that little shoe with the two pearl buttons had, without doubt, been near that seat on the East Cliff where Craig had been killed—present, in all probability, when he had been so mysteriously stricken down.

Was it possible that a woman—the same woman—had assisted in the burglary, and had inadvertently lost her shoe? Perhaps she had taken her shoes off in order to move noiselessly, and in trying to recover them could only regain one!

Lola, I remembered, possessed a very small foot. She was always extremely neat and dainty about the ankles and wore silk stockings and pretty shoes. Was it the print of her foot that I had found near that fatal seat? Was it her shoe that had been found at Beacon House?

Ah! If I could but see her? If she would only call upon me once again!

Day after day I waited, but, alas, she did not come.

That she was most anxious to see me was proved by the fact that she had dared to call at all after what had occurred. She had some strong motive in meeting me again, therefore I lived on in hope that she would return.

The Nightingale! Heavens! What strange memories that one word brought back to me as I sat in the window of my high-up room, gazing over the summer sea.

It was now July, and Cromer was rapidly filling with better-class folk. Now and then I went to London, but only for the day, fearing lest Lola should send me a telegram to meet her. In my absence Rayner always remained on duty.

I had written to her address in the Avenue Pereire, in Paris, but had received no reply. Then I had sent a line to the concierge of the house wherein the flat was situated. To this I had received an ill-scribbled few lines in French, expressing a regret that Mademoiselle had vacated the place some weeks previously and that her present address was unknown.

Unknown! Well, that, after all, scarcely surprised me. Lola's address generally was unknown. Only her most intimate friends ever knew it; and for obvious reasons. She existed always in a deadly fear.

Perhaps it was that very fear which even now kept her from me!

Several times I had advertised in the personal column of the *Matin* in the hope that she might see it and communicate with me, but all to no avail.

In Cromer the sensation caused by the mysterious crime had quite died down.

Frayne, in Norwich, had ceased to make further inquiry, and Treeton now regarded the problem as one that would never be solved. So, with the daily arrival of visitors, Cromer and its tradespeople and landladies forgot the curious affair which had afforded them such a "nine days' wonder."

The month of July passed, and, with the London season over, every one rushed to the seaside. Cromer was filled to overflowing. The narrow streets were crowded with well-dressed folk, and large cars passed one at every turn. Stifled town-dwellers were there to enjoy the strong, healthy breezes from the North Sea, and to indulge in the bathing and the golf.

Yet, though August came, I still kept on my room at the *Paris*, hoping against hope that Lola might yet return.

Quite suddenly, one day, I recollected that curious letter in Italian, signed "Egisto," and addressed to his "Illustrious Master," found at Beacon House.

It had referred to something which had appeared in the Paris *Matin* of March 17. Consequently I sent to Paris for a copy of the paper, and, one morning, the pale yellow sheet arrived.

"The business we have been so long arranging, was successfully concluded last night," the writer of the letter had said, adding that a report of it appeared in the *Matin* on the day of this letter.

Eagerly I searched the paper, which was, as usual, full of sensational reports, for the French newspaper reader dearly loves a tragedy.

The "feature" of the paper is always placed in the right-hand corner near the bottom, and, as I searched, my eyes fell upon the words, in bold capitals: "Motor Bandits: Dastardly Outrage near Fontainebleau."

What followed, roughly translated into English, read—

"By telephone from Fontainebleau. Early this morning we have received information of a dastardly outrage in which two lives have been sacrificed. It appears that, just after midnight, Monsieur Charles Benoy, the well-known jeweller of the Rue de la Paix, was travelling from Paris to his château near Maret-sur-Loire, on the other side of the Forest of Fontainebleau. He was accompanied by his son Pierre, aged twenty-four, and driven by the chauffeur, named Petit. With him, in the car, M. Benoy had in their leather cases four diamond collars of great value, and two pearl necklaces, which he intended to show next day to a certain American gentleman who has recently purchased the ancient Château de Provins, and who was one of the jeweller's customers.

"M. Benoy's intention was to take the jewels over to Provins in his car on the following morning. Apparently all went well on the journey. They passed through Melun, entered the Forest, and at a high speed passed through the little hamlet of Chantoïseau, where they were seen by two gendarmes.

"According to the story of the chauffeur, when about four kilometres beyond Chantoïseau, at a lonely point of the forest, he saw two red lights being waved in the roadway, and reduced his speed on this sign of danger.

"As he did so, however, three men sprang out from the undergrowth. They called upon him to stop, and a revolver was fired point-blank at him. Next moment the bandits fired, without further ado, upon the occupants of the car, but the chauffeur, severely wounded, then fainted, and knew no more until he recovered consciousness in the barracks of the Gendarmerie in Moret.

"What happened, apparently, was that the three assassins, after shooting all three of the occupants of the car, threw the bodies into the roadway, seized the automobile, and drove off with the jewels. M. Benoy and his son were dead when found, the father having two bullet-wounds in his head, while the son had been struck in the region of the heart. The chauffeur, Petit, lies in a critical condition, and only with great difficulty has been able to give an account of the murderous attack.

"Inquiries at M. Benoy's shop, in the Rue de la Paix, have revealed the fact that the jewellery is worth about four hundred thousand francs.

"The car was seen returning through Melun, being driven at a furious pace by the bandits, but, unfortunately, all traces of it, and of the three men, have been lost.

"According to the chauffeur's description of one of the men, who wore motor-goggles as a disguise, the police believe the outrage to be the work of the notorious Jules Jeanjean, the ingenious criminal of whom the police have been so long in search.

"The occupants of the car were treated with inhuman brutality. The bodies of both father and son, together with the number-plates of the car, were thrown unceremoniously into the undergrowth; that of Petit was allowed to lie across the footpath, but for what reason cannot be guessed at.

"From the fact that the number-plates of the car have been found, it would appear that before the bandits moved off they replaced the correct numbers by false ones. No doubt, also, a rapid attempt was made to alter the appearance of the body of the car, because, close by, there were found two pails containing grey paint, and large brushes with the paint still wet in them.

"From this it is seen that the intention of the bandits was to make a long run, perhaps all through the following day, to reach some distant point of safety.

"It will be remembered that Jules Jeanjean was the prime mover in the terrible outrage near Lyons, where three motorists were shot dead and two wounded. Two men named Dubois, and Leblon, were arrested, and before their condemnation confessed that Jeanjean, a dangerous anarchist, had instigated the plot.

"Readers of the *Matin* will not need to be reminded of the many desperate crimes of which this atrocious scoundrel has been the author; of his amazing daring and marvellous cunning; and of the almost uncanny ease with which he, time after time, defies every effort of the police to trace and capture him.

"M. Hamard, Chef de la Sûreté, and several inspectors have left Paris, and are upon the scene of the outrage, while descriptions of the missing jewellery have already been circulated."

CHAPTER XII
LOLA

Several times I re-read the account of the dastardly outrage.

Too well I knew how dangerous and desperate a man was Jules Jeanjean, the studious, and apparently harmless, Belgian doctor, who had lodged in the Overstrand Road, and had strolled about the pier and promenade of Cromer. His name, during the last three years or so, had become well known from end to end of Europe as an Anarchist who defied all the powers of law and order; a man who moved from place to place with marvellous swiftness, and who passed from frontier to frontier under the very noses of the commissaries of police stationed there.

His narrowest escape of capture had been one day in Charleroi, where, while sitting before the *Café des XXV*, he had been recognized by an inspector of the French *Sûreté*, who was in Belgium upon another matter. The inspector called a local agent of police, who suddenly pounced upon him, but in an instant Jeanjean had drawn a revolver, with which he shot the unfortunate policeman dead, and, in the confusion, escaped.

He then wrote an impudent letter to the Prefecture of Police in Paris, telling them that his intention was to serve any other police agent the same who might attempt to arrest him.

I took from my dispatch-box the copy I had made of the letter in Italian, found at Beacon House. In the light of that newspaper report it proved curious and interesting reading.

Who was the writer, Egisto? Evidently one of the conspirators. It was a report to his "Illustrious Master," of what had been done. Who was his Master? Surely not Jules Jeanjean, because one sentence read, "J. arrives back in Algiers to-morrow."

Was it possible that the "Illustrious Master"—the man who actually plotted and directed those dramatic coups—was none other than old Gregory himself!

The letter was certainly a report to the head of an association of dangerous malefactors. Who "H." was, who had "left as arranged," I knew not, but "J." evidently indicated Jules Jeanjean, and the fact that he would arrive back in Algiers on the morrow, showed first, that his hiding-place was on the other side of the Mediterranean; and, secondly, that after the crime a dash had been made to the south to join the mail-boat at Marseilles. The writer, Egisto, had left the other, travelling via Brindisi, to Port Said, so leaving the Paris police to again search for them in vain.

"Does H. know anything, do you think?" was the question Egisto had asked in his letter.

Did "H." indicate Monsieur Hamard, the Chef de la Sûreté?

My own theory was that "H." did indicate that well-known official, whom the gang had so often defied.

The writer, too, declared that "The Nightingale" still sang on blithely.

I knew the singer, the pretty, refined, fair-haired girl, so neat and dainty, with the sweet, clear contralto voice. It was Lola—Lola Sorel!

On the morning of August 24, I was standing with Mr. Day on the well-kept lawn outside the coast-guard station, watching the life-boat being launched for the benefit of the visitors, and in order to collect funds for the Life-boat Institution. The morning was perfect, with bright sunshine, a clear sky and glassy sea. Below us, the promenade and beach were thronged with summer visitors in light clothes, and the scene was one of brightness and merriment.

Amid the cheers of the waiting crowd the life-boat, guided by its gallant crew of North Sea fishermen, wearing their cork belts, went slowly down to the water's edge. The instant it was launched, Mr. Day, who held a huge pistol in his hand, fired a green rocket high into the air—the signal to the Haisboro' Lightship that aid was on its way.

Just as he had done so, a telegraph-boy handed me a message.

I tore it open and read the words—

"Can you meet me at the *Maid's Head Hotel*, Norwich, this afternoon at four? Urgent. Reply, *King's Head Hotel*, Beccles—Lola."

My heart gave a great bound.

From the messenger I obtained a telegraph-form, and at once replied in the affirmative.

Just before four o'clock I entered the covered courtyard of the old *Maid's Head Hotel*, in Norwich, one of the most famous and popular hostelries in Norfolk. John Peston mentioned it in 1472, when its sign was *The Murtel* or *Molde Fish*, and to-day, remodelled with taste, and its ancient features jealously preserved, it is well known to every motorist who visits the capital of Norfolk, the metropolis of Eastern England.

I engaged a small private sitting-room on the first-floor, a pretty, old-fashioned apartment with bright chintzes, and a bowl of fresh roses upon the polished table in the centre. Telling the waiter I expected a lady, I stood at the window to await my visitor.

As I stood there, all-impatient, the Cathedral chimes close by told the hour of four, and shortly afterwards I heard the noise of a car turning from the street into the courtyard.

Was it Lola?

From the room in which I was I could not see either roadway or courtyard, therefore I waited, my ears strained to catch the sound of footsteps upon the stairs.

Suddenly I heard some one ascending. The handle of the door was turned, and next second I found myself face to face with the slim, fair-haired girl whose coming I had so long awaited.

She came forward smiling, her white-gloved hand outstretched, her pretty countenance slightly flushed, exclaiming in French—

"Ah! M'sieu' Vidal! After all this time!"

"It is not my fault, Mademoiselle, that we are such strangers," I replied with a smile, bowing over her hand as the waiter closed the door.

She was a charming little person, sweet and dainty from head to foot. Dressed in a black coat and skirt, the former relieved with a collar of turquoise silk, and the latter cut short, so that her silk-encased ankles and small shoes were revealed. She wore a tiny close-fitting felt hat, and a boa of grey ostrich feathers around her neck.

Her countenance was pale with well-moulded features of soft sympathetic beauty, a finely-poised head with pretty dimpled chin, and a straight nose, well-defined eyebrows, and a pair of eyes of that clear blue that always seemed to me unfathomable.

I drew forward a chair, and she sank into it, stretching forth her small feet and displaying her neat black silk stockings from beneath the hem of her short skirt, which, adorned with big ball buttons, was discreetly opened at the side to allow freedom in walking.

"Well, and why did you not call again upon me in Cromer?" I asked in English, for I knew that she spoke our language always perfectly.

"Because—well, because I was unable," was her reply.

"Why did you not write?" I asked. "I've been waiting weeks for you."

"I know. I heard so," she said with a smile. "I am ve-ry sorry, but I was prevented," she went on with a pretty, musical accent. "That same evening I called upon you, I had to leave Cromer ve-ry hurriedly."

A strange thought flashed across my mind. Had her sudden departure been due to the theft at Beacon House? Had she been present then and lost her shoe?

I glanced at the shoes she wore. They were very smart, of black patent leather, with a strip of white leather along the upper edge. Yes, the size looked to me just the same as that of the little shoe which so exactly fitted the imprint I had made in the sand.

"Why did you leave so quickly?" I asked, standing before her, and leaning against the table, as I looked into the wonderful eyes of the chic little Parisienne.

"I was compelled," was her brief response.

"You might have written to me."

"What was the use, M'sieu' Vidal? I went straight back to France. Then to Austria, Hungary, and Russia," she answered. "Only the day before yesterday I returned to London."

"From where?"

"From Algiers."

Algiers! The mention of that town recalled the fact that it was the hiding-place of the notorious Jules Jeanjean.

"Why have you been in Algiers—and in August, too?"

"Not for pleasure," she replied with a grim smile. "The place is a perfect oven just now—as you may well imagine. But I was forced to go."

"Forced against your will, Lola, eh?" I asked, bending towards her, and looking her full in the face very seriously.

"Yes," she admitted, her eyes cast down, "against my will. I had a message to deliver."

"To whom?"

"To my uncle."

"Not a message," I said, correcting her. "Something more valuable than mere words. Is not that so?"

The Nightingale nodded in the affirmative, her blue eyes still downcast in shame.

"Where was your starting-point?" I asked.

"In St. Petersburg, a fortnight ago. I was given the little box in the *Hôtel de l'Europe*, and that night I concealed its contents in the clothes I wore. Some of them I sewed into the hem of my travelling-coat, and, and——"

"Stones they were, I suppose?" I said, interrupting.

"Yes, from Lobenski's, the jeweller's in the Nevski," she replied. "Well, that night I left Petersburg and travelled to Vienna, thence to Trieste, where I found my uncle's yacht awaiting me, and we went down the Adriatic and along the Mediterranean to Algiers. My uncle was already at home. The *coup* was a large one, I believe. Have you seen reports of it in the English papers?" she asked.

"Certainly," I replied. For a fortnight before I had read in several of the newspapers of the daring robbery committed at the shop of Lobenski, the Russian Court Jeweller, and of the theft of a large quantity of diamonds, emeralds, and rubies. The safe, believed to be impregnable, had been fused by an oxygen acetylene jet, and the whole of its contents stolen. From what Lola had revealed, it seemed that Jeanjean had had no actual hand in the theft, for he had been in Algiers awaiting the booty. But he always travelled swiftly after a *coup*.

"Did the papers say much about it?" asked Lola, with interest.

"Oh, just a sensational story," I replied. "But I never dreamt that you were in Russia, Lola—that you had carried the stones across Europe sewn in your dress!"

"Ah! It is not the first time, as you know, M'sieu' Vidal," she sighed. "There is always danger of some customs officer or agent of police recognizing me. But uncle says I am unsuspected, and hence the work is assigned always to me."

"And you have come to England to see me—eh? Why?" I asked, looking again into her clear blue eyes.

"I have come, M'sieu' Vidal, in order to ask a further favour of you—a request I almost fear to make after your great generosity towards me."

"Oh! Don't let us speak of that," I said. "It is all past and over. I only acted as any other man would have done in the circumstances, Lola!"

"You acted as a gentleman would act," she said. "But, alas! How few real gentlemen are met by a wretched girl like myself," she added bitterly. "Suppose you had acted as thousands would have done. Where should I be now? Spending my days in one of your female prisons here."

"Instead of which you are still the little Nightingale, who sings so blithely, and who is so inexpressibly dainty and charming," I said with a smile. "At the best hotels up and down Europe, Lola Sorel is a well-known figure, always ready to flirt with the idle youngsters, and to make herself pleasant to those of her own sex. Only they must be wealthy—eh?"

She made a quick movement as though to arrest the flow of my words.

"You are, alas! right, M'sieu' Vidal," she replied. "Ah, if you only knew how I hate it all—how day by day, hour by hour—I fear that I may blunder and consequently find myself in the hands of the police—if——"

"Never, if you follow your uncle, Jules Jeanjean," I interrupted. "And, I suppose, you are still doing so?"

She sighed heavily, and a hard expression crossed her pretty face.

"Alas! I am forced to. You know the bitter truth, M'sieu' Vidal—the tragedy of my life."

For a few moments I remained silent, my eyes upon her.

I knew full well the strange, romantic story of that pretty French girl seated before me—the sweet, refined little person—scarcely more than a child—whose present, and whose future, were so entirely in the hands of that notorious criminal.

Why had I not telegraphed to the Paris police on discovering Jeanjean's presence in Cromer? For one reason alone. Because his arrest would also mean hers. He had too vowed in my presence that if he were ever taken alive, he would betray his niece, because she had once, in a moment of despair and horror, at one of his cold-blooded crimes, threatened to give him away.

As she sat there, her face sweet and soft as a child's, her blue eyes so clear and innocent, one would never dream that she was the cat's-paw of the most ingenious and dangerous association of jewel thieves in the whole of Europe.

Truly her story was a strange one—one of the strangest of any girl in the world.

She noticed my thoughtfulness, and suddenly put out her little hand until it touched mine; then, looking into my eyes, she asked, in a low, intense voice—

"What are you thinking about?"

"I am thinking of you, Lola," I replied. "I am wondering what really happened in Cromer, back in the month of June. You are here to explain—eh? Will you tell me?"

Her brows contracted slightly, and she drew her hand back from mine.

"You know what happened," she said.

"I don't. Explain it all to me in confidence," I urged. "You surely know me well enough to rely upon my keeping the secret."

"Ah, no!" she cried, starting up suddenly, a strange light of fear in her eyes. "Never, M'sieu' Vidal! I—I can tell you nothing of that—nothing more than what you already know. Please don't ask me—never ask me again, for I—I can't tell you! It was all too dastardly, too terrible!"

And the girl, with a wild gesture, covered her pale face with her little hands as though to shut out from memory the grim recollection of a scene that was full of bitterness and horror.

"But you will tell me the truth, Lola. Do. I beg of you?" I urged, placing my hand tenderly upon her shoulder.

"No," she cried in a voice scarcely above a whisper. "No. Don't ask me. Please don't ask me."

∴

CHAPTER XIII
RELATES A STRANGE STORY

I stood before Lola, grieved at her distress.

Too well I knew, alas! how deeply she had suffered, of all the bitterness and remorse with which her young life was filled, blighted by an ever-present terror, her youth sapped and her ideas warped by living in an atmosphere of criminality.

Rapidly, as I took her little hands in unspoken sympathy, recollections of our strangely-made acquaintanceship ran through my memory, and before me arose a truly dramatic and impressive scene.

I had first seen Lola, two years before, seated alone at luncheon in the pretty salle-à-manger of the *Hôtel d'Angleterre* in Copenhagen. Many eyes were upon her because of her youth and beauty, and many men sitting at the various tables cast admiring glances at her.

I was with my friend, Jack Bellairs, and we were breaking our journey for a few days in the Danish capital, before going up to Norway salmon-fishing.

Jack first noted her, and drew my attention to the fact that she was alone. At the time, I knew nothing of the two men who were lunching together at another table at the further end of the room, and that the name of one of them was Jules Jeanjean.

The girl, we discovered from the concierge, had been living alone in the hotel for a month, and had become on very friendly terms with a certain very wealthy Hungarian lady, the Baroness Függer, of Budapest. She accompanied the Baroness everywhere, but the reason she was lunching alone that morning was because the Baroness was absent for the day at Elsinore.

During the next day or two we saw the stately old lady, whose chief delight seemed to be the ostentatious display of jewellery, constantly in Lola's company. The girl, though admired everywhere, treated all the men about her with utter unconcern, being most modest and reserved.

On the fourth morning of our stay, at about ten o'clock, the hotel was thrown into the greatest commotion by an amazing report that the Baroness's bedroom had been entered during the night and the whole contents of her jewel-case stolen. The police were at once called, and were mystified by the fact that the Baroness had locked her door before retiring, and that it was still locked when she awoke in the morning. Therefore, it seemed that the jewels had been abstracted immediately before she had entered the room on the previous night—stolen by some one well acquainted with their hiding-place—for the jewel-case was kept for safety at the bottom of a trunk full of soiled linen.

Naturally the police inquired if any of the visitors had left the hotel since the previous night, but no person had left. All the visitors who had been in the hotel the previous day at noon were still there. The night-porter had not noticed anything suspicious, and nobody had heard any unusual sound during the night.

All of us in the hotel were closely interrogated, including Lola, who preserved an air of deepest regret that her dear friend, the Baroness, should have been so ingeniously robbed. Indeed, it was during that interrogation that I had first exchanged words with her.

"I can't understand it," she had declared to me in French. "I was in the Baroness's room until she returned at a quarter to twelve, and I am quite sure the jewels were there because, when she took off her diamond necklace, I got out the case, and placed it with the other jewels."

"The case might then have been already empty," said the Commissary of Police, who was making the investigation.

"It might have been, of course," replied the girl. "But the diamond necklet is no longer there!"

Well, to go into the whole details of the inquiry is unnecessary. Suffice it to say that, though the police searched everywhere, and the Baroness indignantly invoked the aid of her Legation, nothing was ever recovered, and at last I departed for Norway, leaving the Baroness still enjoying the bright companionship of the young and pretty Lola.

The two sedate visitors, one of whom I knew later on as Jules Jeanjean, also remained idling their days in the pleasant city, awaiting the conclusion of a business deal, but, of course, holding no communication with the fair-haired young girl.

After that, quite a year passed, and I found myself, in the course of my erratic wanderings, guest of Lord Bracondale at a shooting-party at Balmaclellan Castle, up in Kirkcudbrightshire—in that wild, lonely, heather-clad land which lies between New Galloway and the Solway Firth.

As is well known, the Earl and Countess of Bracondale surround themselves with a very smart set, and the party in question was a big one. Indeed, most of the rooms in the historic Scottish Castle were occupied, and while there was good sport by day, there was at night much dancing in the fine old ball-room, and much bridge-playing.

In the midst of all the gaiety came the County Ball at Dumfries, to which the whole party went over, the ladies eclipsing each other with their jewels, as the function is always one of the smartest in Scotland.

My room at the castle, a big oak-panelled one, was in the east wing, at the top of a steep flight of spiral stairs set in a corner tower, and on the night following that of the ball, at about half-past two in the morning, I awoke, and lay thinking, when I fancied I heard somebody moving about, outside my door.

I strained my ears to listen.

The room next mine, further along the corridor, was occupied by a Mrs. Forbes Wilson, the widow of the well-known American millionaire, while further beyond slept Lady Oxborough, and beyond these were several other visitors' rooms.

I suppose I must have listened for nearly a quarter of an hour, drowsily wondering who could be on the move, when suddenly I was thoroughly roused by hearing a sharp click. The door of the room adjoining mine had been closed!

This struck me as distinctly curious, because, only at six o'clock the previous evening, Mrs. Forbes Wilson had been called away suddenly to the bedside of her little daughter, who had been taken ill at Wigton, where she was stopping with friends. The widow had taken her maid with her, and left very hurriedly, leaving her luggage behind, and promising to return next day if there was nothing seriously wrong with her child.

Some one was moving about in her room!

I lay there wondering. But as the minutes passed, and I heard no further sound, I began to believe that my imagination had deceived me. I had almost dozed off to sleep again when suddenly a brilliant ray of electricity shot across my room—the light of a small electric torch—and I was immediately aware that my own door had been opened noiselessly, and an intruder had entered.

Quick as thought I sprang out of bed in my pyjamas, but, as I did so, I heard a woman's light scream, while the torch was instantly extinguished.

I was at the door, behind the intruder, and when, next moment, I switched on the light, to my astonishment I found myself confronted with Lola Sorel!

"You!" I gasped, as the girl shrank from me against the wall, her face white as death. "You—Mademoiselle! What is the meaning of this visit—eh?"

"Will you—will you close the door, M'sieur?" she begged in a low whisper, in broken English. "Some one may overhear."

I did as she bade, and slipped on my dressing-gown, which was hanging over the foot-rail of the bed.

"Well?" I asked, with a good deal of severity, for I saw by her manner that she was there for some nefarious purpose. She was dressed in plain black, with a neat little velvet cap, and wore slippers with rubber soles. Her hands were covered with india-rubber gloves, such as surgeons often wear when operating or making post-mortem examinations. Her electric torch was attached to her wrist, while, beneath her dark golf-coat, which fell open, I saw that she wore around her waist a capacious bag of black silk.

"I—I never dreamed that this was your room, M'sieur," the girl declared, terrified. "I—I——"

But she did not conclude her sentence, for she realized how completely she had been trapped. Her pretty countenance betrayed terror in every line, her eyes were staring and haggard, and her hands were trembling.

"I—I—know there is no escape," she said with her pleasing French accent. "You are aware of the truth, M'sieur—of what occurred in Copenhagen. Ah, yes. It is Fate that you and I should again meet—and in these circumstances."

"Please be seated, Mademoiselle," I said. "You have no cause for alarm. Naturally, this encounter has upset you."

I feared that she might faint, therefore I went to the table where, on the previous night, the valet had placed some brandy and a siphon of soda. Mixing a little, I gave it to her to drink.

"This will do you good," I said.

Then, when she had swallowed it, I asked her to explain the reason of her nocturnal visit to the castle.

She looked a pale, pathetic little figure, seated there before me, her fair head bowed with shame and confusion, her terrified eyes staring into space.

"I—I—am entirely in your hands, M'sieur," she stammered at last. "I came here to thieve, because—because I am forced to do so. It was work of peril for all three of us—for me most of all. This room was the last I intended to visit—and in it I found the very last person I wished to meet—you!"

"Tell me more about yourself," I urged. "I'm greatly interested."

"What is there to tell you?" she cried, her eyes filling with bitter tears. "I am a thief—that's all. You are a guest here—and it is your duty to your host to keep me here, and call the police. Jules was watching on the stairs below. By this time he knows you have trapped me, and they have both escaped—without a doubt—escaped with the stuff I handed to them ten minutes ago."

"Jules? Who is he?" I asked quickly.

"Jules Jeanjean—my uncle," she replied.

"Jules Jeanjean!" I ejaculated, "that man!" for the name was synonymous for all that was audacious and criminal.

"Yes, M'sieur."

"And he is your uncle?"

"Yes. At his instigation I am forced to do these things against my will," she declared in a hard, bitter voice. "Ah, if only you knew—if you knew everything, M'sieur, I believe you would have pity and compassion for me—you would allow me one more chance—a chance to escape—a chance to try once more to break away from these hateful men who hold me in the hollow of their hands!"

She spoke so fervently, so earnestly, that her appeal sank deeply into my heart. By her despairing manner I saw that she hoped for no clemency, for no sympathy, especially from me, who had actually been suspected of the robbery in Copenhagen which she and her confederates had committed.

"What have you in that bag?" I asked, indicating the black silk bag beneath her coat.

She placed her small hand into it and slowly and shamefacedly drew forth a splendid collar of large pearls.

"I took it from the next room," she said briefly. "I will replace it if—if only you would allow me to get away," she added wistfully.

"And the other stuff you have stolen?"

"Ah! My uncle has it. He has already gone—carrying it with him!"

"Deserted you—and left you to your fate—as soon as he realized the danger," I remarked. "The coward!"

"Yes. But it was fortunate that you did not come out of this room—upon the stairs," she said.

"Why?"

"Because he would have killed you with as little compunction as he would kill a fly," she replied slowly.

"I quite believe that. His reputation is known all over Europe," I said. "Mine was, no doubt, a fortunate escape."

"Will you let me put these pearls back?" she asked eagerly.

"No. Leave them on the table. I will replace them," I said.

"Then, what do you intend doing with me?" she asked very seriously. "Only allow me to go, and I shall always be grateful to you, M'sieur—grateful to you all my life."

And with a sudden movement she took my hand in hers, and looked so earnestly into my eyes, that I stood before her fascinated by her wonderful beauty.

The scene was indeed a strange one. She pleaded to me for her liberty, pleaded to me, throwing herself wildly upon her knees, covering her face with her hands, and bursting into a torrent of hot, bitter tears.

My duty, both towards my host and towards the guests whose jewellery had been stolen by that silent-footed, expert little thief, was to raise the alarm, and hand her over to the police.

Yet so pitiful was her appeal, so tragic the story she had briefly related to me, so earnest her promise never to offend again, that I confess I could not bring myself to commit her to prison.

I saw that she was but the unwilling cat's-paw of the most dangerous criminal in Europe. Therefore, I gently assisted her to rise to her feet and began to further question her.

In confidence she told me her address in Paris—a flat in the Boulevard Pereire—and then, after nearly half an hour's further conversation, I said—

"Very well, Lola. You shall leave here, and I hope to see you in Paris very shortly. I hope, too, that you will succeed in breaking away from your uncle and his associates and so have a chance to live a life of honesty."

"Ah!" she sighed, gripping my hand with heartfelt thanks, as she turned to creep from the room, and down the stairs. "Ah! If I could! If I only could. *Au revoir*, M'sieur. You are indeed generous. I—I owe my life to you—*au revoir!*"

And, then? Well, she had slipped noiselessly down the winding stair, while I had taken the pearl necklace and replaced it in the room of Mrs. Forbes Wilson.

Imagine the consternation next morning, when it was discovered that burglars had entered the place, and had got clean away with jewellery worth in all about thirty thousand pounds.

I watched the investigations made by the police, who were summoned from Dumfries by telephone.

But I remained silent, and kept the secret of little Lola Sorel to myself.

And here she was, once again—standing before me!

CHAPTER XIV
WHEREIN CONFESSION IS MADE

"Well, Lola," I said at last, still holding her little hand in mine, "and why cannot you reveal to me the truth regarding the mystery of the death of Edward Craig?"

"For a very good reason—because I do not myself know the exact circumstances," was her prompt response, dropping into French. "I know that you have made an investigation. What have you discovered?"

"If you will be frank with me," I said, also in French, "I will be equally frank with you."

"But, have I not always been frank?" she protested. "Have I not always told you the truth, ever since that night in Scotland when you trapped me in your room. Don't you remember?"

"Yes," I replied in a low voice. "I remember, alas! too well. You promised in return for your liberty that you would break away from your uncle."

"Ah, I did—but I have been utterly unable, M'sieur Vidal," she cried quickly in her broken English. "You don't know how much I have suffered this past year—how terrible is my present position," she added in a tone of poignant bitterness.

"Yes, I quite understand and sympathize with you," I said, taking out a cigarette and lighting it, while she sat back in the big old-fashioned horsehair arm-chair. "For weeks I have been endeavouring to find you—after you came to Cromer to call upon me. You have left the Boulevard Pereire."

"Yes. I have been travelling constantly of late."

"After the affair of the jeweller, Benoy—eh? Where were you at that time?"

"In Marseilles, awaiting my uncle. We crossed to Algiers together. Thence we went along to Alexandria, and on to Cairo, where we met our friends."

"It was a dastardly business. I read of it in the *Matin*," I said.

"Brutal—horrible!" declared the girl. "But is not my uncle an inhuman brute—a fearless, desperate man, who carries out, with utter disregard of human life, the amazing plots which are formed by one who is the master of all the criminal arts."

"Then he is not the prime mover of all these ingenious thefts?" I exclaimed in some surprise, for I had always believed Jules Jeanjean to be the head of that international band.

"No. He acts under the direction of another, a man of amazing ingenuity and colossal intellect. It is he who cleverly investigates, and gains knowledge of those who possess rare jewels; he who watches craftily for opportunities, who so carefully plans the *coups*, and who afterwards arranges for the stones to be re-cut in Antwerp or Amsterdam."

"Who is he?" I asked eagerly. "You may tell me in confidence. I will not betray your secret."

"He poses as a dealer in precious stones in London."

"In London?"

"Yes. He has an office in Hatton Garden, and is believed by other dealers in precious stones to be a most respectable member of that select little coterie that deals in gems."

"What is his name?"

The girl was silent for a few seconds. Then she said—

"In Cromer he has been known under the name of Vernon Gregory."

"Gregory!" I gasped in astonishment. "What, to that quiet old man is due the conception of all these great and daring robberies committed by Jules Jeanjean?"

"Yes. My uncle acts upon plans and information which the old man supplies," Lola replied. "Being in the trade, the crafty old fellow knows in whose hands lie the most valuable stones, and then lays his cunningly-prepared plans accordingly—plans that my uncle desperately carries out to the very letter."

This statement much surprised me, for I had always regarded Jeanjean as the instigator of the plots. But now, it appeared, old Gregory was the head of Europe's most dangerous association of criminals.

"Then the jewels found in Gregory's rooms at Cromer were all stolen property?"

"Yes. We were surprised that the police did not discover the real owners," Lola replied. "The greater part of the jewels were taken from the castle of the Grand Duke Alexander of Russia, just outside Kiev, about nine months ago."

"By you?" I asked with a grim smile.

"Not all. Some," admitted the girl with a light laugh. Then she continued: "We expected that when the old gentleman made such a hurried flight from Cromer, the police would recognize the property from the circulated description. But, as they did not, Uncle determined to regain possession of it—which he did."

"Who aided him?"

"Egisto—a man who is generally known as Egisto Bertini."

"The man who rode the motor-cycle?"

She nodded.

"And you assisted," I said. "Why did you leave your shoe behind?"

"By accident. I thought I heard some of the occupants of the house stirring, so fled without having an opportunity of recovering it. I suppose it has puzzled the local police—eh?" she laughed merrily.

"It did. You were all very clever, and my man, Rayner, was rendered insensible."

"Because he was a trifle too inquisitive. He was watching, and did not know that my uncle, in such expeditions, has eyes in the back of his head," she answered. "It was fortunate for him that he was not killed outright, for, as you know, my uncle always, alas! believes in the old maxim that dead men tell no tales."

"The assassin!" I cried in fierce anger. "He will have many crimes to answer for when at last the police lay hands upon him."

"He will never be taken alive," she said. "He will denounce me, and then kill himself. That is what he constantly threatens."

"And because of that you fear to hold aloof and defy him?" I asked. "You live in constant terror, Lola."

"Yes. How can I act—how can I escape them? Advise me," she urged, her face pale and intensely in earnest.

I hesitated. It was certainly a difficult matter upon which to give advice. The pretty girl before me had for several years been the unwilling tool of that scoundrelly gang of bandits, whose organization was so perfect that they were never arrested, nor was any of their booty ever traced.

The four or five men acting under the direction of the master-mind of old Gregory were, in private life, all of them affluent and respected citizens, either in England or in France, while Jules Jeanjean, I afterwards learned, occupied a big white villa overlooking the blue sea three miles out of Algiers. It was a place with wonderful gardens filled with high date-palms and brilliant tropical flowers. There, in his hours of retirement, Jules Jeanjean lived amid the most artistic and luxurious surroundings, with many servants, and a couple of motor-cars, devoting himself to experiments in wireless telegraphy, having fitted up a powerful station for both receiving and transmitting.

The science of wireless telegraphy was indeed his chief hobby, and he spent many hours in listening to the messages from Pold, Poldhu, Clifden, Soller, Paris, Port Said, or Norddeich on the North Sea, in communicating with ships in the Mediterranean, the Adriatic, the Levant, or on the Atlantic.

I was wondering how to advise my little friend. Ever since our first meeting my heart had been full of sympathy and compassion for her, so frail seemed her frame, so tragic her life, and so fettered did she seem to that disreputable gang. Yet, had she not pointed out to me, on the several occasions on which we had met in Paris, the impossibility of breaking the bonds which bound her to that detestable life? Indeed she had, more than once, declared our meetings to be filled with peril for myself.

Her uncle knew me by repute as an investigator of crime, and if he ever suspected me of prying into any affair in which he might be concerned, then my life would most certainly be in jeopardy. Jules Jeanjean never did things by halves. It was, I found, for that reason she had now sought me—to beseech me to relinquish my efforts to fathom the mystery of the death of Edward Craig.

"Do heed what I say, M'sieur Vidal," she exclaimed with deep earnestness. "My uncle knows that you are still in Cromer, and that you have been investigating. In Algiers, a fortnight ago, he mentioned it to me, and declared that very shortly you would cease to trouble him."

"He intends foul play—eh?" I remarked with a grim smile, lighting another cigarette.

"He means mischief," she assured me. "He knows, too well, of your success in other cases in which you have interested yourself," she remarked quickly. "And he fears—fears lest you may discover the secret of the young man's death."

"And if I do?" I asked, looking straight into her face.

"He does not intend that you shall," she replied very earnestly, adding: "Ah! M'sieur Vidal, do heed my words—I beg you. Be warned by me!"

"But, why?" I queried. "I am not afraid of Jules Jeanjean. I have never done him an evil turn. Therefore, why should he conspire to take my life? Besides, I already know of his connexion with the Cromer mystery, the Benoy affair, and others. Could I not easily have sent a telegram to the Prefecture of Police in Paris, when I recognized him in Cromer? But I did not."

"Why?"

"For two reasons. First, I wished to stand aside and watch, and, secondly, I feared to betray him for your sake, Lola."

"Ah!" she exclaimed. "But you are always so generous. You know quite well that he already believes that I have told you the truth. Therefore, he suspects us both and is determined to put an end to your inquisitiveness."

"Unless I act swiftly—eh?" I suggested.

"But think—what would then become of me?" she exclaimed, her eyes open in quick alarm.

"I can't see what you really have to fear," I said. "It is true, Lola, that you live, like your friends, by dishonest methods, but have you not been forced into it by your uncle? Even if you were arrested, the law would treat you with the greatest leniency. Indeed, if necessary, I would come forward and tell the Court all I have known and discovered concerning the baneful influence which has been exercised upon you by the man Jeanjean."

She shook her head mournfully.

"Alas! That would be of no avail," she declared in a low, strained voice.

"Why?"

"Because—because, ah!—you do not know the truth," she faltered, her face pale to the lips.

"Cannot you explain it to me?" I asked, bending down to her, and placing my hand tenderly upon her shoulder.

I felt her shudder beneath my touch, while her big blue eyes were downcast—downcast in shame.

"No. I cannot explain," she replied. "If you knew, M'sieur Vidal, how horrible, how terrible all this is for me, you would not press your question."

"But I do—in your interests," I said with deep earnestness. "I want to help you to escape from these scoundrels—I want to stand as your friend."

"My friend!" she exclaimed blankly. "My friend—ah! that you can never be."

"Why not?"

"You would not wish to cultivate my acquaintance further, M'sieur Vidal, if—if you were aware of the actual truth. Besides, this friendship which you have shown to me may, in itself, prove fatal to you. If you do not exercise the greatest precaution, your reward for saving me, as you did that night at Balmaclellan, will be death!"

"You are apprehensive on my account?" I asked, wondering whether she were really in earnest—or whether beneath her strange warning there lay some subtle motive.

"Yes," was her frank response. "Take great care, or death will come to you at a moment when you least expect it."

For an instant I was silent. Her warning was truly a curious and disconcerting one, for I knew the dangerous character of Jules Jeanjean. That if he threatened, he meant action.

"I do not care for myself, Lola," I said at last. "I am thinking how I can protect you, and rescue you from the hands of these unscrupulous men."

"You cannot," she declared, with a hard, fixed look of desperation. "No, only be careful of yourself, and, at the same time, dismiss me from your thoughts. I—I am unworthy of your regard," she murmured, her voice choked by a sob. "Alas, entirely unworthy!"

"No, no," I urged. "I will not allow you to speak like that, Lola. Ever since you entered my room, on that well-remembered night in Scotland, I have wondered how best I could assist you to lead an honest life; how I could——"

"I can accept no further assistance from you, M'sieur Vidal," she interposed, in a quivering voice. "I repeat that I am utterly unworthy," she cried, and shivered with despair, as she stood erect before me. "And—and—if you only knew the truth—the terrible truth of the past—you would at once, I know, turn and discard me—nay, you would probably ring for the waiter and hand me over to the police without either compunction or regret."

And the girl, known as "The Nightingale," stood before me, her face white and hard, her eyes with a strange light in them, staring straight before her, her breast heaving and falling with emotion which she was trying in vain to suppress.

CHAPTER XV
CONFIRMS CERTAIN SUSPICIONS

For yet another hour we sat together, but Lola would reveal nothing further.

She only repeated that serious warning, urging me to abandon this investigation of the strange affair at Cromer.

She refused to tell me the name under which old Gregory was known in Hatton Garden, and she likewise firmly declined to give me any information concerning the curious code which had been found in Gregory's room. Indeed, she affected ignorance of it, as well as of the mysterious spot in Ealing "where the two C's meet."

"My uncle is in Antwerp," she told me in reply to a question. "I join him to-morrow, and then we go travelling—where, I have no idea. But you know how erratic and sudden our movements necessarily are. The master usually meets my uncle in Antwerp, going there regularly in the guise of a diamond merchant."

"And you will not tell me the master's real name?" I asked persuasively.

"I am not allowed. If you discover it for yourself, then I shall not be to blame," she said, with a meaning smile. "But do, I beg of you, give up the search, M'sieu' Vidal. It can only end fatally if you still persist."

"You have warned me, Lola, and I thank you sincerely for doing so, but I shall continue to act as I have begun."

"At your own peril—a deadly peril!" she ejaculated, with an apprehensive look.

"I must accept the risk," I said quietly. "And I intend to still stand your friend, Lola."

"But you must not, you cannot!" she protested. "Of course I most deeply appreciate all that you have done for me—and how generous you have been, knowing that I am, alas! what I am. But I will not allow you to risk your life further on my account."

"That is really my own affair."

"No. It is mine. I am here to-day, in secret, solely to warn you—to ask you—to give up this inquiry, and allow the matter to rest a mystery," she protested. "Will you not do this for my sake?" she pleaded.

For a few seconds I paused, smiling at her. Then I replied—

"No. I cannot promise that. Young Craig was foully murdered, of that I am confident, and I intend to unravel the mystery."

"Even though it costs you your life?" she asked slowly.

Why, I wondered, was she so frantically anxious for me to abandon the inquiry? Was it really because she feared that her uncle might attempt to rid himself of me, or had she some other hidden motive?

The expression upon her sweet face had altered. It was eager and apprehensive—a curious look, such as I had never witnessed there before.

Deeply in earnest, she was persuading me, with all the arts of which she, as a woman, was capable to give up the investigation—why?

My refusal evidently caused her the greatest anxiety—even deadly fear. She would, however, reveal nothing more to me. Therefore, I told her point-blank that I would make her no promise.

"But you will think over my words," she said earnestly. "You will be forewarned of the evil that is intended!"

"If there is evil, then I will combat it," I replied briefly. "My first concern is yourself, Lola. Do you remember our confidential talks when we strolled together in the Bois—when you told me all your troubles, and your fears?"

"Yes," she replied in a strange, dreary voice. "But—but, I did not tell you all. You do not know," she added in a whisper.

"Tell me all," I urged. "I know you are—well, let us say it quite plainly—a thief."

"Ah! If I were only *that*, I might dare to look you in the face—to crave your sympathy—your interest—your generosity once again. But I cannot. No! I cannot," and she burst into tears.

"Are we not friends?" I queried. "And between friends surely there may be confidences."

"To a certain degree, yes. But there is a limit even to confidences between friends," was her slow, thoughtful reply, as she dried her eyes with a little wisp of lace.

I was disappointed. I had fully expected to obtain from her some clue which might lead to a solution of the mystery of Craig's death. But she was obdurate.

"Lola," I said, taking her trembling hand again, "I wish to tell you something."

"Well, what is it?" she asked.

"Simply this. I think I ought to tell you that, near that seat on the cliff at Cromer, where Craig was found, there was discovered a clear print of a lady's shoe," and I watched her countenance narrowly.

Her face went paler in an instant, and in her eyes showed a quick look of terror. But in a second she had recovered herself, and said—

"That is interesting. Do you think that its presence there gives any clue to the assassin?"

"I don't know," was my reply. I stood before her in wonder. Her perfect sang-froid was truly amazing. "But," I went on, "curiously enough, the same lady's shoe was found in Beacon House, after Gregory's property had been carried off. It fitted exactly the imprint in the sand near the seat."

The only sign that her mind was perturbed by my knowledge was a slight twitching at the corners of her pretty mouth. Yes, she preserved an astounding calm.

"That is curious," she remarked with unconcern.

"Very," I declared, still gazing fixedly into her white face. "And can you tell me nothing further regarding this affair?" I asked, bending to her, and speaking in a whisper.

She shook her head.

I did not suspect—nay, I could not bring myself to believe—that Edward Craig had fallen by her hand. Yet the facts were strange—amazingly strange—and her demeanour was stranger still.

We had tea together. She poured it out, and handed it to me daintily, with a sweet smile upon her lips. Then after a further chat, she drew on her long gloves, settled her skirts and prepared to leave.

"A letter addressed to the Poste Restante at Versailles will always find me," she said, in reply to my request for an address. "I use the name Elise Leblanc."

I made a rapid note of it upon my shirt-cuff, and having paid the bill, we descended, and walked together, through the busy streets of Norwich, to the Thorpe Station, where I saw her into the evening express for London.

"*Au revoir*, M'sieu' Vidal," she said, as she held my hand, before entering the first-class compartment. "Do heed my warning, I beg of you. Do not further imperil yourself. Will you?"

"I cannot promise," I replied with a smile.

"But you must not persist—or something will most surely happen," she declared. "*Au revoir!* If we meet again it must be in the strictest secrecy. My uncle must never know."

"*Au revoir!*" I said as the porter closed the door, and next moment the train moved off.

I saw her face smiling, and a white-gloved hand waving at the window, and then "The Nightingale" had gone.

A fortnight went by. I had packed my traps, and leaving Cromer, returned to my rooms in London, and then crossed to Paris, where I spent a week in close, anxious inquiry.

Paris in August is given over to the Cookites and provincials, and most of my friends were absent.

The Prefecture of Police was, however, the chief centre of my sphere of operations, for in that sombre room, with its large, littered writing-table, its telephones, its green-painted walls, and green-baize covered door, the private cabinet of my friend Henri Jonet—the famous Chief Inspector of the Sûreté—I sat on several occasions discussing the activity of Jeanjean and his clever gang.

Jonet was a sharp-featured, clean-shaven man of about forty-five, short and slightly stout, with a pair of merry dark eyes, his hair carefully brushed and trousers always well creased. He was something of a dandy in private life, even though he so often assumed various disguises, passing very frequently as a camelot, or a respectable workman. Of his successes in detection of crime all the world knew.

Next to the Chef de la Sûreté, Chief Inspector Jonet was the most famous police official in Paris, or even in France. In the course of the past few years he had many times dealt unsuccessfully with crimes in which the amazing Jules Jeanjean had been implicated.

I had on many occasions assisted him in his investigations into other matters, and, therefore, on the sultry afternoon, when I called and presented my card, I was shown up immediately into his private bureau—that dismal and rather depressing room, which I so well remembered.

We sat smoking together for a long time before I approached the subject upon which I had called to consult him.

He sat back in his chair enjoying the excellent Bogdanoff cigarette, a fellow to which he had handed to me, and recalling a strange affair that, a year ago, had occupied us both—a theft of bonds from a private bank in the Boulevard Haussmann.

Outside, the afternoon was blazing hot, therefore the green sun-shutters were closed, and the room was in semi-darkness. Jonet's big writing-table was piled with reports and correspondence, as well as one or two recently-arrived photographs of persons wanted by the police authorities of other European countries.

Now and then the telephone buzzed, and he would reply, and give instructions in a quick, sharp voice. Then he turned to me again and continued our conversation.

"The Benoy affair in March last was a sensational one—the murder of the jeweller while in his motor-car in the Forest of Fontainebleau—you remember," I remarked presently in French, leaning back in my chair and puffing at my cigarette. "You made no arrest, did you?"

"Yes, several. But we didn't get the culprits," he replied with a dry smile. "It was our friend Jules Jeanjean again, without a doubt. But he and his accomplices got clean away in the stolen car. It was found two days later a mile out of Mâcon, painted grey, and bearing another number. The bandits evidently took train."

"Where to?"

"Who knows? Back to Paris, perhaps," was his reply, flicking the ash from his cigarette. "Yet, though we made a close search, we found no trace whatever of the interesting Jules. *Sapristi!* I only wish I could lay hands upon him. He is undoubtedly the most daring and dangerous criminal in the whole of Europe," Jonet went on. "Of late we have had reports of his doings from Germany and Russia, but he always escapes. A big jewel robbery in Petersburg is his latest clever exploit. Yet how he disposes of his booty always puzzles me. He must get rid of it somewhere, and yet we never find any trace of it."

I said nothing. From his words I saw how utterly ignorant even Jonet was of the truth, and how little he suspected the actual fact that Jeanjean was not the originator of those ingenious crimes but merely the instrument of another and a master-brain.

The great police official drew a long sigh, and expressed wonder as to whether the elusive jewel-thief and assassin would ever fall into the hands of justice.

"At present he seems to bear quite a charmed life," he declared with a smile. "He openly defies us each time—sometimes even going the length of writing us an insulting letter, denouncing us as incompetent and heaping ridicule upon the whole department of the *Sûreté*. It is that which makes my officers so intensely keen to capture him."

"I fear you will never do so," I remarked.

"Why?"

"Because Jeanjean is too clever to be caught. He is wary, rich, and takes every precaution against surprise."

"You know him—eh?"

"Yes," I admitted. "But what is the latest information you have regarding him?"

Jonet took up the telephone and gave instructions for the dossier of the great criminal to be brought to him.

In a few moments a clerk entered bearing three formidable portfolios full of reports, photographs, lists of stolen jewellery, and other matters concerning the career of the man who had constantly baffled all attempts to capture him.

Jonet opened one of the portfolios and scanned several sheets of closely-written reports. Then he said—

"It seems that he, with a young girl, said to be a niece of his, were in Russia just prior to the great robbery from a jeweller in Petersburg. No doubt they were implicated in it. The girl, travelling alone, passed the frontier at Wirballen on the following day, but the telegram from the Petersburg police arrived at the frontier too late, and in Germany she disappeared."

"And what about Jeanjean?" I asked.

The famous Chief Inspector read on for a few moments. Then he replied—

"He was seen on the day of the theft, together with an Italian, believed to be one of his accomplices, but after that nothing further was heard of him until four days later. Then an inspector at Lille recognized him from his circulated photograph, but not being quite certain, and also knowing that, if the suspect were actually the man wanted, he would be armed, and recollecting the affair at Charleroi, he did not care to make a pounce single-handed. He went back to the police-station, but while he was looking for the photograph, his man, evidently seeing he was suspected, made his escape."

"And have you a photograph of the girl?" I asked anxiously.

"She has never been arrested, therefore we have no official portrait," was his reply. "But last summer, one of my assistants, a young man named Rothera, was in Dinard at the *Hôtel Royal*, keeping observation in another matter, when one evening he saw a young girl, who was staying in the hotel with an elderly aunt, meet in the Casino a man who greatly resembled

Jeanjean. The pair went out and had a long stroll, speaking confidentially together. Meanwhile Rothera, like the inspector at Lille, went to the local bureau de police to turn up the description of the wanted man. Having done so, and having satisfied himself that it was actually the master-criminal so long wanted, he took three men and waited in patience in the country road along which the pair had strolled. Two hours elapsed, when, to their dismay, the young girl returned alone. Jeanjean, it was afterwards discovered, had a motor-car awaiting him about four kilometres away along the Dinan road. Rothera said nothing to the girl, but next day got into conversation with her in the hotel. He was exceedingly attentive through several succeeding days, and being an amateur photographer, asked to be allowed to take a snapshot of her. He had satisfied himself that, from her description, she was that female accomplice of the notorious jewel-thief, of whom we possessed no portrait. She, quite unsuspecting, believed Rothera to be an idle young man of means. He took the picture—and here it is," added the Inspector, and passed over to me a photograph of post-card size.

It was Lola. Lola, in a pretty white summer gown, lolling lazily in a long cane chair upon the beach at Dinard, and laughing merrily, her hat flung upon the ground, and her book in her lap. A pretty scene of summer idleness.

CHAPTER XVI
"WHERE THE TWO C'S MEET"

So Lola's portrait was in the hands of the French police. The fact jarred upon me.

But I was careful not to betray any of the agitation I felt, and after gazing upon it in silence I remarked in a light tone to Jonet—

"That is the only portrait you've got—eh? Rather good-looking, isn't she?"

"Good-looking! Ah, mon cher Vidal, extremely beautiful, I call her," declared the Inspector, taking the picture and gazing upon it. "Really," he added, "it hardly seems possible that such a pretty girl should be such a hardened and expert thief as she is reported to be."

"I thought Jeanjean was the thief," I said with a pretence of surprise.

Jonet lit a fresh cigarette, after offering me one. Then he said—

"It is on record here," and he tapped the damning portfolio that lay under his hand, "that in at least half a dozen cases the methods have been the same. The Nightingale—as the girl, whose real name is Lola Sorel, but who has a dozen aliases—is called by her friends, goes with her maid to one of the smartest hotels, say at Carlsbad, Nice, Aix, Trouville, or London, Berlin, anywhere, where there are usually wealthy women. She is a modest little person, and makes a long stay, keeping her blue eyes well open for any visitor possessed of valuable jewellery. Having fixed upon one, she carefully cultivates the lady's acquaintance, is extremely affable, and soon becomes on such intimate terms with her that she is admitted to her bedroom, and is then able to discover where the lady's jewels are kept—whether the case is sufficiently small to be portable, and if not, what kind of lock it has. Every detail she carefully notes and passes on to Jeanjean, who, when the *coup* is ready, appears from nowhere. He is too wary to stay in the same hotel."

"Then the girl has a maid with her!" I exclaimed.

"Invariably," was Jonet's reply. "But the methods by which the robberies are carried out are varied. In some cases the pretty Lola has simply seized an opportunity to transfer her 'friend's' jewel-case to her own room, whence it has been abstracted in her absence by Jeanjean. In other cases while she has been out with the owner of the jewels, motoring, or shopping, or at the theatre, Jeanjean, having had the tip from his niece, has slipped in and secured the valuables. Again this method has been varied by Lola stealing the best piece from the victim's room and in the night handing it to Jeanjean from her bedroom window, as was done at Cannes last winter, when the Princess Tynarowski lost her diamond collar after a brief acquaintance with the fascinating Lola. The latter remained in the hotel for nearly a fortnight following the theft and left still enjoying the greatest friendship of the unsuspecting victim."

"Then this girl must be very clever and daring," I exclaimed.

"Yes. She is the tool of that scoundrel Jeanjean," declared Jonet, closing the dossier. "Poor girl. Probably she acts entirely against her will. The brute has her in his power, as so many girls are in the power of unscrupulous men in the criminal under-world. They, in their innocence, commit one crime, perhaps unconsciously, and for years afterwards they are threatened with exposure to us; so, in order to purchase their liberty, they are forced to become thieves and adventuresses. Ah, yes, mon cher Vidal, that is a curious and tragic side of criminal life, one of which the world never dreams."

"Then you do not believe this girl is really a criminal from instinct?" I asked eagerly.

"No. She is under the all-compelling influence of Jeanjean, who will not hesitate to take a life if it suits him; the man who has set at naught every law of our civilized existence."

"Her position must be one full of terror," I said.

"Yes. Poor girl. Though I have never seen her, to my knowledge, yet I, even though I am a police functionary, cannot help feeling pity for her. Think what a girl forced into crime by such a man must suffer! Rothera in his report says she is extremely refined and full of personal charm."

"That is why wealthy women find her such a pleasant and engaging companion, I suppose."

"No doubt. Most middle-aged women take an interest in a pretty girl, especially if she can tell a good story of her unhappiness with her parents, or of some sorrowful love affair," remarked Jonet. "I expect she can romance as well as you can, my friend," he laughed. "And you are a professional writer."

"Better, in all probability," I rejoined, also laughing. "At any rate it seems that, by her romances, this fellow Jeanjean reaps a golden harvest."

"And I dare say her profits are not very much," said the police official. "He probably pays all her hotel bills, and gives her a little over for pocket money."

"And the maid?"

"Ah! She must be one of the gang. They would never risk being given away by one who was not in the swim. The maid, if she were in ignorance of what went on, would very quickly scent some mystery, for each time her young mistress found a new friend in an hotel she would notice that jewels invariably were reported missing, and a hue and cry raised. No. The maid is an accomplice, and at this moment I am doing all I can to fix the interesting pair."

"And you will arrest them?"

"Of course," he replied determinedly. "I sympathize with the pretty little thief, yet I have my duty to perform. Besides, if I have the interesting little lady here before me for interrogation, I shall, I think, not be very long before I discover our friend Jeanjean in his secret hiding-place."

I did not answer for several minutes.

A trap had evidently been laid for Lola, and, in her own interests, she should be warned.

Continuing, I further questioned my friend, and he told me some astounding stories of Jeanjean's elusiveness. I, however, said nothing of what I knew. I remained silent regarding the curious affair in Cromer, and as to my knowledge that the pretty villa near Algiers concealed the man for whom all the police of Europe were in search.

My chief concern was for Lola, and that same evening I wrote to her at the Poste Restante at Versailles giving her warning of what was intended. She was probably in Brussels, but in due course would, no doubt, receive my letter, and see me again, as I requested.

On two other occasions I saw Jonet, but he had no further information regarding Jeanjean and his gang. The chief point which puzzled him seemed to be the fact that not a single stone, out of all the stolen jewels, had been traced.

"The receiver is an absolute mystery," he declared. "Perhaps the stuff goes to London."

"Perhaps," I said. "Have you made inquiry of Scotland Yard?"

"Oh, yes. I was over there a month ago. But they either know nothing, or else they are not inclined to help us." Then with a faint smile he added,

"As you know, mon cher ami, I have no very great admiration for your English police. Their laws are always in favour of the criminal, and their slowness of movement is astounding to us."

"Yes. Your methods are more drastic and more effective in the detection of crime," I admitted.

"And in its prevention," he added.

That day was the twenty-sixth of August, and as I walked along the Rue de Rivoli back to the *Hotel Meurice*, I suddenly remembered the mysterious tryst contained in that letter found in the pocket of Edward Craig. The appointment at the spot, "where the two C's meet," at Ealing.

I left Paris that night by the mail-train, crossed from Calais to Dover, and at noon next day alighted at Ealing Broadway station.

I had never been in Ealing before, and spent several hours wandering about its quiet, well-kept suburban roads, many of them of comfortable-looking detached villas. But I found the district a perfect maze of streets, therefore I went and sat on one of the seats in the small park in front of the station, wondering how best to act.

Two clear days were still before me ere the meeting which had apparently been arranged with old Gregory—the man with the master-mind.

"Where the two C's meet."

I lunched at the *Feathers Hotel* near the station, and all that hot afternoon wandered the streets, but failed to discover any clue. What "C's" were meant? Possibly two persons whose initials were C were in the habit of meeting at some spot, or in some house at Ealing—and Ealing is a big place when one is presented with such a problem.

Fagged and hungry, I returned to my rooms in Carlos Place, off Berkeley Square, where Rayner was awaiting me. He knew the object of my search, and as he admitted me, asked if I had been successful.

"No, Rayner, I haven't," I snapped. "I can see no ray of daylight yet. The appointment is an important one, no doubt, and one which we should watch. But how?"

"Well, sir," he replied, as I cast myself into my big arm-chair, and he got out my slippers, "we could watch the two railway stations at Ealing, and see if we detect old Gregory, or any of the others."

"They might go to Ealing in a tram or a taxi," I suggested.

"Yes, sir. But there'll be no harm in watching the trains, will there?" my man remarked. "If he went in a taxi he might leave by train."

"True," I said, and after a few seconds' reflection, added, "Yes. We'll try the trains."

So, on the night of the twenty-ninth, at about nine o'clock in the evening, I took up my post in the small arcade which formed the exit of the station and there waited patiently.

I was in a shabby tweed suit, with patched boots, and a cloth golf-cap, presenting the appearance of a respectable workman, as I smoked my short briar-pipe and idled over the *Evening News*.

As each train arrived I eagerly scanned the emerging passengers, while pretending to look in the shop window, but I saw nobody whom I knew.

The expression, "Where the two C's meet," kept running through my mind as I stood there in impatient inactivity. It was already past nine, and, in three-quarters of an hour, the fateful meeting, for somehow I felt that it was a fateful meeting, would be held.

The two "C's." The idea suddenly flashed across my mind, whether the spot indicated could be the junction of two roads, or streets, the names of which commenced with "C." Yet, how could I satisfy myself? If I searched Ealing again for roads commencing with a "C," I could only do so in daylight, too late to learn what I so dearly wished.

Of a porter I inquired the time of arrival of the next underground train and found that I had eight minutes. So I dashed along to the *Feathers Hotel*, where I obtained a map of the Ealing district and eagerly scanned it to find streets commencing with "C."

For some minutes I was unsuccessful, until of a sudden I noticed Castlebar Road, and examining the map carefully saw, to my excitement, that at an acute angle it joined another road, called Carlton Road, a triangular open space lying between the two thoroughfares.

It was the spot in Ealing where the two C's met!

I glanced at the clock.

It still wanted a quarter to ten, therefore I drained my glass hastily and, leaving the hotel, struck across the small open space opposite the station, in which, in a direct line, lay the junction of the two roads.

The evening was dark and sultry, with every indication of a thunderstorm. I remembered Rayner's vigil, but alas! had no time to go to him and explain my altered plans.

Along the dark, rather ill-lit, suburban road I hurried until, before me, I saw a big electric-light standard with four great inverted globes.

It showed a parting of the ways.

I looked at my watch as I passed a street-lamp, and saw that it wanted two minutes to ten.

And as I looked on ahead I saw, standing back in the shadow of the trees, on the left-hand, a dark figure, but in the distance I could not distinguish whether a man or a woman waited there.

I hurried forward, full of eagerness, to witness the secret meeting, and with an intention of watching and following those who met.

Yet, could I have foreseen the due result of such inquisitiveness, I scarcely think that I would have dared to tread ground so highly dangerous.

CHAPTER XVII
REVEALS ANOTHER PLOT

Approaching from Ealing Broadway, the huge electric-light standard, which was also a sign-post, shed a bright glow across the junction of the two roads. The thoroughfare on the right was Castlebar Road and on the left Carlton Road. In the latter road stood half a dozen big old trees, relics of a day when Ealing was a rural village and those trees formed a leafy way.

Beyond the sign-post, placed at the end of the triangle, lay a small open space of grass, and behind it a pleasant house with many trees in its spacious grounds.

At that hour silence reigned in that highly respectable suburban neighbourhood, and, as I went forward, I noticed that the figure beneath the trees was that of a man, who, emerging from the shadow, crossed the road leisurely and passed across the grass into the Castlebar Road, on the right hand.

He was dressed in dark clothes with a light grey felt hat, but so far was I away that to see his features was impossible, though the zone of light from the sign-post revealed his figure plainly.

Once he halted and looked in my direction, on hearing my footsteps, I suppose, but then continued his leisurely stroll.

I was upon the left-hand pavement, and in order not to attract the man's attention, passed along by the garden walls of the series of detached villas, for about two hundred yards, until the road ran in a curve round to the left, and thus I became hidden from his view.

When I found that I had not attracted the attention of the waiting man in the grey hat, I halted.

Was that the spot indicated? Was he one of those keeping the long-arranged appointment?

Ten o'clock had struck fully five minutes before, therefore, treading noiselessly, I retraced my steps until I could cautiously peep around the corner and see over the triangular plot of grass to the Castlebar Road.

Yes, the man was still standing there awaiting somebody. I could see the glowing end of his cigar.

Fortunately, he had his back turned towards me, gazing in the direction of the Broadway in apparent expectation. This allowed me to slip along a few yards, and entering the garden gate of one of the villas, I crouched down behind the low stone wall which separated the garden from the footway.

Kneeling there, I could watch without being seen, for fortunately the stranger opposite had not seen me.

I suppose I must have been there fully ten minutes. Several people passed within a few inches of me quite unsuspicious of my presence. In Castlebar Road a few people went along, but none interested the watcher.

Of a sudden, however, after straining his eyes for a long time in the direction whence I had come, he suddenly threw away his cigar and started off eagerly.

A few moments later I witnessed the approach of a short, thinnish man, wearing a black overcoat, open, over his evening clothes, and an opera hat.

And as he approached I recognized him. It was none other than Gregory himself!

The two men shook hands heartily, and by their mutual enthusiasm I realized that they could not have met for some considerable time.

They halted on the kerb in eager consultation, then both with one accord turned and strolled together in the direction of the station.

Next moment I had slipped from my hiding-place and was lounging along at a respectable distance behind them.

How I regretted that I had had no time to hail Rayner, for he would have had no difficulty in keeping observation upon the pair, while I, at any moment, might be recognized by the cunning, clever old fellow to whose inventiveness all the *coups* of the notorious Jules Jeanjean were due.

He seemed to walk more erect, and with more sprightliness, than at Cromer, where his advanced age and slight infirmity were undoubtedly assumed. In his present garb he really looked what he was supposed to be—a wealthy dealer in gems.

Engaged in earnest conversation, Gregory and his companion walked together along the dark road until they came to a taxi-stand near the station, when, entering the first cab, they drove rapidly away.

The moment they had left, I leapt into the next cab and, telling the driver to keep his friend in sight, we were soon moving along after the red tail-light of the first taxi.

The chase was an exciting one, for we whizzed along dark roads, quite unfamiliar to me, roads lying to the south of Ealing towards the Thames. My driver believed me to be a detective from my garb, and I did not discourage the belief.

Suddenly we turned to the right, when I recognized that we were in the long, narrow town of Brentford, and travelling in the direction of Syon House, the main road to Hounslow and Staines. At Spring Grove, which I had known slightly in years gone by, we turned again to the right, and were soon passing through a district of market-gardens and solitary houses.

On the way I had leaned out of the window and instructed the taxi-driver to keep well behind the other cab, so as not to be discovered. Therefore, in carrying out my orders, he suddenly put on his brakes and stopped, saying—

"They're going into that house yonder, sir. See?"

I nipped out quickly and saw that in the distance the other taxi had pulled up and the two men had alighted before a garden gate.

"Put out your lights, go back to the end of the road, and wait for me," I said.

Then I hurried forward to ascertain what I could.

The taxi, having put down its two fares and been dismissed, turned and passed me as I went forward. At last I had run the sly old fox, Gregory, to earth, and I now meant to keep in touch with him.

On approaching the house I found it to be a good-sized one, standing back, lonely and deserted, in a weedy garden, and surrounded by big, high elms. From the neglect apparent everywhere, the decayed oak fence, and the grass-grown path leading to the front door, it was plain that the place was unoccupied, though in two windows lights now shone, behind dark-green holland blinds.

The place seemed situated in the centre of some market-gardens, without any other house in the near vicinity. A dismal, old-fashioned dwelling far removed from the bustle of London life, and yet within hearing of it, for, as I stood, I could see the night-glare of the metropolis shining in the sky, upon my right, and could hear the roar of motor-buses upon the main road through Spring Grove.

For a few moments I stood up under the shadow of a big bush which overhung the road, my eyes upon the lower window where the fights showed. The house was half-covered with ivy and had bay-windows upon each side of the front door, which was approached by a short flight of moss-grown steps.

That I was not mistaken in my surmise that the house was uninhabited was proved by the "To Let" notice-board which I discerned lying behind the fence, thrown down purposely, perhaps.

Was old Gregory an intruder there? Had he purposely thrown down that board in order that any person, seeing lights in the window, would not have their suspicions sufficiently aroused to cause them to investigate?

The house was a dark, weird one. But what would I not have given to be inside, and to overhear what was being planned!

Vernon Gregory was, according to Lola, the instigator of all those marvellously ingenious thefts effected by Jeanjean. Was another great robbery being planned?

Perhaps the man in the grey hat had travelled from afar. Possibly so, because of the long time in advance the appointment had been made.

All was silent. Therefore I crept over the weedy garden until I stood beneath the bay window in which a light was shining.

I could hear voices—men's voices raised in controversy. Then, suddenly, they only conversed in whispers. What was said, I could not distinguish. They were speaking in French, but further than that I could catch nothing.

Sometimes they laughed heartily at something evidently hailed as a huge joke. I distinctly heard Gregory's tones, but the others' I could not recognize. As far as I could gather they were strangers to me.

Was the place, I wondered, one of old Gregory's hiding-places? Though he conducted his business in Hatton Garden, where he was well known, his private address, Lola had told me, had always been a mystery, such pains did he take to conceal it.

Was that lonely house his place of abode? Had he met his friend in Ealing and taken him there in order to place before him certain plans for the future?

I looked at the grim old house, with its mantle of ivy, and reflected upon what quantities of stolen property it might contain!

That the man I knew as Vernon Gregory was head of an association of the cleverest jewel-thieves in the world, had been alleged by Lola, and I believed her. His deep cunning and clever elusiveness, his amazing craftiness and astounding foresight had been well illustrated by his disappearance from Cromer, even though his flight had been so sudden that he had been compelled to abandon his treasures. Yet as I stood there, upon the carpet of weeds, with my ears strained, I could hear his familiar voice speaking in slow measured tones, as he was explaining something in elaborate detail.

What was it? I stood there in a fever of excitement and curiosity.

Yet I had one satisfaction. I had run him to earth at last.

Presently the voices of the men were again raised in dissension. Gregory had apparently made some statement from which the others—how many there were, I knew not—dissented. They spoke rapidly in French, and I could hear one man's mouth full of execrations, a hard, hoarse voice of one of the lower class.

Then I distinctly heard some one say in English—

"I don't believe it! He knows nothing. Why take such a step against an innocent man?"

"Because, I tell you, he knows too much!" declared Gregory, now speaking loudly in English. "He was at Cromer, and discovered everything. Ah! you don't know how shrewd and painstaking he is. Read his books and you will see. He is the greatest danger confronting you to-day, my friends."

I held my breath. They were discussing me!

"I object," exclaimed the man who had first spoken in English. "He has no evil intentions against us."

"But he knows the Nightingale, and through her has learnt much," Gregory replied promptly.

"What?" gasped the unseen speaker. "Has she told him anything? Has the girl betrayed us?"

"Ask her," the old man urged. "She's upstairs. Call her."

Lola was there—in that house!

CHAPTER XVIII
DONE IN THE NIGHT

I heard the stranger's voice call—

"Lola! Lola! Come here. We want you."

I heard her rather impatient reply, and then, a few moments later, she descended the stairs and entered the room where the gang had been discussing me.

Some quick words in French were exchanged. Then I heard her cry—

"I tell you, I refuse!"

A man's voice protested.

"No, You shall not!" she declared in a loud, defiant voice. "If you do, then the police shall know!"

"Oh!" exclaimed old Gregory, whose voice I recognized. "Then you object, Mademoiselle, eh?"

"Yes. I do object, M'sieu'!" she cried. "If any attempt is made against him, then I shall myself inform the police. Remember, M'sieu' Vidal is my friend."

"Your lover, perhaps," sneered the old man.

"No," she cried in loud, angry protest. "He is not my lover! Would he love a girl like myself—a girl who has been brought by you, and your friends, to what I am?"

"Well, you are a very pretty girl, and sometimes uncommonly useful to your uncle," replied old Gregory tauntingly.

"Of use to you!" she cried. "Yes, I know I am! And when you have no further use for me, then—then—an accident will happen to me, and I shall trouble you no further—an accident like that which you intend shall befall Mr. Vidal!"

I crouched against the window, my ears glued to the glass. I tried to picture to myself the scene within—how the young girl I had befriended in such curious circumstances was standing before them, defying them to make any attempt to put me out of action.

"You speak like a little fool, Lola," old Gregory declared. "You lead the life of a lady of means. You travel with a maid, and all you have to do is to be pleasant to people, and keep your eyes and ears open. For that you receive very handsome rewards, and——"

"And you make a million francs a year, M'sieur Gregory," she interrupted. "Ah! when the police trace these marvellous plots to their source, they will be surprised. One day the papers will be full of you and your wicked doings—mark me!"

"You are mad, you ungrateful little minx!" shouted the old man in furious anger. "If you try to prevent me carrying out any of my schemes, depend upon it you will rue it. I'm not a man to be played with!"

"Neither am I to be played with, though I am only a girl!" she retorted. "I'm desperate now—rendered desperate by you and your blackguardly gang."

"Because you fear for this novelist friend of yours—this prying person who is so fond of investigating other people's affairs, and using the material for his books, eh?"

"Yes. I fear for him, because I know what is intended."

"I tell you it's a matter which does not concern you," said the man with the master-mind, as I listened attentively.

"It does. He is my friend," she exclaimed in French. "I know that you intend he shall die—and I will warn him."

"You will, will you!" shouted Gregory, and I heard him spring to his feet. "Repeat that, at your peril!"

"I do repeat it!" said the girl wildly. "He shall not be harmed!"

"Eh? So you are ready to betray us, are you!" said the old man in a hard, hissing voice.

"Yes," she cried in defiance. "I will, if you so much as touch a hair of his head."

"You will! Then take that!" screamed the old man, while, at the same instant, I heard a heavy blow struck, followed by a woman's scream, and a loud noise as she fell upon the floor.

"*Dieu!*" I heard a man's voice exclaim. "Why—master—you've killed her!"

Then as I stood there, breathless, I heard some further conversation in low tones. The ruffians were discussing the tragedy—for a tragedy I felt it to be. A defenceless girl struck down by old Gregory—her lips closed for ever because she had sought to protect me!

These men feared me! This thought, despite the horror and anger with which I was seething, flashed through my mind like fire. They believed that I knew more than I really did.

But it was a moment for action. Old Gregory had deliberately struck down that unfortunate girl who had been trained until she had become an expert thief, made a cat's paw and tool for that dangerous gang of criminals.

Creeping along the wall of the house, I managed to find and noiselessly place against the window a rustic garden-chair, and discovering also a heavy piece of wood. I prepared to make a dramatic entry into the room where this tragedy had happened, and the conspiracy against my life was being hatched.

Again I listened. The voices were now so low that I could not catch the words uttered.

Then standing on a level with the window-sill, I raised my arm and with the block of wood smashed one of the huge, long panes to fragments.

The crash was startling, no doubt, but ere they could recover from it I had dashed the holland blind aside and stepped boldly into the room, my big Browning revolver in my hand, and my back instantly against the wall.

The scene there was truly a strange one.

It was a dingy, old-fashioned drawing-room furnished in early Victorian style, with ponderous walnut furniture, a brown threadbare carpet, ugly arm-chairs, a what-not, and wax flowers under a glass dome, in the fashion beloved by our grandmothers. By the fireplace was a cosy corner, the upholstery of which was tattered and moth-eaten, while the stuffing of some of the chairs appeared through the corners of the cushions. Near where I stood was an old chintz-covered couch, and beyond, an arm-chair, of the same inartistic description.

The place smelt damp and musty, and in places the faded grey paper was peeling from the walls.

Three men were there. Gregory, and two others, strangers. The old man's appearance had greatly altered from what it was when I had seen him wandering about in Cromer. Then he had worn his white hair and beard long, and with his broad forehead, his pointed chin, and wide-brimmed slouch hat presented the picturesque appearance such as twenty years ago used to be affected by literary men or artists.

But now, as he stood before me, startled by my sudden appearance, I saw that he wore both beard and hair much shorter, and, though he could not alter his height, his facial expression was considerably different.

In an instant I realized that I saw him now as he naturally was, while in Cromer he had so disguised himself as to appear many years older than was actually the case.

His two companions were rather well-dressed men of perhaps thirty, one of whom, a foreigner, wore a small pointed brown beard, while the other, clean-shaven, was unmistakably an Englishman. Thieves they were both, assuredly, yet in the street one would have passed them by as respectable and rather refined citizens.

"You! Vidal!" cried Gregory, starting back when I sprang so unceremoniously into their midst.

"Yes, Vidal, Mr. Gregory!" I cried, striving to remain calm. Yet how could I, when my eyes fell upon the form of Lola, who, dressed in a dark-brown walking-costume, was lying huddled up in a heap on the floor, a few feet from where I stood.

Blood was upon the bosom of her dress. She had been struck down brutally with a knife!

"I may tell you, Gregory," I said, as coolly as I could, "that I have been listening to your interesting conspiracy to kill me. Well, do so now, if you dare! My friends are outside. They will be charmed to meet you, I assure you, especially after the foul deed you committed only a few minutes ago."

The three men started and exchanged glances. I saw by their faces that they were frightened. Yet I dared not lower my pistol, or bend down to Lola, for they would have jumped upon me instantly.

As I spoke, I pushed forth my weapon threateningly, covering them with it determinedly. But it required all my nerve to face them.

"You are an assassin, sir!" I cried, "and I have caught you redhanded."

"You haven't caught us yet," remarked the foreigner, defiantly, speaking English with a strong accent; and the expressions upon the faces of all three were villainous.

My thoughts were not of myself, but to avenge that murderous blow which had been struck at the poor defenceless girl. They were scoundrels, without pity and without compunction, who held human life cheaply whenever the existence of a person stood in the way of their schemes.

And I knew that they intended that I, too, should die.

But they were not quite sure whether I had the police waiting outside or not. My bluff had worked. I saw how they hesitated. Even Gregory was taken aback by my boldness in entering there and facing them.

"I may tell you," I said, still keeping my back to the wall and my useful Browning ready for business, "that I have discovered much more concerning your interesting doings and your intentions than you imagine."

"Lola has told you!" burst forth old Gregory. "Well, she won't have further opportunity of doing so."

"And you will not have further opportunity of engineering your remarkable thefts, my dear sir," I replied quite coolly. "The police desire to see you, and to question you about a certain little affair at Cromer, remember. You are extremely clever, Mr. Gregory—or whatever your real name may be—but I tell you that you are at last unmasked. To-morrow the papers will be full of your interesting career, and one diamond-broker will disappear from Hatton Garden for ever."

"Listen," cried the master-criminal to his companions, his face now white as paper. "Hark what that little chit of a girl has been saying! Was I not right to strike her down?"

"Quite," admitted his two companions.

"And now you will pay the penalty, my dear sir," I declared. "I intend that you shall."

"Put that revolver down," Gregory commanded. "Let us talk. You are clever, Mr. Vidal, and I—well, I confess you have the whip hand of us."

His companions looked at each other, dismayed at these words of the Master. He had actually admitted defeat!

For a few seconds I did not reply. I was reflecting, and it struck me that this pretence of being vanquished might only be a ruse. Gregory was far too clever and defiant a criminal to be beaten single-handed by the man he so sincerely hated and feared.

"No," I replied with a grim smile. "It is war between us, Mr. Gregory—not peace. Therefore, I shall hold my revolver here until my friends arrive. They will not be long, and I shall not suffer from fatigue, I assure you."

Gregory, quick-witted and shrewd, cast a rapid glance around as he stood before me, a smart figure in his well-cut evening clothes, with a fine diamond glistening in his pleated shirt-front.

"Well," he exclaimed after a brief pause, "if you deliberately take on the duties of the police, and pry into affairs which do not concern you, then you must take the consequences."

"For that very reason I have entered here," I said, "to become witness of your dastardly crime. You have killed that girl—killed her because you feared she would betray you."

"She has betrayed us," he retorted. "And she deserves all she has got."

"You infernal brute!" I cried. "If it were not that it would be deliberate murder, I'd put a bullet through you in return."

"Try it," he laughed jeeringly. "This quixotic temperament of yours will be your undoing."

"I befriended that unfortunate girl," I said. "And she has appreciated what I did."

"The little fool ran her head into a noose, I know," was his reply. "But even though you befriended her, it gave her no right to betray us."

"Nor any right to you to strike her down," I said, glancing at the white face of the prostrate form.

"Ah! You are her champion!" he laughed. "But you wouldn't be if you knew the truth. She wasn't the innocent little person she led you to believe she was."

"No," I cried angrily. "You shall say nothing against your victim's honour, curse you! I only thank Heaven that I'm here to-night—that I know the truth regarding this tragedy. Your intention was—the intention of all three of you, no doubt, was—to get rid of the evidence of your crime. But that will now be impossible."

As I uttered that last sentence, the bearded Frenchman made a movement towards the door.

"Halt!" I cried in a loud, imperious voice. "Come back here. Do not attempt to leave this room or I'll shoot you," and as he glanced at me he found himself looking into the barrel of my weapon.

"Come," said Gregory. "Enough of this fooling! It's a drawn game between us, Mr. Vidal. Why not let us discuss the future quietly and without any ill-feeling on either side. I admit what I have done—killed the traitress."

"And by Heaven! you shall pay the penalty of your crime!" I cried.

"Oh, shall I?" he laughed with a nonchalant air. "We shall see."

Next instant I heard a sharp click in the passage outside and the room was plunged in darkness. The electric light had been switched off by one of Gregory's confederates out in the hall.

I heard the door opened, and voices shouted wildly in French.

"Just in time," I heard the new-comer cry.

"Ah, Jules!" gasped Gregory. "You are late. Where have you been? Where are you?"

And, by the shuffling of feet, I knew that the men were groping about in the darkness.

Jules Jeanjean was there, in that room!

"*Dieu!* You were nearly trapped, all of you," I heard him cry. "Where is he?" he asked, referring to myself. "He shall not live to blab. Mind he doesn't get out by the window."

But I still stood with my back against the wall, my pistol raised in self-defence.

A few moments elapsed—moments that seemed like hours—when of a sudden my eyes were blinded by the ray of an electric torch which threw a strong light upon me from the doorway.

Ere I could realize my peril, there was a red flash, followed by a loud explosion, and I felt a hot, stinging sensation in my throat.

Then next second the blackness of unconsciousness fell upon me, and I knew no more.

CHAPTER XIX
RECORDS FURTHER FACTS

How long I remained there, or what subsequently happened to me, I did not learn till long afterwards.

I only knew, when I again awoke to consciousness, that it was day, and I found myself in a narrow bed, with two nurses in blue linen dresses, and white caps and aprons, standing near me, while two doctors were gazing into my face with keen, anxious expressions.

At first they would tell me nothing, even though, with a great effort, I asked what had happened. Bandages were around my throat and across my left shoulder, and I felt a nausea and a giddiness that I knew arose from chloroform, and therefore that some operation had been performed. I slowly struggled back to a knowledge of things about me.

"It's all right, Mr. Vidal," the youngest of the two doctors assured me. "Try and sleep. Don't worry. Everything is all right."

I felt uncommonly drowsy, and again slept, and not until night had fallen did I re-open my eyes.

A night-nurse was seated at my bedside, reading by a green-shaded lamp. The little room was in darkness, and I think I startled her when I suddenly spoke.

"Where am I, Nurse?" I inquired in a thin, weak voice, and with difficulty.

"This is the Cottage Hospital at Hounslow," was the reply. "You've been here two days, but you are much better now. Don't talk, however, for the doctor has forbidden it."

"But I want to know what has happened," I protested.

"Well, I don't exactly know," the dark-haired young woman answered. "I only know what I've been told. That is, that a taxi-driver who took you to some house beyond Spring Grove, grew tired of waiting for you, and on going to the house found you in one of the rooms, dying."

"Dying!" I gasped. "Ah! yes, I remember," I added, as recollections of that fateful night arose within my memory.

"Yes. You were suffering from a serious bullet-wound in the throat," she went on. "The window of the room was smashed, but your friends had all fled."

"My friends!" I echoed. "Who said they were my friends?"

"The taxi-driver said so, I believe."

"Where is he?"

"He has promised to come to-morrow, to see you."

"But was not a lady found in the same room?" I inquired eagerly, trying to raise myself. "She had been killed—deliberately struck down!"

"Yes. I've heard that a lady was found there."

"Was she brought here, with me?"

"No" was the nurse's reply. "She was removed, but to what place I've not heard."

Lola was dead! Ah! The sight of that white, upturned face, so delicate and sweet, and of that dark, ugly stream of blood across the bosom of her dress, haunted me. I recollected those hideous moments when, being on my guard against the assassins, I alas! had no opportunity of lending her aid.

She was found dead, apparently, and they had removed her body—probably to the nearest mortuary to await an inquest.

All my thoughts became confused when I realized the tragic truth. The nurse saw that I was upset and urged to try to sleep again. Indeed she gave me a draught which the doctor had ordered and, presently, though much against my inclination, I again dozed off.

It was once more day—a warm, sunny day—when I became thoroughly alive to things about me. The doctors came and expressed satisfaction at my improvement, dressed my wound, which I confess was very painful, and declared that I had had a very narrow escape.

"A quarter of an inch further to the left, Mr. Vidal," one of the surgeons remarked, "and we couldn't have saved you."

Towards noon the taxi-driver, cap in hand, came up to my bedside to inquire how I was. His name was Stevens. The nurse would not, however, allow me to put many questions to him.

"You were such a long time gone, sir, that I thought I'd just come up and see if you wanted me any more. I had to get over to Acton to the garage, for I'd had a long day," he told me. "I'd just got to the garden gate when I heard a pistol shot and, entering the garden, and seeing the window smashed, I suspected something wrong. I got in at the window and found the room in darkness. A light was burning in the hall and the door was open. Quickly I found the electric switch and, turning it, saw you lying on the floor close beside the body of a young lady."

"Did you see the other men?" I asked eagerly.

"At first sir, I believed it to be a case of murder and suicide," answered Stevens, "but a moment later, as I stood in the room horrified at the discovery, I heard several persons leave the house. I tried to raise an alarm, but nobody heard me, so they got clean away. I examined the young lady and yourself, then I rushed out for help. At the bottom of the road I went towards my cab, but as I did so, I heard the engine started and the red tail-lamp moved off, away from me. Those fellows that had run from the house were inside. Yes, sir, them vagabonds had stolen my cab!"

"What did you do then?" I asked excitedly.

"Why, I yelled after 'em, but nobody heard me, until presently I came across a copper and told him what was up. We soon got another taxi and went back to the house, and there we found you both a-lying as I'd left you."

"Was the lady alive?" I queried huskily.

"Yes. She was a-breathing slightly, and as we thought she was injured worse than you, the copper took her off at once to the Brentford Hospital by herself, as there wasn't room for both of you in the cab. On the way he sent another taxi back for me and I brought you here."

"But is the young lady alive now?" I asked.

"I believe so, but I'm not quite sure. She was last night when I called at the hospital, but she was dreadful bad, and in great danger, they told me."

"Ah!" I sighed. "I only hope and pray that she may recover to face and condemn her brutal enemies."

"Was she a friend of yours, sir?" asked the man with some curiosity.

"Yes, a great friend," was my reply.

"But who tried to kill you, sir?" Stevens asked. "Those blokes as escaped seemed to be a pretty desperate lot. My cab ain't been found yet," he added.

"They were her enemies as well as mine," I replied vaguely, for I had no intention of telling him the whole story, though I thanked him sincerely for his prompt help. Had it not been for him I fear that Lola and myself would never have lived through the night. Jeanjean would have taken good care that the lips of both of us were closed for ever.

"Well, sir, you've had a pretty narrow shave of it," Stevens declared. "There's something very queer about that house, it seems. People say that though the place, as was to be let furnished, had nobody a-living in it, strange lights have been seen a-moving about it, and in the windows now and again and always very late at night."

"Will you do a favour for me, Stevens?" I asked.

"Certainly, sir."

Then I gave him instructions first to go to the hospital where Lola was lying, to inquire how she was. Then he was to go on to my flat in Carlos Place, tell Rayner all that had occurred, and order him to come to me at once.

Just then the nurse kindly, but very firmly intervened, and the taxi-driver rose from the chair at my bedside and left.

For some hours I dozed. Then woke to find the faithful Rayner standing by me, much concerned.

"I've had an awful fright, sir," he said. "When you didn't come home for forty-eight hours, I went to Vine Street Police Station and reported that you were missing. Inspector Palmer, of the C.I. Department, knows you well, sir, and he quickly stirred himself. But I heard nothing till that taxi-driver came and told me you were here. He explained how you'd been shot at a house in Spring Grove, Isleworth. I hope you're all right again, sir?"

"Yes, Rayner, so far," I answered rather feebly. "I've a bit of pain in my throat, but they've bandaged me up all right, and I'll soon be about again. That fellow you knew as Dr. Arendt, in Cromer, plugged me."

"What! The man Jeanjean!"

"The same," I said. "Gregory was there, too. I tracked them into their den, and this is what I got for my trouble," I added grimly.

"Well, sir, I'm no end glad you escaped. They're a desperate crowd and you might very easily have gone under. Can I do anything?"

"Yes. Take a message for me to the Brentford Hospital, to Mademoiselle Sorel."

"The lady the taxi-man told me about?" Rayner asked.

"Yes. An attempt was made upon her life," I replied. "Go there, take some nice flowers, and send up a message from me expressing a hope that she's better, and say that I will see her as soon as ever I'm able."

"Very well, sir. I'll be off at once," he replied.

But for some time longer he sat with me, while I gave him instructions regarding various matters. Then he left, promising me to quickly return and bring me news of Lola.

He was absent about a couple of hours, and on re-entering told me that he had seen the Sister in charge, who had given Lola my flowers and my message and had received one in return from her. This was that she felt much better, and that until we met and consulted it would be best to take no action against the assassins.

That same evening, with the doctor's sanction, a tall, clean-shaven man in grey tweeds approached my bed and, seating himself, announced that his name was Warton, and that he was an Inspector of the Criminal Investigation Department.

He brought out a business-like book and pencil and in a rather abrupt manner commenced to interrogate me regarding the events of that night when I so narrowly escaped being murdered.

From his methods I judged that he had risen from a constable. He was bluff and to the point. He told me he was attached to the Brentford Station, and I set him down as a man of similar mental calibre to Frayne.

No good could accrue at that moment from any full explanation, so, after listening to him for some little time, I pretended to be very unwell and only answered his questions with plain "yes" or "no."

It was not likely that I would tell all I knew to this local detective. Had Henri Jonet been present it would have been a different matter, but I saw at a glance that Warton was a very ordinary type of police-officer.

He asked me what took me to the house in Spring Grove on that fateful night. To this I merely replied with the one word—

"Curiosity."

Then he asked—

"Did you know the lady who was found stabbed a few feet from you?"

"Yes. I had met her," was my reply.

"Do you know the circumstances in which she was struck down?"

"I was not present then, therefore I could know nothing," was my evasive response.

"But the men in the house were friends of yours, were they not?" he asked.

"No. They were not," was my prompt reply.

"Then, who were they?" he asked, scribbling down my answers with his stumpy pencil.

"I—I don't feel well enough to be questioned like this," I complained to the Sister, who was standing by. "I've committed no crime, and I object to the police making a cross-examination as though I were a criminal. I appeal to you, Sister."

The middle-aged woman in her cool linen uniform, with a silver medal upon her breast, looked hard at me for a moment. Then, realizing the situation, she turned to the detective, and said—

"You must come to-morrow. The patient still suffers much from shock, and I cannot allow him to be questioned further. He is too weak."

"Very well, Sister," replied Warton, as he closed his pocket-book. "I'll come to-morrow. But a strange mystery envelopes that house in Spring Grove, Mr. Vidal," he added, turning back to me. "You'll be surprised when you go there and see for yourself."

"Perhaps Mr. Vidal may be well enough to do so in a few days," said the Sister. "We shall see."

And with that the police-officer was forced to depart.

CHAPTER XX
ANOTHER DISCOVERY IS MADE

On several occasions during the weary week that followed Inspector Warton called and saw me, but I always managed, by one subterfuge or another, to evade the more pointed of his questions.

The three men who had attacked Lola and myself that night knew from the papers that we both still lived as witnesses against them.

The nurses would not allow me to see the papers, but from Rayner I learnt that the more sensational section of the London Press had published reports headed, "Novelist Found Shot." Indeed, a great many reporters had called at the hospital, but had been promptly sent empty away.

At last, one morning, I was declared convalescent and sufficiently well to be removed to my chambers. Therefore Rayner ordered Stevens to bring his taxi for me, and we left the hospital.

Though still feeling far from well, I was all curiosity to see the house in Spring Grove by daylight, so we called at the police-station and a stout sergeant of the T. Division accompanied us with the key, the place being still in the hands of the police.

As we pulled up in that unfrequented side-road I saw how mysterious and desolate the place was in the warm sunshine—an old red-brick Georgian house, with square, inartistic windows, standing solitary and alone, half covered by its ivy mantle, and surrounded by a spacious garden dotted with high trees, and neglected and overgrown with weeds.

As we walked over the moss-grown flags leading to the steps, I noticed the window I had smashed in making my entry that night.

The constable unlocked the door and we found ourselves in a wide, spacious hall, its stone flags worn hollow and containing some old-fashioned furniture. The atmosphere of the house was musty and close, and long cobwebs hung in festoons in the corners.

The room on the right, the one in which I had been found, I remembered well. It was just the same as when I had stood there in the presence of the

Master and the notorious Jules Jeanjean. Upon its brown threadbare carpet were two ugly stains in close proximity to each other—the spots where both Lola and I had lain!

I saw the wall against which I had stood in defiance. An evening overcoat still lay upon a chair—the coat which old Gregory had abandoned in his hurried flight, when Stevens, the taxi-driver, had so opportunely appeared upon the scene.

"Nothing's been touched, sir," remarked the fat sergeant. "We've been waiting for you to see the place, and to tell us what you know."

I exchanged glances with Rayner.

"I know very little," I replied. "I simply fell in with a very dangerous set. They were evidently plotting something, and believing that I had overheard, attempted to put me out of the way."

"And the lady?"

"I imagine the same sort of thing happened to her. They considered she knew too much of their movements and might betray them."

"But what were they plotting?"

"They spoke in French, so I couldn't catch."

"Oh! They were foreigners—eh?" exclaimed the sergeant in surprise. "Coiners or anarchists, perhaps."

"Perhaps," I said. "Who knows?"

"Ah. I've heard that two strangers have been seen up and down here in the night time," continued the sergeant. "We've got their description from a constable who's been doing night-duty. He says he'd know 'em again. Once he saw a woman with 'em, and he believes it was the young lady now in the hospital."

"He saw them together—eh?"

"He says so."

Then I changed the conversation, and I followed him from room to room through the dirty, neglected house, which nevertheless, with slight signs here and there, showed marks of recent occupation.

Two of the beds in the upstairs rooms had been slept in, and there was other evidence in both kitchen and dining-room that, as I had surmised, it had been the secret hiding-place of the man who posed in Hatton Garden as a substantial and respectable dealer in precious stones.

No doubt he came there late at night, and if he remained during the day he never went out.

Surely the place was one where he might effectively conceal himself from the police; yet to live in such a house, and in that manner, certainly showed a daring and audacity unequalled. He, of course, never knew when a prospective tenant might come to visit it, or the agents in Hounslow might send to inspect its condition.

"You had a very narrow escape here, sir," said the sergeant as we descended the stairs. "Will you step outside? I want to show you something."

We all went out by the kitchen door into the weedy garden where, behind a low wall, lay a mound of newly-dug earth. By its side I saw a rough, yawning hole about five feet long by three broad.

"That's the grave they'd prepared for you, sir, without a doubt! By gum! It was lucky that taxi-driver got up here just in time, or they'd have flung you in and covered you up, dead or alive!"

I stood aghast, staring at the hole prepared for the concealment—not of my body—but that of Lola. They had had no inkling of my expected presence, hence that prepared grave had been for her—and her alone!

She had been invited there by old Gregory, who had intended that she should die, and ere morning broke all trace of the crime would have been removed.

Yes. The fat sergeant spoke the truth. Had not Stevens fortunately come to that house at the moment he did, we should both have been flung into that gaping hole and there buried. In a week the weeds of the garden would have spread and all traces of the soil having been moved would have been obliterated.

How many secret crimes are yearly committed in the suburbs of London! How many poor innocent victims of both sexes, and of all ages, lie concealed beneath the floors of kitchens and cellars, or in the back gardens of the snug, old-fashioned houses around London? Once, Seven Dials or Drury Lane were dangerous. But to-day they are not half so dangerous to the unwary as our semi-rural suburbs. The clever criminal never seeks to dissect, burn, or otherwise get rid of his victim save to bury the body. Burial conceals everything, and the corpse rapidly moulders into dust.

If the walls of the middle-class houses of suburban London could speak, what grim stories some of them could tell! And how many quiet, respectable families are now living in houses where, beneath the basement floor, or in the little back garden, lie the rotting remains of the victim of some brutal crime.

It is the same in Paris, in Brussels, in Vienna, aye, in every capital. The innocent pay the toll always. Men make laws and cleverer men break them. But God reigns supreme, and sooner or later places His hand heavily upon the guilty.

Ask any of the heads of the police of the European Powers, and they will tell you that Providence assists them to bring the guilty to justice. It may be mere chance, mere coincidence, vengeance of those who have been tricked, jealousy of a woman—a dozen motives—yet the result is ever the same, the criminal at last stands before his judges.

The great detective—and there are a dozen in Europe—takes no kudos unto himself. He will tell you that his success in such and such a case is due to some lucky circumstance. Ask him who controlled it, and he will go further and tell you that the punishment meted out to the assassin by man is the punishment decreed by his Creator. He has taken a life which is God-given—hence his own life must pay the penalty.

Rayner, as he looked into the hole which had been so roughly dug, was inclined to hilarity.

"Well, sir," he exclaimed. "It's hardly long enough for you, is it?"

"Enough!" I said. "Had it not been for Stevens, I should have been lying down there with the earth over me."

"I was afraid I shouldn't get my fare," said the taxi-driver, simply. "I didn't know you, sir, and I had four-and-sixpence on the clock—a lot to me."

"And a good job, too," declared Rayner. "If it had only been a bob fare you might have gone back to Acton and left Mr. Vidal to his fate."

"Ah! I quite agree," Stevens said. "It was only by mere chance, as I had promised my wife to be home early that night, it being our wedding-day, and we had two or three friends coming in."

"Then your wedding anniversary saved my life, Stevens!" I exclaimed.

"Well, if you put it that way, sir, I suppose it really did," he replied with a laugh. "But this preparation of a grave is a surprise to me. They evidently got it ready for the young lady—eh?"

I paused. My blood rose against the crafty old Gregory and his associates. They knew of Lola's friendship with me, and they had deliberately plotted the poor girl's death. They had actually dug a grave ready to receive her!

Within myself I made a solemn vow that I would be even with the man whom the mysterious Egisto had addressed as "Master."

Surely I should have a strange and interesting story to relate to my friend Jonet in Paris.

I glanced at the surroundings. About the oblong excavation was a tangled mass of herbage, peas and beans with fading leaves, for it was in the corner of a kitchen-garden, which in the fall of the previous year had been allowed to run wild. And in such a position had the grave been dug that it was entirely concealed.

That it had been purposely prepared for Lola was apparent. She had been invited there to her death!

Had it not been for my fortunate presence, combined with the fact that Stevens had called just at the opportune moment, then the dainty little girl who, against her will, was the cat's paw of the most daring and dangerous gang of criminals in Europe, would be lying there concealed beneath that long tangle of vegetables and weeds.

"The house has been to let for nearly three years," the sergeant informed me. "But this hole has only been recently dug, a little over a week, we think. It was probably on the evening previous to your adventure, sir."

"Probably," I said, for the earth looked still fresh, though the rain had caked it somewhat. Two spades were lying near, therefore, I conjectured, the work had been accomplished by two men. The two I had seen with Gregory, I presumed.

"We're making inquiries regarding the intruders," the sergeant went on. "I only wish Mr. Warton were here, but he had to go up to the Yard this morning. Can't you give any description of the people you saw here?"

"I thought you had described them, Stevens," I said, addressing the taxi-driver.

"So I have, sir. But in the dark I wasn't able to see very much."

"Well," I exclaimed, in reply to the sergeant, "I, too, did not have much opportunity of seeing them. The electric light was switched off the moment I entered and I was shot by the aid of an electric torch. I had no means of defending myself. I fired at the light at the time, it's true, but the scoundrel evidently held it away from him, knowing that I might shoot."

I did not intend to assist the police. The Criminal Investigation Department never showed very great eagerness to assist me in any of my investigations.

"But you saw the men?"

"Yes. As I have already told Inspector Warton."

"What brought you here?"

"I followed two of the men from Ealing."

"I know. But for what reason did you follow them?"

"Because I believed that I recognized them."

"But you were mistaken, eh?" asked the fat sergeant as we still stood at the edge of the grave.

"I hardly know," I answered vaguely, "except that a dastardly attempt was made upon my life because I had pried into the men's business."

The sergeant was silent for a few moments, and I had distinct suspicion that, from the expression upon his face, he did not believe me.

Then he remarked in a slow, reflective tone—

"I suppose, Mr. Vidal, you know that the young French lady who was found here has made a statement to Inspector Warton?"

"What!" I gasped. "What has she told him?"

"I don't know, except that he's gone up to Scotland Yard to-day regarding it."

I held my breath.

What indiscretions, I wondered, had Lola committed!

CHAPTER XXI
EXPLAINS LOLA'S FEARS

After leaving the house in which I had so narrowly escaped death, I dropped the sergeant at Spring Place station and, with Rayner, drove over to Brentford, where, at the hospital, I stood beside Lola's bed.

She looked a pale, frail, pathetic little figure, clad in a light blue dressing-jacket, and propped up among the pillows. When she recognized me she put forth a slim white hand and smiled a glad welcome.

"I have been so very anxious about you, Lola," I said after the nurse had gone. "You know, of course, what happened?"

"Yes," she answered weakly in French. "I am so very sorry that you should have fallen into the trap as well as myself, M'sieur Vidal. They induced me to call there for one purpose—to kill me," she added in English, with her pretty French accent.

"I fear that is so," was my reply. "But did you not receive my warnings? The Paris *Sûreté* are searching for you everywhere, and Jonet is most anxious to find you."

"Ah, I know!" she exclaimed with a slight laugh. "Yes, I got your kind letters, but I could not reply to them. There were reasons which, at the time, prevented me."

She looked very sweet, her fair, soft hair in two long plaits hanging over her shoulders, the ends being secured by big bows of turquoise ribbon.

Yes, she was decidedly pretty; her big, blue, wide-open eyes turned upon me.

"I wrote to Elise Leblanc at Versailles," I said, for want of something else to say.

"I got the letters. I was in Dresden at the time."

"With your uncle?"

"No. He has been in Vienna," was her brief response.

"But he was at that house in Spring Grove."

"Yes. It was a trap for me—a dastardly trap laid for me by old Gregory," she cried in anger. "He intended that I should die, but he never expected you to come so suddenly upon the scene."

"How was it that Jeanjean arrived there also?" I asked.

"He came there to consult the Master," she replied. "A huge affair was being planned to take place at the offices of one of the best known diamond dealers in Hatton Garden. Gregory, being in the diamond trade, knows most of the secrets of the other dealers, and in this case had learned of the arrival of three very fine stones, among the most notable diamonds known to the world. For three months he had carefully laid his plans of attack, and on the night in question had called his confederates together, as was his habit, in order to put his plans finally before them, and to allocate each his work. Through my uncle, however, I knew of the proposed robbery, and the old man, fearing me, had decided that it would be in their interests if I died. Hence the attack upon me."

"A most base and brutal one!" I cried. "But thank Heaven! Lola, you are recovering. I overheard all that you said regarding myself."

She flushed slightly, but did not reply.

"To-day I have heard that you have made a statement to the police," I went on in a low voice so that I should not be overheard by the nurse who stood outside the door of the small two-bedded ward, the second bed being unoccupied.

"Yes. An agent of police came and questioned me," was her reply, "but I did not tell him much—at least, nothing which might give them any clue—or which would jeopardize either of us. I had heard that you were recovering, and therefore I thought you would prefer to unmask Gregory and his associates yourself, rather than leave it to the London police. Besides, they have escaped and I have no idea where they may now be."

"Quite right," I replied, much relieved at her words. "You acted wisely, for had you told them the truth they would in all probability have arrested you."

She smiled faintly.

"Yes. That was one of the reasons which caused me to exercise discretion. I felt that we should soon meet again, M'sieur Vidal," she added. "They say that I shall be discharged from here in about a week."

"I hope so," I declared earnestly. "You had a very narrow escape from those fiends."

"I was quite unsuspicious when I went there," she said. "That house has been our meeting-place for the past eighteen months or so. Sometimes we met at Gregory's flat in Amsterdam, and sometimes at the tenantless house in Spring Grove, or at one which has been to let at Cricklewood, and also at a house in West Hampstead."

"The spot 'where the three C's meet' at Ealing is the usual rendezvous, I suppose?"

"Yes, the place is easy of access, quiet, and entirely unsuspicious. I have met my uncle there sometimes when in London, and sometimes Gregory or the others. The conference usually took place there, and then we went together in a taxi to one or other of the meeting-places which Gregory had established."

"As soon as you have quite recovered we will lay a trap and secure the whole gang," I whispered confidently.

"Ah! I fear that will not be easy," she exclaimed, slowly shaking her head. "We shall be too well watched."

"And we can watch also," I remarked. "I know that from to-day I shall be kept under close supervision because they will fear me more than ever. But I shall manage to evade them, never fear. As soon as you leave hospital we must join forces and exterminate this gang of assassins."

She drew a long breath, bent her fair brows and looked straight across at the pale-green wall. I could see that she was not at all confident of escape. She knew how clever, designing and unscrupulous was the old man Gregory; how cheaply her uncle, Jules Jeanjean, held human life.

"Where is Gregory now, I wonder?" I exclaimed.

"Who knows? They are all in France or Belgium, I expect. They may be in Amsterdam, but I do not think so, as they might suspect me of making a statement to the police."

"What did you tell the police?"

For a moment she hesitated.

"Simply that I was enticed there by a young man whom I knew in Paris, and found myself in the company of several men who were undoubtedly thieves. These men I described. I stated that I was pressed to act as their decoy, and on refusal was struck down."

"Then they will be already searching for the men!" I exclaimed, remembering that Warton had that morning gone up to consult his chief at Scotland Yard.

"They will be searching for men whose descriptions do not tally with those of my uncle and his friends," she whispered frankly, with a mischievous smile.

"Tell me, Lola," I asked, after complimenting her upon her astuteness, "do you recognize the names of Lavelle, Kunzle, Geering, or Hodrickx?"

She started, staring at me.

"Why? What do you know of them?" she inquired quickly, an apprehensive look upon her pretty face.

"They are associates of your uncle, are they not—in fact, members of the gang?"

"Yes. But how did you discover their true names?"

Then I explained how, after poor Craig's death, I had found the paper with the elaborate calculations, and the list of names with corresponding numbers.

"They are code-numbers, so that mention of them can be made in telegrams or letters, and their identity still concealed."

"And what were the columns of figures?" I asked, describing them.

"Probably either the calculations of weights and values of precious stones, or calculations of wave-lengths of wireless telegraphy in which Gregory experiments," she replied. "After a *coup* Gregory always valued the stolen gems very carefully before they were sent to Antwerp or Amsterdam to be re-cut and altered out of recognition. At one *coup*, a year ago, when at Klein's, the principal jeweller in Vienna, the night-watchman was killed and the safe opened with the acetylene jet. We got clear away with jewels valued at three-quarters of a million francs. Afterwards, I motored from Vienna to Antwerp, carrying most of the unset stones and pearls in the radiator of my car. The prying *douaniers* at the frontiers never suspect anything there, nor in the inner tube of a spare wheel. Besides, I was the daughter of the Baronne de Lericourt, travelling with her maid, therefore nobody suspected, and Kunzle, a young Dane, acted as my chauffeur."

"In which direction did your uncle travel?"

"To Algiers, by way of Trieste, and home to his hobby, wireless telegraphy. He has high aerial wires across the grounds of his villa, and can receive on his delicate apparatus messages from Clifden in Ireland, Trieste, Paris, Madrid, London, Port Said, and stations all over Europe."

"Can he transmit messages?" I asked.

She sighed slightly, her wound was giving her pain.

"Oh, yes. His transmitter is very powerful, and sometimes, at night, he can reach Poldhu in Cornwall."

"Then your uncle is, apparently, a skilled scientist, as well as a daring criminal!" I said, surprised.

"*Oui*, M'sieur. He is just now experimenting with a wireless telephone, and has already heard from Algiers, across the Mediterranean, to Genoa, where his friend, the man Hodrickx, has established a similar station. It was Hodrickx you saw at Spring Grove."

"And the wireless is sometimes used for their nefarious purposes, I suppose?"

"Probably. But that is, of course, their own secret. I am told nothing," was her reply, dropping into French. "Sometimes, when at home, my uncle sits for hours with the telephones over his ears, listening—listening attentively—and now and then, scribbling down the mysterious call-letters he hears, and referring to his registers to see whose attention is being attracted. Every night, at twelve o'clock, he receives the day's news sent out from Clifden in Ireland to ships in the Atlantic."

"It must be an exceedingly interesting hobby," I remarked.

"It is. If I were a man I should certainly go in for experimenting. There is something weirdly mysterious about it," she said with a sweet expression.

"If he can speak by telephone across the Mediterranean to Genoa, then, no doubt, such an instrument is of greatest use to him in the pursuit of his shameful profession," I said.

"I expect it is," she answered rather grimly, regarding me with half-closed eyes. "But, oh! M'sieu', how can I bear the future? What will happen now? I cannot tell. For me it must be either a violent death, at a moment when I least expect it, or—or——"

"Leave it all to me, Lola," I interrupted. "I'll leave no stone unturned to effect the arrest of the whole gang."

"Do be careful of yourself," she urged, with apprehension. "Remember, they intend at all hazards to kill you! Gregory and my uncle fear you more than they do the police. Ever since you unearthed that mystery in Brussels, they have held you in terror. The evidence you gave in the Assize Court against the man Lefranc showed them that you entertained suspicion of who killed the jeweller, Josse Vanderelst, in the Avenue Louise. And for that reason you have since been a marked man," she added, looking very earnestly into my face.

"I assure you I have now no fear of them, Lola. I will extricate you from the guilty bonds in which they hold you, if you will only render me assistance."

For a moment she remained thoughtful, a very serious expression upon her fair face.

"*Bien!* But if the men are arrested they will at once turn upon me," she argued. "Then I too will stand in the criminal dock beside them!"

"Not if you act as I direct," I assured her, placing my hand upon hers, which lay outside the coverlet.

Then, after a brief pause, during which I again looked straight into her great blue eyes, I suddenly asked—

"Where can I find trace of old Gregory? As soon as I am a little better I shall resume my investigations, and run the whole gang to earth."

"I do not know where he lives. My uncle once remarked that he was so evasive that he changed his abode as often as he did his collars. His office, however, is in Hatton Garden over a watchmaker's named Etherington, on the second floor. You will find on a door, 'Loicq Freres, Diamond Dealers, Antwerp.' Mr. Gregory Vernon, not Vernon Gregory, poses as the London manager of the firm of 'Loicq Freres,' who, by reason of their wealth and the magnitude of their purchases and sales, are well known in the diamond trade. So, by carrying on a genuine business, he very successfully conceals his illegitimate one of re-cutting stones and re-placing them upon the market."

"Good!" I said, enthusiastically, in English. "I shall endeavour to trace his hiding-place, for most certainly he is no longer in London, now that he knows that his attempt upon you was unsuccessful."

"And the police are now looking for mythical persons!" she laughed merrily, displaying her white, even teeth.

Yes, the more I saw of my dainty little divinity, the greater I became attracted by her, even though force of circumstances had, alas! compelled her, against her will, to become an expert jewel-thief, who by reason of her charm, her beauty, and her astuteness, had passed without suspicion.

What a strange and tragic career had been that of the frail little creature now smiling so sweetly at me! My heart went out in sympathy towards her, just as it had done ever since that memorable night when I had gripped her slim waist and captured her in my room.

The nurse entered, so I rose from my chair, and clasping Lola's little hand, bade her *au revoir*, promising to return again in two days' time, and also suggesting that when she became convalescent I should take her down to some friends of mine at Boscombe to recuperate.

My suggestion she adopted at once, and then I turned, and thanking the nurse for all her kindness, left the hospital.

CHAPTER XXII
THE ROAD OF RICHES

When my doctor first allowed me forth on foot it was fully a week later.

I had driven to Brentford in a taxi on three occasions to visit Lola, taking her fresh flowers, grapes and other dainties. Each time I recognized a marked improvement in her.

I felt certain that every movement of mine was being watched, but neither Rayner nor myself could discover any one spying upon us. I had always flattered myself that nobody could keep observation upon me without I detected them, and I certainly felt considerable chagrin at my present helplessness.

Rayner, a shrewd, clever watcher himself, was up to every ruse in the science of keeping observation and remaining unseen. Yet he also failed to discover any one.

Therefore, one morning I left Carlos Place in a taxi and drove to King's Cross Station, where I alighted, paid the man, and went on to the main line departure platform. Thence I passed across to the arrival platform, so as to evade any pursuer, though no one had followed me to my knowledge, and then I drove down to Brentford.

Though still weak, I that afternoon accompanied the dainty little invalid down to Bournemouth, where I saw her comfortably installed with a very worthy family—a retired excise officer and his wife and daughter, living at Boscombe—and, after a night at the *Bath Hotel*, I returned to London to resume my investigations.

Through three days following I felt very unwell and unable to go out, the journey to Bournemouth having rather upset me in my weak state. Indeed, it was not before another week that one afternoon I alighted from a taxi at Holborn Circus and strolled leisurely down Hatton Garden in search of the watchmaker's Lola had indicated.

I found it with but little difficulty, about half-way down on the left-hand side.

A stranger passing along Hatton Garden, that dreary, rather mean street, leading from busy Holborn away to the poverty-stricken district of Saffron Hill, with its poor Italian denizens and its Italian church, would never dream that it contained all the chief wholesale dealers in precious stones in London. In that one street, hidden away in the safes of the various dealers, Jew and Gentile, are gems and pearls worth millions.

The houses are sombre, grimed, and old-fashioned, and there is an air of middle-class respectability about them which disguises from the stranger the real character of their contents. The very passers-by are for the most part shabby, though, now and then, one may see a well-dressed man enter or leave one of the houses let out in floors to the diamond dealers.

It is a street of experts, of men who pay thousands of pounds for a single stone, and who regard the little paper packets of glittering diamonds as the ordinary person would regard packets of seed-peas.

Many a shabby man with shiny coat, and rather down at heel, passing up the street, carries in his pocket, in a well-worn leathern wallet, diamonds, rubies or emeralds worth the proverbial king's ransom.

On that autumn afternoon the sun was shining brightly as I passed the house where "Gregory Vernon's" office was situated. Seldom, indeed, does the sun shine in Hatton Garden or in Saffron Hill, but when it does it brings gladness to the hearts of those sons and daughters of the sunny Italy, who are wearing out their lives in the vicinity. To them, born and bred in the fertile land where August is indeed the Lion Month, the sun is their very life. Alas! it comes to them so very seldom, but when it does, the women and children go forth into the streets bare-headed to enjoy the "bella giornata."

And so it was then. Some Italian women and children, with a few old men, white-haired and short of stature, were passing up and down the Road of Riches into which I had ventured.

I knew not, of course, whether old Gregory was still in London. He might be at his upper window for aught I knew. Therefore I had adopted the dress of a curate of the Church of England, a disguise which on many an occasion had stood me in good stead. And as I loitered through the road, with eyes about me on all hands, I presented the appearance of the hard-worked curate of a poor London parish.

Before the watchmaker's I halted, looking in at the side door, where I saw written up with the names in dark, dingy lettering, "Loicq Freres, Second Floor."

Beyond was a dark, well-worn stair leading to the other offices, but all looked so dingy and so dismal, that it was hard to believe that within were stored riches of such untold value.

I did not hesitate long, but with sudden resolve entered boldly and mounted the stairs.

On the second floor, on a narrow landing, was a dingy, dark-brown door on which the words "Loicq Freres" were painted.

At this I knocked, whereupon a foreign voice called, "Come in."

I entered a clerk's room where, at a table, sat a man who, when he raised his head and sallow face, I recognized instantly as the mysterious motor-cyclist of Cromer, the man Egisto Bertini, who had so cleverly evaded me on the night of my long vigil on the Norwich road, and who had assisted Gregory, or Vernon as he called himself, to remove the jewels from Beacon House.

He did not, of course, recognize me, though I knew his face in an instant. He rose and came forward.

"Is Mr. Gregory Vernon in?" I asked, assuming a clerical drawl.

"No, sare," replied the dark-eyed Italian. "Can I gif him any message?" he asked with a strong accent.

The reply satisfied me, for my object in going there was not to see the man whose real name was Vernon, but to get a peep at the unsuspicious headquarters of the greatest criminal in Europe.

"Ah, I—I called to ask him to be good enough to subscribe to an outing we are giving to the poor children of my parish—that of St. Anne's. We have much poverty, you know, and the poor children want a day in the country before autumn is over. Several kind friends——"

"Meester Vernon, he will not be able to make a subscription—he is away," broke in the Italian.

My quick eye had noticed that opposite me was a door of ground-glass. A shadow had flitted across that glass, for the short curtains behind it were inadvertently drawn slightly aside.

Some one was within. If it were Vernon, then he might have a secret hole for spying and would recognize me. Thereupon I instantly altered my position, turning my back towards the door, as though unconsciously.

"I'm sorry," I said. "Perhaps you could subscribe a trifle yourself, if only one shilling?" and I took out a penny account book with which I had provided myself.

"Ah, no," was his reply. "I haf none to gif," and he shook his head and held out his palms. "Meester Vernon—he reech man—me, no! Me only clerk!"

"I'm sorry," I said. "Perhaps you will tell Mr. Vernon that the Reverend Harold Hawke called."

"Yes, sare," replied the expert motor-cyclist, whom I knew to be one of the clever gang. And he pretended to scribble something upon a pad. He posed as a clerk perfectly, even to the shabbiness of his office-coat. He presented the appearance of a poor, under-paid foreign clerk, of whom there are thousands in the City of London.

Standing in such a position that old Mr. Vernon could not see my face, I conversed with the Italian a few moments longer as I wished to make some further observations. What I saw surprised me, for there seemed every evidence that a *bona fide* trade was actually conducted there.

The shadow across the private office had puzzled me. I entertained a strong suspicion that old Vernon was within that room, and the man, Egisto Bertini, had orders to tell all strangers that his master was absent.

If he feared arrest—as no doubt he did, knowing that Lola might make a statement to the police—then it was but natural that he would not see any stranger.

No. I watched Bertini very closely as I chatted with him, feeling assured that he was lying.

So I apologized for my intrusion, as a good curate should do, and descended the dark, narrow stairs with the firm conviction that Gregory Vernon was actually in his office.

In the street I walked leisurely towards Holborn, fearing to hurry lest the crafty old man should be watching my departure. Having turned the corner, however, I rushed to the nearest telephone and got on to Rayner.

He answered me quickly, and I gave him instructions to dress instantly as a poor, half-starved labourer—for my several suits of disguise fitted him—and to meet me at the earliest moment at Holborn Circus, outside Wallis's shop.

"All right, sir," was the man's prompt reply. "I'll be there inside half an hour."

"And, Rayner," I added, "bring my small suit-case with things for the night, and an extra suit. Drop it at the cloak-room at Charing Cross on your way here. I may have to leave London."

"Anything interesting, sir?" he asked, his natural curiosity rising.

"Yes. I'll tell you when we meet," was my answer, and I rang off.

I have always found clerical clothes an excellent disguise for keeping observation. It may be conspicuous, but the clergyman is never regarded with any suspicion, where an ill-dressed man who loiters is in peril of being interfered with by the police, "moved on," or even taken into custody on suspicion of loitering for the purpose of committing a felony. England is not exactly the "free country" which those ignorant of our by-laws are so fond of declaring.

Having spoken to Rayner, I returned to the corner of Hatton Garden, and idling about aimlessly, kept a sharp eye upon the watchmaker's shop.

If my visit to the offices of Loicq Brothers had aroused any suspicion in the mind of Gregory Vernon, then he would, no doubt, make a bolt for it. If not, he would remain there till he left for his home.

In the latter case I should certainly discover the place of his abode, and take the first step towards striking the blow.

On the one hand, I argued that Vernon would never dare to remain in England after his brutal attack upon Lola, knowing that the police must question her. Then there was the tell-tale excavation in the garden at Spring Grove—the nameless grave ready prepared for her! But, on the other hand, I recollected the subtle cunning of the man, his bold audacity, his astounding daring, and his immunity hitherto from the slightest suspicion.

The flitting shadow upon the ground-glass was, I felt confident, his silhouette—that silhouette I had known so well—when he had been in the habit of passing the *Hôtel de Paris*, at Cromer, a dozen times a day.

The afternoon wore on, but I still remained at the Holborn end of Hatton Garden, ever watchful of all who came and went. Rayner was longer than he had anticipated, for he had to drive down to Charing Cross before coming to me. But at last I saw a wretched, ill-dressed, pale-faced man alight from a bus outside Wallis's drapery shop, and, glancing round, he quickly found me.

I walked round a corner and, when we met, I explained in a few brief words the exact situation.

Then I instructed him to pass down Hatton Garden to the Clerkenwell Road end and watch there while I maintained a vigilance in Holborn. When Vernon came out we would both follow him, and track him to his dwelling-place.

I told Rayner of Bertini's presence there as a clerk, whereupon my man grew full of vengeful anger, expressing a hope that later on he would meet the Italian face to face and get even for the treatment meted out to him on that memorable night at Cromer.

We had walked together to the end of the Road of Riches in earnest discussion, when, on suddenly glancing along the pavement in the direction of the watchmaker's, I recognized the figure of a well-dressed man coming in our direction.

I held my breath, for his presence there was entirely unexpected.

It was Jules Jeanjean.

CHAPTER XXIII
FOLLOWS THE ELUSIVE JULES

The man of a hundred aliases, and as many crimes, was walking swiftly in our direction, and I only just had time to nip back and cross to the street refuge in the centre of Holborn Circus.

Rayner recognized him in an instant, and I had just time to exclaim—

"There's Jeanjean! Take him up, but be careful. Got your revolver?"

"Trust me, sir," Rayner laughed. "I don't forget Cromer."

"Be careful," I whispered, and next instant we had separated.

I saw Jeanjean gain the end of the drab thoroughfare and glance around apprehensively. He was dressed smartly in a well-cut suit of blue serge and wore a grey hat of soft felt, and a pair of yellow wash-leather gloves, like those poor Craig had habitually affected. His quick, shifty eyes searched everywhere for a few seconds, then he turned into the bustle of the traffic in Holborn and walked westward in the direction of Oxford Street.

A moment later Rayner, a poor wretched-looking figure, penurious and ill, crossed from the opposite side of the road and lounged slowly after Jeanjean until I lost them amidst the crowd.

I was divided in my intentions, for if I followed the pair I should miss the Italian clerk, and as he undoubtedly was a member of the interesting association, I felt that it would be judicious to follow and ascertain where he lived.

For nearly two hours, nevertheless, my vigilance remained unrewarded. Office-boys came forth from the various houses laden with letters, and middle-aged clerks carried in black bags packets of precious stones in order to insure them for transmission by post. Then as the dusk crept on, the offices and workshops in the vicinity emptied their workers, who hurried home by train or motor-bus, while in a constant stream came weary Italians, painfully and patiently dragging piano-organs and ice-cream barrows on their way to their quarters at the other end of the road, their day's wanderings over.

A perfect panorama of London life passed by me as I stood there watching in vain.

At length, about seven o'clock, when it had grown dark and the street-lamps had been lit, I saw the figure of the Italian emerge from the door, and turning his back towards me, he walked in the direction of Clerkenwell Road.

In eagerness I took a few quick steps after him, but halted as a sudden suggestion arose within me. If Jeanjean had been there it was for consultation with his chief—the man he regarded as his master—the master-mind of that daring and dangerous association. Was it possible, therefore, that these two men had left the place at long intervals, because of the suspicion in which they held the curate who had called for a subscription? Was it possible that Gregory Vernon, alias Gregory, and alias a dozen other names, no doubt, was still safe in his high-up dingy little office wherein lay concealed stolen gems of untold value?

Rayner was, without doubt, hot upon the track of the elusive bandit whose *empreintes digitales*, and whose *clichés* and *relevés* were so carefully preserved in that formidable dossier at the Prefecture of Police of the Seine. Rayner was a past master in the art of observation, and I felt convinced that ere long I should learn where Jeanjean made his headquarters in London.

Therefore, after a second's reflection, I decided not to follow Bertini, but to still remain on and watch for the clever old rascal to whose plots so many jewel robberies in Europe, with and without violence, were due. By some vague intuition I felt that if Jeanjean dared to go to the offices of Loicq Freres, then certainly the elder man would have no hesitation. But their daring was astounding in face of the circumstances.

Perhaps, so completely and entirely did they hold Lola in their grip, that they felt confident she dare not reveal the truth. Was it not a fact, alas! that the sweet, dainty little girl was actually a thief, forced into crime and trained by her uncle to act the part of decoy, her very innocence disarming suspicion? Her youth was her protection, for nobody would believe that she was actually a clever adventuress and a professional thief.

Ah! how I pitied her, knowing all that I did. How often recollections arose in my mind of that never-to-be-forgotten night in Scotland when she had inadvertently entered my bedroom, and I had seized her—of her piteous appeal to me, and of her expression of heartfelt thanks when I allowed her her liberty. Yes, assuredly Lola Sorel was to be pitied, not blamed. She had been struggling all along to free herself from those bonds of guilt which had bound her to that unscrupulous brutal gang of malefactors who were undoubtedly the most dangerous criminals in Europe. But, alas! all in vain. They had held her in their inexorable grip until, fearing lest she should appeal to me and make revelations, the sinister-faced old rascal who ruled them had ruthlessly struck her down and left her for dead.

Such a formidable band as that, constituted as it was, and with enormous funds at command, could hold the police in contempt. Money was of no object, and Lola had once told me how police officials, both in Berlin and in Rome, had been judiciously "squared" by a certain obscure lawyer who had an office in the Italian capital, and who, being a member of the gang, conducted their legal affairs—which mainly consisted in the obtaining of information concerning the whereabouts of jewels in the possession of private families, and in bribing any obnoxious police official, from a *sous-prefet* down to a humble *agent*.

Bribery among the Continental police is far more rife than is generally supposed. Poor pay, especially in Italy, is the prime cause. There are, of course, black sheep in every flock, even in England, but in the southern countries the aspect of the flock is much darker than in the northern ones. Many a law-breaker to-day pays toll to the police, even in our own London, and from the street bookmaker in the East End slums to the keeper of the luxurious gaming-house near Piccadilly Circus, hundreds of men are allowed to carry on their nefarious practices by sending anonymous presents to the private addresses of those who might trouble them.

So it is even in matters criminal. There is not a single member of the Criminal Investigation Department who has not been sorely tempted at one time or another. And perhaps in the light of certain recent prosecutions, and the allegations of Mr. Keir Hardie, big names—the names of certain men who are leaders of our present-day life and thought—are suppressed, and grave scandals concealed by the judicious application of gold.

My watch proved a wearying one, especially in my weak state.

With the darkness there were fewer people in the streets. The City traffic had now died down, and at eight o'clock Hatton Garden had become practically deserted.

I had been chatting to the constable on duty, who, on account of my clerical attire, had not viewed me with any suspicion, when of a sudden Rayner alighted from a taxi and approached me.

"Well?" I asked eagerly, when we were together.

"He gave me the slip, sir," exclaimed my man breathlessly. "He's devilish clever, he is, sir."

"You surely knew that before, Rayner," I said, reproachfully.

"Yes, and I took every precaution. But he did me in the end."

"How?"

"Well, when he left here, he walked as far as Gamage's very leisurely. Then he took a taxi up to Baker Street Station. I followed him, and saw that he took a ticket to Swiss Cottage, where he took another taxi along the Finchley Road, alighting at the end of a rather quiet thoroughfare of superior houses called Arkwright Road. He went into one of them, a new red-brick house, called Merton Lodge."

"You were near when he entered?" I asked.

"Quite. I watched the door open to admit him, but couldn't see who opened it," he replied. "Then I waited for nearly two hours, concealing myself in the area of an unoccupied house close by. The road was so quiet and unfrequented that I dare not show myself. The house seemed smart and well-kept, with a large garden behind."

"No one came out?"

"Nobody. But at last I grew impatient and got out on to the pavement, when, a few seconds later, the door opened, and a middle-aged, dark-eyed man came out straight up to me. He had a Hebrew cast in his features. Without ado, he asked me with indignation why I was watching his house. Whereupon I told him I was waiting for a friend who had entered there. In reply, he denied that any friend of mine was there. He said, 'I object to my house being watched like this, and if you don't be off, I shall telephone for the police, and have you arrested for loitering. I believe you intend to commit a burglary.'"

"Ah! that was rather disconcerting, eh, Rayner?"

"Yes, sir. What could I do? I saw I'd been spotted, and so the game was up. Well, a thought occurred to me, and I replied to him, 'Very good. Telephone at once. I'll be pleased to have a constable here to help me.' It was a bold move, but it worked. He believed me to be a detective, and his tone altered at once. 'I tell you,' he said, 'I have nobody in my house. Nobody has come in since I returned home at five o'clock. You may search, if you wish!' I smiled and said, 'Oh, so you don't now suspect me of being a thief?' 'Well,' he replied, 'if you think your friend is here, come over and satisfy yourself.'"

"Clever of him—very clever," I remarked. "But there might have been a trap! Jeanjean would set one without the slightest hesitation."

"Just what I suspected, sir," replied Rayner. "At first I hesitated, but I had my revolver with me, so I resolved to search the place. Just as I crossed the road a constable turned the corner idly, and in a moment I was beside him. In a few words I asked him to accompany me, at the same time slipping a couple of half-crowns into his hand, much to the chagrin of the occupier of the house. To the constable I explained that I had reason to believe that a friend of mine was hidden in the house and I had been invited to search. So together we went in, and while the constable remained in the hall, I went from room to room with the dark-faced Hebrew. The place was well furnished, evidently the abode of a man of wealth and taste. He was something of a student, too, for in a corner of the small library at the rear, on the ground-floor, was a table, and on it several queer-looking electrical instruments and a telephone receiver. From room to room I went, and found nobody. Indeed, there was nobody else in the house except a sallow-looking youth, the son of the man who had invited me in. The back premises, however, told their own tale. At the end of the dark garden was a door in the wall, leading to a narrow lane beyond the tradesmen's entrance. By that way Jules Jeanjean had escaped nearly two hours before!"

"So he has eluded you, as he always does," I remarked regretfully.

"Yes. But the owner of Merton Lodge no doubt knows him and gives him shelter when he's in London," Rayner said.

"He may, but, if I judge correctly, Jeanjean knew he was followed from the first, and simply led you there to mystify you. He entered by the front door and went out at once by the back one," I said. "In all probability he only knows the owner of Merton Lodge quite slightly. If not, why did the Hebrew come out so boldly and ask you to search?"

"Bluff," declared Rayner promptly.

"No, not exactly," I remarked. "If Jeanjean knew he was followed he would never have gone to a house where he could be again found, depend upon it. No. He perhaps told the person who opened the door to him some cock-and-bull story, and only remained in the house a minute or two. To me, all seems quite clear. He led you on a wild-goose chase, Rayner," I laughed, as we stood together in Holborn.

Yet scarcely had these words left my mouth when there passed close by us a thin, old gentleman in black, and wearing a silk hat. His grey hair and beard were close-cropped, but his broad forehead and narrow chin could not be disguised.

I held my breath as I recognized him at a glance. He had not noticed me, for my back had been towards him. Yet my heart beat quickly, for might he not have identified me by my clerical hat!

It was the man I had suspected of lying closely concealed in his office— old Gregory Vernon, the dealer in stolen gems.

CHAPTER XXIV
MAKES A STARTLING DISCLOSURE

He crossed Holborn, walking leisurely, and smoking a cigar, and continued down St. Andrew Street and along towards Shoe Lane, I strolling after him at some distance behind.

At that hour the thoroughfare was practically deserted, therefore concealment was extremely difficult. Yet by his leisurely walk I felt convinced that in passing he had, fortunately, not recognized me.

Behind me came Rayner to see, as he swiftly put it, "that no harm came" to me.

The old man in the full enjoyment of his cigar, and apparently quite happy that if his offices were watched his two confederates would have taken off the watchers, strolled along St. Bride Street as far as the corner of Ludgate Hill, when he hailed a taxi and drove westward. His example I quickly followed, leaving Rayner standing on the kerb, unable to follow, as no third cab was in sight.

Up Fleet Street we drove quickly and along the Strand as far as Charing Cross, when the taxi I was pursuing turned into Northumberland Avenue and pulled up before the *Hôtel Metropole*.

I drew up further along, at the corner of the Embankment, at the same time watching the old man pay the driver and enter, being saluted by the uniformed porter, who evidently knew him.

For about five minutes I waited. Then I entered the hotel, where I also was well known, having very often stayed there.

Of the porter at the door, who touched his hat as I went in, I asked the name of the old gentleman who had just entered.

"I don't know his name, sir. He often stays here. They'll tell you at the key-office."

So I ascended the stairs into the hall, and made inquiry of the sharp-eyed, dark-faced man at the key-counter.

"Oh, Mr. Vernon, you mean, sir? Been in about five minutes. He's just gone up in the lift—Room 139*a*, first-floor—shall I send your name up, Mr. Vidal?"

"No, I'll go up," I said. "You're sure he is up in his room?"

"Quite sure, sir. He took his key about five minutes ago."

"Is he often here?"

"Every month," was the reply. "He usually spends about a week with us, and always has the same room."

"What is he? Have you any idea?"

"I've heard that he's a diamond-broker. Lives in Paris, I fancy."

"Has he many callers?"

"One or two business men sometimes; but only one lady."

"A lady!" I echoed. "Who?"

"Oh, a very pretty young French girl who comes sometimes to see him," replied the clerk. Then, after reflection, he added: "I think the name is Sorel—Mademoiselle Sorel."

I started at mention of the name.

"Does she come alone?" I asked. "Excuse me making these inquiries," I added apologetically, "but I have strong reasons for doing so."

"Once she came alone, I think about six weeks ago. But she generally comes with a tall, rather ugly, but well-dressed Frenchman of about forty-five, a man who seems to be Mr. Vernon's most intimate friend."

I asked for a further description of her companion, and decided that it was Jules Jeanjean.

"Is the hotel detective about?" I asked.

"Yes. He's somewhere down on the smoking-room floor. Do you want him?" he asked, surprised.

I replied in the affirmative. Whereupon a page was at once dispatched, and returned with an insignificant-looking man, an ex-sergeant of Scotland Yard, engaged by the hotel as its private inquiry agent.

He knew me well, therefore I said—

"Will you come up with me to 139*a*. I want to see a Mr. Vernon, and there may be a little trouble. I may have to call in the police."

"What's the trouble, sir?" he asked in surprise, though he knew me to be an investigator of crime.

"Only a little difference between us," I said. "He may have a revolver. Have you got one?"

The detective smiled, and produced a serviceable-looking Colt from his hip-pocket, while I drew a long, plated, hammerless Smith & Wesson, which has been my constant companion throughout my adventurous life.

Then together we ascended in the lift, and passed along the corridor till we found the room which the clerk had indicated.

I tapped loudly at the door, at the same moment summoning all my self-possession. I was about to secure one of the most cunning and clever criminals on earth.

There was no answer. Yet I distinctly heard some one within the room.

Again I knocked loudly.

Then I heard footsteps advancing to the door, which was thrown open, and a chambermaid stood there.

"I'm sorry, sir," she said apologetically.

I drew back in dismay.

"Is Mr. Vernon in here?" I asked breathlessly.

"Mr. Vernon—the gentleman in this room, sir?"

"Yes. He has come up here, I know."

"He did come in a few minutes ago, and took a small leather case, but he went out again at once."

"Went out? You saw him?"

"Yes. He was coming out just as I came in, sir," replied the girl.

"Gone!" I gasped, turning to the ex-sergeant.

"He must have gone down the stairs, sir," the man suggested.

With a glance round the room, which only contained a suit-case, I dashed down the stairs and into the hall.

Of the porter at the door I asked a quick question.

"No, sir," he replied. "Mr. Vernon hasn't gone out this way. He may have gone out by the door in Whitehall Place."

I rushed through the hotel and, at the door indicated, the man in uniform told me that Mr. Vernon had left on foot five minutes before, going towards Whitehall.

I hurried after him, but alas! I was too late.

Again, he had evaded me!

So I returned to my rooms utterly fagged by the long vigil, and feeling thoroughly ill. Indeed, in my weak state, it had been a somewhat injudicious proceeding, yet I felt anxious and impatient, eager to strike a crushing blow against the daring band who held poor Lola so completely in their power.

The result of my imprudence, however, was another whole week in bed, and a further confinement to my room for a second week. Meanwhile Rayner was active and watchful.

Observation upon the offices of Loicq Frères showed that only an English clerk was left in charge, and that neither Vernon, Jeanjean nor Bertini had since been there. Vigilance upon Merton Lodge, in Hampstead, also resulted in nothing. It was clear, therefore, that the trio had become alarmed at my visit to Hatton Garden, even though I had exercised every precaution to avoid recognition.

As I sat in my big arm-chair, day after day, unable to go out, I carefully reviewed all the events of the past, just as I have set them down in these pages. Somehow—how it came to pass, I cannot tell—I found myself thinking more than ever of Lola Sorel, the sweet-faced, innocent-looking girl whose career had been fraught with so much tragedy, apprehension and bitterness.

Every day, nay, every hour, her pretty, fair face arose before my vision— that pale, delicately-moulded countenance, with the big, blue, wondering eyes, larger and more perfect than the eyes of any woman I had ever before met in the course of my adventurous career.

Time after time I asked myself why my thoughts should so constantly revert to her. Sleeping or waking, I dreamed ever of that dainty little figure with its sweet, rather sad face, the pathetic countenance of the pretty Parisienne who had so gradually fascinated and entranced me.

Within myself, I laughed at my own feelings of sympathy towards her. Why should I entertain any regard for a girl who, after all, was only a thief—a girl whose innocence had decoyed men, and caused women to betray the whereabouts of their jewels, so that her associates could rob them with impunity?

From the moment when I had seized her in my bedroom at Balmaclellan I had pitied her, and that pity had now deepened into keen sympathy for her, held, as she was, in those bonds of guilt, yet struggling always to free herself, like a poor frightened bird beating its wings against the bars.

Had I fallen in love with her? Time after time I asked myself that question. But time after time did I scout the very idea and laughed myself to ridicule.

The thought that I loved Lola Sorel, beautiful as she was, seemed utterly absurd.

Yes. During that fortnight of forced inactivity I had plenty of time to carefully analyse the whole situation, to examine every detail of the mystery surrounding the death of Edward Craig and, also, to formulate fresh plans.

One fact was evident—that Vernon and his friends intended that Lola should die. In addition, so subtle were they, I knew not when some secret and desperate attack might not be made upon myself.

Foul play was intended. Of that I had no doubt.

The autumn days were passing. Business London had returned from the country and the sea, and even the blinds of houses in Berkeley Square were, one after another, being raised, indicative of the fact that many people in Society were already again in town.

I exchanged letters with Lola almost daily. She was very happy and had greatly improved, she said, and also expressed a hope that we should soon meet, a hope which I devoutly reciprocated.

My one great fear, however, was that some dastardly attack might be made upon her if any of the bandits succeeded in discovering her hiding-place. For that reason I sent Rayner to Bournemouth in secret to watch the house, and to ascertain whether any signs of intended evil were apparent.

He remained there a week, until one morning in October I received an urgent telegram from him asking me, if I were well enough, to lose no time in coming to Bournemouth. He gave no reason for the urgency of his message, but gravely apprehensive, I took the next train from Waterloo, arriving in Bournemouth about four o'clock. Rayner refused to meet me openly, so I drove to the *Grand Hotel*, where he was staying, and found him in his room awaiting me.

"There's something up, sir," he said very seriously, when I had closed the door. "But I can't exactly make out what is intended. Mademoiselle does not, of course, know I'm here. She went to the Winter Gardens with two young ladies last night, and they were followed by a man—a stranger. He went behind them to the concert, and sat in the back seats watching them, and when they walked home, he followed."

"Have you ever seen him before?"

"Never, sir."

"Is he young or old?"

"Young, and looks like a gentleman."

"A foreigner?"

"No, an Englishman, sir," was my man's reply. "I dare say if we go along to Boscombe to-night, and watch the house, we might see him. He's up to no good, I believe."

I readily adopted Rayner's suggestion.

As soon as darkness fell, we took the tram eastward, and at length alighted at the end of a quiet road of comfortable red-brick villas, in one of which Lola was residing, a road which ran from the highway towards the sea.

Separating, I passed up the road, while my man waited at the corner. The house of my friends stood in its own small garden, a neat, artistic little red-and-white place with a long verandah in front and a pleasant garden full of dahlias. As I passed it I saw that many of the rooms were lit, and I was eager to go and ring at the door and meet Lola, after our long separation.

But I remembered I was there to watch and to ward off any danger that might threaten. Therefore I turned upon my heel, and finding a hedge, behind which lay some vacant land, I hid myself behind it and waited, wondering what had become of Rayner.

All was quiet, save for the rumble of electric trams passing along the main road to Bournemouth. From where I lurked, smoking a cigarette, I could hear a woman's sweet contralto voice singing gaily one of the latest songs of the Paris Café concerts, which ran—

"*C'est la femme aux bijoux,*
Celle qui rend fou,
C'est une enjôleuse,
Tous ceux qui l'ont aimée,
Ont souffert, ont pleuré.

Ell' n'aime que l'argent,
Se rit des serments,
Prends garde à la gueuse!
Le cœur n'est qu'un joujou,
Pour la femme aux bijoux!"
La femme aux bijoux!

The words fell upon my ears, causing me to ponder. Was she not herself "*La femme aux bijoux*"! How strangely appropriate was that merry *chanson* which I had so often heard in Paris, Brussels, and elsewhere.

Suddenly the train of my reflections was interrupted by the sound of a light footstep coming in my direction, and, peering eagerly forth, I discerned the figure of a rather smart-looking man advancing towards me.

I watched him come forward, tall and erect, into the light of the street-lamp a little to my left. He was well dressed in a smart suit of dark brown with well-creased trousers, and wore a soft Hungarian hat of dark-brown plush. On his hands were wash-leather gloves and he carried a gold-mounted stick.

As he came nearer I saw his face, and my heart gave a great leap. I stared again, not being able to believe my own eyes!

Was it, indeed, any wonder? How would you, my reader, have felt in similar circumstances? I ask, for the man who came past me, within a couple of feet from where I stood concealed, all unconscious of my presence, was no stranger.

It was Edward Craig—Edward Craig, risen from the dead!

CHAPTER XXV
IS MORE MYSTERIOUS

I stood there aghast, staggered, open-mouthed. The man was walking slowly towards the house whence issued the gay *chanson*, the house where, in the great bay window, shone a bright light across the tiny strip of lawn which separated it from the roadway.

I watched him like a man in a dream. As he approached the house he trod lightly on tip-toe, unaware of my presence behind the bushes. In a flash the recollections of that strange affair by the North Sea, in Cromer, recurred to me. I remembered that green-painted seat upon the cliff, where the coast-guard, in the early dawn, had found him lying dead, of his strange disguise, and of the coroner's inquiry which followed. I remembered too, all too well, the puzzling incidents which followed; the presence of the notorious Jeanjean in that quiet little cliff-resort; the disappearance of the man of master-mind; the discovery of his hoard of gold and gems, and how, subsequently, it had been spirited away in a manner which had absolutely flabbergasted the astute members of the Norfolk Constabulary, unused as they were to cases of ingenious crime.

Truly it was all amazing—utterly astounding.

I watched Craig's receding figure in startled wonder, holding my breath, and trying to convince myself that I had been mistaken in some resemblance.

But I was not. The man who had passed me was Edward Craig in the flesh—the man upon whose death twelve honest tradesmen of Cromer had delivered their verdict—the man who had been placed in his coffin and buried.

Was ever there incident such as this, I wondered? Had ever man met with a similar experience?

By the light of the street-lamp I saw him glance anxiously up and down that quiet, dark road. Then satisfying himself that he was unobserved, he crept in at the gate, crossed the lawn noiselessly, and peered in at the window through the chink between the windowframe and the blind.

For fully five minutes he remained with his eyes glued to the window. In the light which fell upon him I saw that his face had assumed an angry, vengeful look, and that his gloved hands were clenched.

Yes. He certainly meant mischief. He was watching her as she sat, all unconsciously, at the piano, singing the gay *chansons* of the boulevards, "Mimi d'Amour," "Le tic-tac du Moulin," "Petit Pierre," and others, so popular in Paris at the moment.

The family of the retired excise-officer knew but little French, but they evidently enjoyed the spontaneous gaiety of the songs.

That Edward Craig, after his mysterious death, should reappear as a shadow in the night was certainly most astounding. At first I tried to convince myself that only a strong resemblance existed, but his gait, his figure, his face, the manner in which he held his cane, and the slight angle at which he wore his hat—the angle affected by those elegant young men who in these days are termed "nuts"—were all the same.

Yes. It was Edward Craig and none other!

And yet, who was the man who so suddenly lost his life while masquerading in the clothes of old Gregory Vernon?

Aye, that was the question.

With strained eyes I watched and saw him change his position in order to obtain a better view of the interior of the room. There was no sign of Rayner, who, I supposed, had not risked following him, knowing that I was lurking close to the house.

That his intentions were evil ones I could not doubt, and yet the light shining upon his countenance revealed a strange, almost fascinated expression, as his eyes were fixed into the room, and upon her without a doubt.

The music had not ceased. Her quick fingers were still running over the keys, and in her sweet contralto she was singing the catching refrain—

"*Mimi d'amour,*

Petite fleur jolie,

Oui pour toujours

Je t'ai donné ma vie.

Les jours sont courts

Grisons-nous, ma chérie,

Petit' Mimi jolie,

Mimi d'amour!"

Her voice ceased, and, as it did so, the silent watcher crept away, gaining the pavement and walking lightly in my direction.

As he passed, within a couple of feet of where I was concealed, I was able to confirm my belief. There was no doubt as to his identity. By this discovery the cliff-mystery at Cromer had become a more formidable and astounding problem. Who could have been the actual victim? What facts did Lola actually know?

So well organized and so far extended the ramifications of the criminal association of which Gregory Vernon was the head and brains, that I became bewildered.

I stood gazing over the hedge watching Craig disappear back towards the main road, where at the corner a small red light now showed.

When he had got a safe distance from me, I emerged and, crossing the road quickly, hastened after him. Rayner was in waiting and would, no doubt, take up the chase.

Yet when he approached the corner I saw that he suddenly crossed to where the red light showed, and entering the car, which was evidently waiting for him, was driven swiftly off to the right in the direction of Christchurch.

Rayner met me in breathless haste a few moments after the car had turned the corner, saying—

"I didn't know that car was waiting for him, sir. It only pulled up a moment ago."

"Was anybody in it?"

"Only the driver."

"Did you take the number?"

"Yes, sir. It's local, we'll soon find out its owner."

"You must do so," I said. "The police will help you. But do you know who that man was?"

"No, sir. He's a stranger to me," Rayner replied.

"Well," I said, "he's Edward Craig."

"Edward Craig!" echoed Rayner, staring at me as we stood at the street corner together. "Why, that's the man who was murdered at Cromer!"

"The same."

"But he died. An inquest was held."

"I tell you, Rayner, that Edward Craig—the man who is supposed to be nephew of old Gregory Vernon—is still alive. I could identify him among ten thousand."

Rayner was silent. Then at last he said—

"Well, sir, that's utterly astounding. Who, then, was the man who was killed?"

"That's just what we have to discover," I replied. "We must find out, too, why he wore old Vernon's clothes on that fatal night."

Thoughts of the footprint, and the tiny shoe which had so exactly fitted it, arose within me, but I kept my own counsel and said nothing.

Having told Rayner to inquire of the police regarding the mysterious car, and to return to the hotel and await me, I retraced my steps along that quiet, eminently respectable road, inhabited mostly by retired tradespeople from London or the North of England, who live in their "model" villas or "ideal homes" so pleasantly situated, after the smoke and bustle of business life.

When I entered the pretty little drawing-room where Lola was, she sprang to her feet to receive me, holding out her small white hand in glad welcome.

In her smiling, sweet face was a far healthier look than when I had taken leave of her, and returned to London, and in reply to my question, she declared that she felt much stronger. The sea air had done her an immense amount of good. Yes, she was a delightful little person who had been ever in my thoughts.

She anxiously inquired after my health, but I laughingly declared that I was now quite right again.

Her hostess, Mrs. Featherstone, with her daughter, Winifred, and a young fellow to whom the latter was engaged, were present, so I sat down for a chat, all four being apparently delighted by my unexpected visit. Mr. Featherstone had, I found, gone to London that morning and would not return for three days.

Presently mother and daughter, and the young man, probably knowing that I wished to speak with Mademoiselle alone, made excuses and left the room.

Then when the door had closed I rose and walked over to where Lola, in a simple semi-evening gown of soft cream silk, was reclining in an armchair, her neat little shoes placed upon a velvet footstool.

"To-night," I said in a low voice in French, as I stood near her chair, my hand resting upon it. "To-night, Lola, I have made a very startling discovery."

"A discovery!" she exclaimed, instantly interested. "What?"

"Edward Craig is still alive!" I answered. "He did not die in Cromer, as we have all believed."

"Edward Craig!" she echoed, amazed. "How do you know? I—I mean—*mon Dieu!*—it's impossible!"

"It seems impossible, but it is, nevertheless, a fact, Lola," I declared in a low, earnest tone as I bent towards her. I had watched her face and, by its expression, knew the truth. "And you," I added, slowly, "have been aware of this all along."

"I—I——" she faltered in French, opening her big blue eyes widely, as the colour mounted to her cheeks in her confusion.

"No," I interrupted, raising my hand in protest. "Please do not deny it. You have known that Craig did not die, Lola. You may as well, at once, admit your knowledge."

"*Certainement*, I have not denied it," was her low reply.

"How did you know he was alive?" I asked.

"Well," and then she hesitated. But, after a few seconds' reflection, she went on: "After that affair at Lobenski's in Petersburg, I was leaving at night for Berlin, by the Ostend rapide, with some of the stolen stones sewn in my dress, as I told you, when, just as the train moved off from the platform, I fancied I caught sight of him. But only for a second. Then, when I came to consider all the facts, I felt convinced that my eyes must have deceived me. Edward Craig was dead and buried, and the man on the railway platform must have only borne some slight resemblance to him."

Was she deceiving me? I wondered.

"Have you since seen the same man anywhere else?" I asked her, seriously.

"Well, yes," she replied slowly. "Curiously enough, I saw the same person once in Paris, and again in London. I was in a taxi going along Knightsbridge on the afternoon of the day when I afterwards walked so innocently into the trap at Spring Grove. He was just coming out of the post-office in Knightsbridge, but did not notice me as I passed. I turned to look at him a second time, but he had gone in the opposite direction and his back was towards me. Yet I felt certain that he was actually the same man whom

I had seen as the Ostend Express had left Petersburg. And now," she added, looking straight into my eyes, "you tell me that Edward Craig still lives!"

"He does. And he has been here—at this house—to-night!"

"At this house!" gasped the Nightingale, starting instantly to her feet, her face as pale as death.

"Yes. He has been standing on the lawn outside, peering in at this window, watching you seated at the piano," I explained.

"Watching me!"

"Yes," I replied. "And, if my surmise is correct, he is certainly no friend of yours. He has watched you during the *coup* in Petersburg, again in Paris, and in London, and now he has discovered your hiding-place," I answered. "What does it all mean?"

Deathly pale, with thin, quivering lips, and hands clasped helplessly before her, she stood there in an attitude of deadly fear, of blank despair.

"Yes," she whispered in a low, strained voice, full of apprehension. "I believed that he was dead, that——"

But she halted, as if suddenly recollecting that her words might betray her. Her bosom, beneath the laces of her corsage, rose and fell convulsively.

"That—what?" I asked in a soft, sympathetic voice, placing my hand tenderly upon her shoulder, and looking into her wonderful eyes.

"Oh! I—I——" she exclaimed in a half-choked voice. "I thought him dead. But now, alas! I find that my suspicions are well grounded. He is alive—and he has actually been here!"

"Then you are in fear of him—in deadly fear, Lola," I said. "Why?" And I looked straight at my dainty little friend.

She tried to make response, but though her white lips moved no sound escaped them. I saw how upset and overwrought she was by the amazing information I had conveyed to her.

"Tell me the truth, Lola—the truth of what happened in Cromer," I urged, my hand still upon her shoulder. "Do not withhold it from me. Remember, I am your friend, your most devoted friend."

She trembled at my question.

"If the dead man was not Edward Craig, then, who was he?" I asked, as she had made no reply.

"How can I tell?" she asked in French. "I thought it was Craig. Was he not identified as Craig and buried as him?"

"Certainly. And I, too, most certainly believed the body to be that of Craig," I answered.

For a few moments there was a dead silence. Then I repeated my question. I could see that she feared that young man's visit even more than she did either her uncle or the old scoundrel Vernon.

For some mysterious reason the fact that Craig still lived held her in breathless suspense and apprehension.

"Lola," I said at last, speaking very earnestly and sympathetically, "am I correct in my surmise that this man, whom both you and I have believed to be in his grave, is in possession of some secret of yours—some weighty secret? Tell me frankly."

For answer she slowly nodded, and next moment burst into a torrent of hot, bitter tears, saying, in a faltering voice, scarce above a whisper—

"Yes, alas! M'sieur Vidal. He—he is in possession of my secret—and—and the past has risen against me!"

CHAPTER XXVI
HOT-FOOT ACROSS EUROPE

By Lola's attitude I became more than ever mystified. I tried to induce her to tell me the exact position of affairs, but she seemed far too nervous and unstrung. The fact that Craig had found out her hiding-place seemed to cause her the most breathless anxiety.

That he knew some guilty secret of hers seemed plain.

It was eleven o'clock before I rose to go, after begging her many times in vain to tell me the truth. I felt confident that she could reveal the strange mystery of Cromer, yet she steadfastly refused.

"You surely see, Lola, that we are both in serious peril," I said, standing before the chair upon which she had sunk in deep dejection. "These daring, unscrupulous people must, sooner or later, make a fatal attack upon us, if we do not deliver our blow against them. To invoke the aid or protection of the police is useless. They set all authority at defiance, for they are wealthy, and the ramifications of their society extend all over Europe."

"I know," she admitted. "Vernon has agents in every country. I have met many of them—quite unsuspicious persons. My uncle has introduced me to people at whose apparent honesty and respectability I have been amazed."

"Then you must surely realize how insecure is the present position of both of us," I said.

"I do. But disaster cannot be averted," was her sorrowful response.

"Unless you unite with me in avenging the attack made upon us at Spring Grove."

"What is the use?" she queried. "They have all left London."

"What?" I exclaimed quickly. "You know that?"

"Yes," she replied. "I know they have."

"How?"

"By an advertisement I saw in the paper three days ago," she answered. "They use a certain column of a certain paper on a certain day to distribute general information to all those interested."

"In a code?"

"In a secret cipher—known only to the friends of M'sieur Vernon," she said. "They always look for his orders or his warnings on the eighteenth of each month. My uncle is back at Algiers."

"Where is Vernon?"

"Ah! I do not know. Perhaps he is with my uncle."

"But the young man, Craig. Why is he watching you? It can only be with evil intent."

She drew a long breath, but said nothing. And to all my further questions she remained dumb, so that when I bent over her outstretched hand and left, I felt annoyed at her resolute secrecy—a secrecy which must, I felt, result fatally.

And yet by her manner I was confident that she was still prevented by fear from revealing everything to me. Yes, after all, I pitied her deeply.

At the *Grand* I found Rayner awaiting me. He had already learnt from the police that the car in which Craig had driven away belonged to a garage in Bournemouth.

On going there he had found the car had just returned. It had been hired for the evening by Craig himself, who had first driven out to Boscombe and was afterwards driven to Christchurch, where he had caught the express for London.

He had, therefore, gone.

This news I scribbled in a note to Lola, and before midnight Rayner had delivered it at Mr. Featherstone's house.

Then I retired to rest full of strange thoughts and serious apprehensions. The revelations of that night had indeed been astounding. Craig was alive, and his intentions were, undoubtedly, sinister ones.

But who was the man who had met with such a mysterious death and had been buried as "Mr. Gregory's nephew?"

At eleven o'clock next morning I took the tram along to Boscombe and rang at the door of the house where my delightful little friend was living.

The neat maid who answered amazed me by saying—

"Mademoiselle left for London by the eight o'clock train this morning, sir. She packed all her things after you left last night, and ordered a cab by telephone."

"Didn't she leave me any message?" I asked Mrs. Featherstone, when I saw her a few moments later.

"No, none, Mr. Vidal," replied the old lady. "After you had gone, and she received your note, she became suddenly very terrified, why, I don't know. Then she packed, and though we tried to persuade her to stay till you called, she declined. All she said, besides thanking us, was that she would write to you."

"Most extraordinary!" I exclaimed. "I wonder what caused her such sudden fear?"

Could it have been that she had discovered any one else watching the house? Strange, I thought, that she had not sent me word of her intended departure. She could so easily have spoken to me on the telephone.

Well, two hours later, I followed her to London, and began an inquiry of hotels where I knew she had stayed on previous occasions—the *Cecil*, the *Savoy*, the *Carlton*, the *Metropole*, the *Grand*, and so forth. But though I spent a couple of hours on the telephone, speaking with various reception clerks, I could get no news of Mademoiselle Sorel.

Yet, was it surprising? She would hardly, in the circumstances, stay in London in her own name.

Ten days went by. By each post I expected news of Lola, but none came, and I felt confident that she had gone abroad.

I wired and wrote to Mademoiselle Elise Leblanc, at the Poste Restante at Versailles. But I obtained no reply. At last I went down to Cromer and remained at the *Hôtel de Paris* for nearly a week, carefully going over all the details of the mystery with Mr. Day and Inspector Treeton, who were, of course, both as much puzzled as I was myself.

The autumn weather was perfect. The holiday crowd had left, and Cromer looked her brightest and best in the glorious sunshine and golden tints of the declining year. On the links I played one or two most enjoyable rounds, and once or twice I sat outside the Golf Club and smoked and chatted with men I knew in London.

Daily I wondered what had become of Lola.

Time after time I visited that green-painted seat near which the dead man had been found and where I had discovered the imprint of Lola's shoe. But, beyond what I have already recorded in the foregoing pages, I could discover absolutely nothing. The identity of the man who had masqueraded in the clothes of the master-criminal was entirely enshrouded in mystery.

The law had buried Edward Craig, and in the cemetery, on the road to Holt was a plain head-stone bearing his name and the date of his death.

How could I have been mistaken in his identity? That was the chief fact which held me puzzled and confused. I had looked upon his face, as others had done, and all had agreed that the man who died was actually Craig.

I told Treeton nothing of my discovery, but one day, as I stood at the window of the hotel gazing across the sea, I made a sudden resolve, and that evening I found myself back again in my rooms in London, with Rayner packing my traps for a trip across the Channel.

My one most deadly fear was that Lola might, already, have fallen into one or other of the pitfalls which were, no doubt, spread open for her. The crafty, unscrupulous gang, with Vernon at their head, were determined that we both should die.

On the morning of my arrival from Cromer I left Charing Cross by the boat-train, and that same evening entered the long, dusty *wagon-lit* of the night rapide for Marseilles.

Marseilles! How many times in my life had I trod the broad Cannebière, drank cocktails at the Louvre et Paix, ate my boullibuisse at the little underground café, where the best in the world is served, or sauntered along the double row of booths placed under the trees of the boulevard—shops where one can buy anything from a toothpick to a kitchen-stove. Yes, even to the blasé cosmopolitan, Marseilles is always interesting, and as I drove along from the station up the Cannebière, I found the place full of life and movement, with the masts of shipping and glimpses of huge docks showing at the end of the broad, handsome thoroughfare.

From the station I drove direct to the big black mail-boat of the French Transatlantic Company, and by noon we had swung out of the harbour past the historic Château d'If, our bows set due south, for Algiers. Lola had told me that Jeanjean had fled to his hiding-place. And I intended to seek him and face him.

There were few passengers on board—one or two French officers on their way to join their regiments, a few commercial men; while in the third class I saw more than one squatting, brown-faced Arab, picturesque in his white burnouse and turban, placidly smoking, with his belongings tied in bundles arranged around him on the deck. The sea in the Gulf of Lyons was rough, as it usually is, yet the bright autumn weather on land had seemed perfect. As soon, however, as we were away from the gulf and in the open sea, following for hours in the wake of an Orient liner on her way to Australia, the weather abated and the voyage became most enjoyable.

As a student of men, I found the passengers in the steerage far more interesting than those in the saloon. Among the former was a knot of young, active-looking men of various nationalities, who leaned over the side watching the crimson sunset, and smoking and chattering, sometimes trying to make each other understand. I saw they were in charge of a military officer, and one of them being a smart, rather gentlemanly young Englishman—the only other Englishman on board, as far as I could gather—I spoke to him.

"Yes," he laughed, "my comrades here are rather a queer lot. We've all of us come to grief in one way or another. Bad luck, that's it. I speak for myself. I had a commission in the Hussars, but the gambling fever bit me hard, and I went a little too often to Dick Seddon's snug little place in Knightsbridge. Then I came a cropper, the governor cut up rough, and there was only one thing left to do—to hand in my papers, go to Paris, and join the French Foreign Legion. So, here I am, drafted to Algeria as a private with my friends, who are all in the same glorious predicament. See that fair-bearded chap over there?" he added, pointing to a well-set-up man of thirty-five who was just lighting a cigarette. "He's a German Baron, captain of one of the crack regiments in Saxony—quite a decent chap—a woman, I think, is at the bottom of his trouble."

And so, while the Arabs knelt towards Mecca, and touched the decks with their foreheads, we chatted on, he telling me what he knew concerning each of his hard-up companions who, under names not their own, were now on their way to serve France, as privates, in the "Legion of the Lost Ones," and start their careers afresh.

At last, after a couple of days, the blue coast of Africa could be discerned straight ahead, and gradually, as I stood leaning upon the rail and watching, the long white front of Algiers, with its breakwater, its white domes of mosques, and high minarets, and its heights crowned by white villas, came into view.

The city, dazzling white against the intense blue of the Mediterranean, presented a picture like the illustration to a fairy tale, and I stood watching, the sunny strip of African shore until at last we dropped anchor in the shelter of the bay, and presently went ashore in a boat.

I followed my traps across the sun-baked promenade to the nearest hotel—the old-fashioned *Régence*, in The Place—and after a wash, and a marzagran at the café outside, I inquired my way to the Prefecture of

Police, where, on presenting an open letter, which Henri Jonet, of the *Sûreté*, had given me a couple of years before, and which had often served as an introduction, I was received very cordially.

To the French detective-inspector I said—

"I am making an inquiry, and I want, M'sieur, to ask you to allow me to have one of your men. I am meeting an individual who may prove desperate."

"There is danger—eh? Why, of course, M'sieur, a man shall accompany you." And he shouted through the open window to one of his underlings who was seated on a bench in the inner courtyard.

I made no mention of the name of Jules Jeanjean. Had I done so the effect would, I know, have been electrical.

But when I got outside with the dark-eyed, sunburnt little man in a shabby straw hat and rather frayed suit, I exclaimed in French—

"There is a villa somewhere outside the town where some experiments in wireless telegraphy are being conducted. Do you happen to know the place?"

"Ah! M'sieur means the Villa Beni Hassan, out near the Jardin d'Essai. There are two high masts in the grounds with four long wires suspended between them."

"Who lives there?"

"The Comte Paul d'Esneux."

"Is he French?" I asked, at the same time inquiring his description.

From the latter, as the detective gave it to me, I at once knew that the Comte d'Esneux and Jules Jeanjean were one and the same.

"Non, Monsieur," replied the man. "He is a great Belgian financier. He comes here at frequent intervals, and carries on his experiments with wireless telegraphy. It is said that he has made several discoveries in wireless telephony, hence the Government have given him permission to establish a station with as great a power as that at Oran."

"And he is often experimenting?"

"Constantly. It is said that he can actually transmit messages to Paris and England. Last year, when the station at Oran was injured by fire, the Government operators came here, took his instruments over and worked them. The installation is, I believe, most up-to-date."

"*Bien!*" I said. "Then let us go up there, and see this Comte d'Esneux."

And together we entered a ramshackle fiacre in The Place, and drove away out by the city gate to the white, dusty high-road, along which many white-robed Arabs and a few Europeans were trudging in the burning glare of the African sun.

When I had mentioned the Count as the person whom I wished to see, I noticed that the detective hesitated, and, with a strange look, regarded me with some apprehension.

Did he suspect? Was he suspicious of the truth concerning the actual identity of the wealthy Belgian financier who dabbled in wireless?

Were rumours already afloat, I wondered?

Had the ever-active Jonet at last succeeded in establishing the secret hiding-place of the notorious Jules Jeanjean—the prince of European jewel-thieves?

CHAPTER XXVII
OPENS A DEATH-TRAP

The Villa Beni Hassan, a great red-and-white house of Moorish architecture, with three large domes, and many minarets, and long-arched windows of stained glass, I found standing high up, facing the azure sea, amid a wonderful tropical garden full of tall, feathery palms, dark oleanders, fiery pointsettias, and a perfect tangle of aloes, roses, giant geraniums and other brilliant flowers.

A high white wall hid it from the dusty highway, its position being between the road and the sea with spacious, well-kept grounds sloping away down to the golden beach. Truly it was a princely residence, one of the finest in the picturesque suburbs of Algiers. That afternoon beneath the blazing African sun, shining like burnished copper, all was still in the fiery heat, which, after the coolness of autumn in England, seemed overpowering.

At length the ricketty fiacre pulled up before great gates of ornamental iron-work, the tops of which were gilded, and on ringing, a gigantic Arab janitor in blue and gold livery appeared from the concierge's lodge, and salaamed.

In Arabic my companion explained that we wished to see the Comte, whereupon he opened the gates, and on foot we proceeded up the winding, well-kept drive, bordered by flowers, and shaded by palms of various species. On our left, across a sun-baked lawn, in the centre of which a big handsome fountain was playing, I caught sight of an aerial mast of iron lattice nearly a hundred feet high, and across from it to another similar mast were suspended four thin wires, kept apart by wooden crosses.

I held my breath. I was actually upon the domain of the most daring criminal known to the European police.

"There are the wires of the wireless station," the detective exclaimed. "But why, M'sieur, do you wish to see the Comte?" he asked with sudden curiosity.

"To ask him a plain question," was my brief and, I fear, rather snappish reply. "But tell me," I added, "have you ever seen his niece here visiting him?"

"Mademoiselle Sorel, M'sieur means. Yes, certainly. She has often been here — young, about nineteen — *très petite*, and very pretty. She lives in Paris."

"Yes. When was she here last?"

"Ah! I have not seen her here for several months," replied the man in the shabby straw hat. "I saw the Comte only yesterday. I was in Mustapha Pasha when he went past in his grey automobile. He had with him the tall elderly Englishman who sometimes visits here, a M'sieur Vernon, I think, is his name."

"Vernon!" I exclaimed with quick satisfaction. "Is he here?"

"I believe so, M'sieur. He was here yesterday."

As he uttered the words we turned the corner, and the great white Moorish house, with the broad dark-red bands upon the walls, and dark-red decorations over the arched corridors, came into view.

Boldly we approached the front door, before which was a great arched portico lined with dark-blue tiles, delightfully cool after the sun without. Yet scarcely had we placed our feet upon the threshold when a tall servant, with face jet-black and three scars upon his cheeks, his tribal marks, stood before us with a look of inquiry, silently barring our further passage.

Beyond we saw a cool courtyard, where vine were trailing overhead, and water plashed pleasantly into a marble basin.

Again the detective explained that we wished to see the Comte d'Esneux, whereupon the silent servant, bowing, motioned us to enter a small elegantly furnished room on the left of the courtyard, and then disappeared, closing the door after him.

The room, panelled in cedar-wood, was Moorish in character, the light filtering in through long windows of stained glass. Around the vaulted ceiling was a symmetrical device in Arabesque in gold, red and blue, while about the place were soft Moorish divans and silken cushions, with rich rugs on the floor, and a heavy brass arabesque lamp suspended from the centre of the ornamented ceiling. The place was full of the subtlest perfume of burning pastilles, and, in a cabinet, I noted a collection of rare Arab gold and silver jewellery.

And this was the home of the motor-bandit of the Forest of Fontainebleau — the man who had shot dead the Paris jeweller, Benoy, with as little compunction as he killed a fly.

I strode around the room, bewildered by its Arabian Nights aspect. Truly Jules Jeanjean lived in a style befitting an Eastern Prince.

"Hush!" I exclaimed, and we both listened to a loud crackling. "That," I said, "is the sound of wireless telegraphy. A message is being sent out across the sea."

Jeanjean was evidently in a room in the vicinity.

Suddenly the noise ceased. The door-keeper, who had not asked our names, had evidently sent in the message that two strangers desired to see his master.

But it was only a pause, for in a few seconds the message was resumed. I could easily distinguish the long and short cracks of the spark across the gap, as the electric waves were sent into the ether over the Mediterranean to Europe.

I happen to know the Continental Morse code, for I had dabbled in wireless telegraphy two years before. So I stood with strained ears trying to decipher the tapped-out message. I heard that it was directed to some station the call-letters of which were "B. X." But the message was a mere jumble of letters and numerals of some pre-arranged code.

I listened attentively till I heard the rapid short sound followed by four long sounds, and another short one, which indicated the conclusion of the message.

Then we both waited breathlessly. Who was B. X., I wondered?

I felt myself upon the verge of a great and effective triumph. I would give Jeanjean into custody upon a charge of murder, and if Vernon were still there, he should also be captured at the point of the revolver.

Those seconds seemed hours.

In a whisper I urged my companion to hold himself in readiness for a great surprise, and to have his revolver handy — which he had.

I laughed within myself at the great surprise the pair would have.

The heavy atmosphere of the room where, from a big old bowl of brass with a pierced cover, ascended the blue smoke of perfume being burnt upon charcoal ashes, became almost unbearable. The pastilles as burnt by the Orientals is pleasing to the nostrils unless some foreign matter be mixed with them, or the smoke is not allowed to escape. In this case the round-headed stained glass windows were fully twelve feet from the ground, had wire-work in front of them, and apparently did not open. The designs of dark-blue, purple, red and yellow were very elegant, and they were probably very ancient windows brought from some fairy-like palace of the days before the occupation of Algeria by the French.

Again I gazed around the delightfully luxurious apartment, so essentially Moorish and artistic. Amid such surroundings had lived Lola—the girl who had fled from me and disappeared.

What would the world say when it became known that that magnificent house, almost indeed a palace, was the home of the man of a hundred crimes, the daring and unscrupulous criminal, Jules Jeanjean?

I was listening for a repetition of the wireless signals to B.X., but could distinguish nothing. Probably he was receiving their reply, in which case there would be no sounds except in the head-telephones.

"*Mon Dieu!*" gasped my companion, whose name he had told me was Fournier. "This atmosphere is becoming suffocating!"

I agreed, and tried to extinguish the fire within the brazier. Unfortunately I failed to open the lid, which was held down by some spring the catch of which I could not detect.

Indeed, the thin column of blue smoke grew darker and denser, as we watched. The room became full of a perfume which gradually changed to a curious odour which suffocated us.

We both coughed violently, and upon me grew the feeling that I was being asphyxiated. My throat became contracted, my eyes smarted, and I could only take short, quick gasps.

"Let's get out of this," I exclaimed, reaching to open the door.

But it was locked.

We were caught like rats in a trap.

In an instant we both realized that we were imprisoned, and began to bang violently upon the heavy doors of iron-bound and unpolished oak, shouting to be let out. The fool of an Arab had secured us there while he went to announce our visit to his master.

I took up a small ebony and pearl coffee-table inlaid with a verse from the Koran, and raising it frantically above my head, attacked the locked door. But when it struck the oak it flew into a dozen pieces. Fournier took up a small chair with equally futile result, and then in silence we exchanged glances.

Could it be, that on our approach to the house, we had been recognized by the owner and invited into that room which, with its rising fumes, was nothing less than an ingenious death-trap.

I remembered the sinister grin upon the villainous black face of the silent servant.

Again and again we attacked the door, for we knew that our lives depended upon our escape. We shouted, yelled and banged, but attracted no attention. We threw things at the windows, but they were protected by the wire-work.

Then a sudden thought occurred to me.

Swiftly I bent down and examined the large keyhole. The key had been taken and, it seemed to me, the heavy bolt of the lock had been shot into a deep socket in the framework of the door.

Without a word I motioned Fournier to stand back, and finding that the barrel of my revolver was, fortunately, small enough to insert into the keyhole, I pushed it in and pulled the trigger.

A loud explosion followed, and splinters of wood and iron flew in all directions. The bolt of the lock was blown away and the door forced open.

Next second, with revolvers in our hands, we stood facing two black faced servants, who drew back in alarm as we rushed from that lethal chamber.

Fournier, excited as a Frenchman naturally would be in such circumstances, raised his weapon and shouted in Arabic that he was a police-officer, and that all persons in that house were to consider themselves under arrest. Whereupon both men, Moors they were most probably, fell upon their knees begging for mercy.

My companion exchanged some quick words with them, and they entered into a conversation, while at the same moment, casting my eyes across the beautiful, blue-tiled, vaulted hall, I looked through an open door into the room which the Count d'Esneux used for his experiments in wireless.

At a glance I recognized, by the variety of the apparatus, the size of the great spiral transmitting helix, by the pattern of the loose-coupled tuning inductance, the big variable condensers, those strange-looking circular instruments of zinc vanes enclosed in a round glass, used for receiving, the electrolytic detector, and the big crystal detector, a gold point working over silicon, carborundum, galena, and copper pyrites—that the station must have a very wide range. The spark-gap was bigger than any I had ever before seen, while there was a long loading coil enabling any distant station using long wave-lengths to be picked up, as well as the latest type of potentiometer, used to regulate the voltage and current supplied to the detectors.

At a glance I took in the whole arrangement, placed as it was, upon a long table beneath a window of stained glass at the further end of that luxurious little Moorish chamber. Apparently no cost had been spared in its installation, and I fully believed that with it the notorious criminal could communicate with any station within a radius of, perhaps, two thousand miles.

Fournier had questioned the native servants rapidly, and received their replies, which were at first unsatisfactory. I saw by the fear in their faces that he had threatened them, when suddenly one of them excitedly made a statement.

"*Diable!*" cried the detective in French, turning to me. "The Count recognized us, and had us locked in that death-chamber while he and the Englishman, M'sieur Vernon, got away!"

"Escaped!" I gasped in dismay. "Then let us follow."

A quick word in Arabic, and the two servants, without further reluctance, dashed away along the big hall, through several luxuriously-furnished rooms full of soft divans, where the air was heavy with Eastern perfumes and the decorations were mostly in dark red and blue. Then across a small cool courtyard paved with polished marble, where another fountain plashed, and out to the sun-baked palm-grove which sloped from the front of the house away to the calm sapphire sea.

Excitedly the men pointed, as we stood upon the marble terrace, to a white speck far away along the broken coast of pale brown rocks, a speck fast receding around the next point, behind which was hidden the harbour of Algiers.

"By Gad!" I cried, gazing eagerly after it, "that's a motor-boat, and they are making for the town! We mustn't lose an instant or they will get away to some place of safety."

So together we dashed back to the road as fast as our legs could carry us, and drove with all possible speed back to the town, in order to reach the harbour before the fugitives could land.

CHAPTER XXVIII - DESCRIBES A CHASE

The driver, with the southerner's disregard of the feelings of animals, lashed his weedy horse into a gallop, as up-hill and down-hill we sped, back to the town.

Entering the city gate, the man scattered the dogs and foot-passengers by his warning yells in Arabic, until at last we were down upon the long, semi-circular quay, our eager eyes looking over the blue, sun-lit sea.

No sign could we discern of the motor-boat, but Fournier, with his hand uplifted, cried—

"See! Look at that white steam-yacht at the end of the Mole—the long, low-built one. That belongs to the Count. Perhaps he has already boarded her!"

I looked in the direction my companion indicated, and there saw lying anchored about half a mile from the shore a small white-painted yacht, built so low that her decks were almost awash, with two rakish-looking funnels, and a light mast at either end with a wireless telegraph suspended between them. The French tricolour was flying at the stern.

From the funnels smoke was issuing, and from where I stood, I could see men running backwards and forwards.

"She's getting under weigh," I cried. "The fugitives must be aboard. We must stop them."

"How can we?" asked the Frenchman, dismayed. "Besides, why should we—except that we were nearly suffocated in that room."

"That man you know as the Comte d'Esneux is the most dangerous criminal in all Europe," I told him. "To the Prefecture of Police in Paris—to you in Algiers also—he is known as Jules Jeanjean!"

"Jules Jeanjean!" choked out the man in the shabby straw hat. "Is that the actual truth, M'sieur?"

"It is," I replied. "And now you know the cause of my anxiety."

"Why, there is a reward of four hundred thousand francs for his capture, offered by companies who have insured jewels he has stolen," he cried.

"I know. Now, what shall we do?" I asked, feeling myself helpless, for at that moment I saw the motor-boat draw away from the yacht, with only one occupant, the man driving the engine. It had turned and was speeding along the coast back in the direction of the villa, white foam rising at its elevated bows.

"What can we do?" queried my companion. "That yacht is the fastest privately owned craft in the Mediterranean. It is the *Carlo Alberta*, the Italian torpedo-boat built at Spezzia two years ago. Because it did not quite fulfil the specifications, it was disarmed and sold. The Count purchased her, and turned her into a yacht."

"But surely there must be some craft on which we could follow?" I exclaimed. "Let's see."

We drove down to the port, and after a few rapid inquiries at the bureau of the harbour-master, found that there was lying beyond the Mole, a big steam-yacht belonging to an American railway magnate named Veale. The owner and some ladies were on board, and he might perhaps assist the police and give chase.

Quickly we were aboard the fast motor-boat belonging to the harbour authorities, but ere we had set out, the *Carlo Alberta*, with long lines of black smoke issuing from her funnels, had weighed anchor and was slowly steaming away.

Silas J. Veale, of the New York Central Railroad, a tall, very thin, very bald-headed man in a smart yachting suit, greeted us pleasantly when we boarded his splendid yacht. When he heard our appeal he entered into the adventure with spirit and gave the order to sail at once.

Beside us, on his own broad white deck, he stood scanning the low-built, rapidly disappearing *Carlo Alberta* through his binoculars.

"Guess they'll be able to travel some! We'll have all our work cut out if we mean to keep touch with them. Never mind. We'll see what the old *Viking* can do."

Then he shouted another order to his captain, a red-whiskered American, urging him to "hurry up and get a move on!"

As we stood there, three ladies, his wife and two daughters, the latter respectively about twenty-two and twenty, all of them in yachting costumes, came and joined us, eagerly inquiring whither we were bound.

"Don't know, Jenny," he replied to his wife. "We're just following a couple of crooks who've got slick away in that two-funnelled boat yonder, and we mean to keep in touch with them till they land. That's all."

"Then we're leaving Algiers!" exclaimed the younger girl regretfully.

"Looks like it, Sadie," was his reply. "The police have requested our aid, an' we can't very well refuse it." Then turning to me he exclaimed, "Say, I wonder where they're making for?"

"They are the most elusive pair of thieves in Europe," I replied. "They are certain to get away if we do not exercise the greatest caution."

The ladies grew most excited, and as the vessel began at last to move through the water, the chief officer shouting at her men, the girl whose name was Sadie, a smart, rather good-looking little person, though typically American, exclaimed to me, as she fixed her grey eyes on the fleeing vessel—

"Do you think they are faster than we are?"

"I fear so," was my reply. "But your father has promised to do his best."

"What crime is alleged against the men?" inquired Mrs. Veale, in a high-pitched, nasal tone.

"Murder," replied Fournier, in French, understanding English, but never speaking it.

"Murder!" all three ladies echoed in unison. "How exciting!"

And exciting that chase proved. Old Mr. Veale entered thoroughly into the spirit of the adventure. With Fournier, I took off my coat and, descending to the engine-room, assisted to stoke, we having put to sea short-handed, three men being ashore. Amateur stoking, of course, is not conducive to speed, but Veale himself, his coat also off, and perspiring freely, directed our efforts.

Still our speed was not up to what it should have been. Therefore the owner of the yacht went along to the storeroom, and dragging out sides of cured bacon, chopped them up, and with the pieces fed the furnaces, until we got up sufficient steam-pressure, and were moving through the calm, sun-lit waters at the maximum speed the fine yacht had attained on her trials.

As the golden sun sank away in the direction of Gibraltar, the fugitive vessel held on her course to the north-east, straight to where the nightclouds were rising upon the horizon. Far away we could see the long line of black smoke lying out behind her upon the glassy sea. And though we had every ounce of pressure in our boilers, yet with heart-sinking we watched her slowly but very surely, getting further and further away from us, growing smaller as each half-hour passed.

The fiery sun sank into the glassy sea, and was followed by a wonderful crimson afterglow, which shone upon our anxious faces as, ever and anon, we left our work in the stifling stokehold, and went on deck for a breath of fresh air.

Fournier's face was grimy with coal-dust, and so was mine, while Veale himself also took his turn in handling the shovel.

The chase was full of wildest excitement, which was certainly shared by the three ladies, to whom the hunting of criminals was a decided novelty.

With the aid of a whisky and soda now and then, and on odd ham sandwich, we worked far into the night.

The captain reported that before darkness had fallen the *Carlo Alberta* had, according to the laws of navigation, put up her lights. But an hour after the darkness became complete she must have either extinguished them or had passed through a bank of mist. For fully half an hour nothing was seen of the lights, though most of the men on board were eagerly on the watch for a sight of them. Suddenly, however, they again reappeared.

Then our captain, after consultation with Mr. Veale, decided to try a ruse. He extinguished every light in the ship, but still held on his course, following the distant yacht. For quite an hour we went full-speed ahead with all lights extinguished, keeping an active look-out for shipping, or for obstacles.

We did this in order that the fugitives should believe we had given up the chase. Though their vessel was so fast, it was apparent that something must have happened to them, for they had not drawn away from us so far as we had expected. An ordinary steam-yacht, however swift she may be, can never hold her own with a destroyer.

"Guess she's got engine-trouble," remarked the American captain as I stood with him upon the bridge, peering into the darkness. "We may overhaul her yet if you gentlemen keep the furnaces a-going as you have been. Hot job, ain't it?"

"Rather," I laughed. "But I don't mind as long as we can get alongside that boat." And then I returned to my place in the stokehold, perspiring so freely that I had not a stitch of dry clothing upon me.

Half an hour later I was again on deck for a blow, and saw that the fugitive steamer had perceptibly increased the distance between us. Had her engines been working well she would, no doubt, have been well out of sight two hours after we had left Algiers. Yet, as it was, we were still following in her wake, all our lights out, so that in the darkness she could not see us following.

The whole of that night was an exciting one. All of us worked at the furnaces with a will, pouring in coal to keep up every ounce of steam of which our boilers were capable. No one slept, and Mrs. Veale, now as excited as the rest, brought us big draughts of tea below.

In the stokehold the heat became unbearable. I was not used to such a temperature, neither were the railway magnate nor the detective. The latter was all eagerness now that he knew who was on board the vessel away there on the horizon.

"She's making for Genoa, I believe," declared the captain, towards four o'clock in the morning. "She's not going to Marseilles, that's very evident. If only we had wireless on board we might warn the harbour-police at Genoa to detain them, but, unfortunately, we haven't."

"And they have!" I remarked with a grin.

Dawn came at last, and the spreading light revealed us. From the two low funnels of the escaping vessel a long trail of black smoke extended far away across the sea, while from our funnel went up a whirling, woolly-looking, dunnish column, due to our unprofessional stoking.

All the bacon had been used, as well as other stores, to make as much steam as possible, yet even though the *Carlo Alberta* had plainly something amiss with her engines, we found it quite impossible to overhaul her.

The day went past, long and exciting. The captain held to his opinion that our quarry was making for Savona or Genoa. The weather was perfect, and the voyage would have been most enjoyable had not the race been one of life and death.

To Veale and his party I related some of the marvellous exploits of the criminal pair, and told how cleverly they had escaped us from the Villa Beni Hassan. I described the dastardly attempt made upon my life, and that of Lola, and my narrative caused every one on board to work with a will in order to break up the desperate gang.

As we had feared, when night again fell the vessel we were chasing showed no lights. Only by aid of his night-glasses could our captain distinguish her in the darkness, but fortunately it was not so cloudy as on the previous night, and the moon shone from behind the light patches of drifting vapour much, no doubt, to Jeanjean's chagrin, for it revealed their presence and allowed us to still hang on to them.

Our American captain was a tough-looking fellow, of bull-dog type, and full of humorous remarks concerning the fugitives.

I recollected what Lola had told me in regard to her uncle's wireless experiments with a friend of his in Genoa. Yes. Finding themselves pressed by us they, no doubt, intended to land at that port. How devoutly we all wished that their engines would break down entirely. But that was not likely in a boat of her powerful description. Yet something was, undoubtedly, interfering with her speed.

The second day passed much as the first. We were already within sight of the rocky coast near Toulon, and in the track of the liners passing up and down between Port Said and Gib'. We passed two P. and O. mail steamers, and a yellow-funnelled North German Lloyd homeward bound from China. Still we kept at our enemies' heels like a terrier, though the seas were heavy off the coast, and a strong wind was blowing.

Fournier suffered from sea-sickness, so did Mr. Veale's second daughter, but we kept doggedly on, snatching hasty meals and performing the monotonous, soul-killing work of stoking. The run was as hard a strain as ever had been put upon the engines of the *Viking*, and I knew that the engineer was in hourly dread of their breaking down under it.

If she did, then all our efforts would be in vain.

So he alternately nursed them, and urged them along through the long, angry waves which had now arisen.

Another long and weary night passed, and again we both steamed along with all lights out, a dangerous proceeding now that we were right in the track of the shipping. Then, when morning broke, we found we were off the yellow Ligurian coast, close to Savona, and heading, as our captain had predicted, for Genoa. The race became fiercely contested. We stood on deck full of excitement. Even Fournier shook off his sea-sickness.

Soon the high, square lighthouse came into view through the haze, and we then put on all the speed of which we were capable in a vain endeavour to get closer to the fugitives. But again the black smoke trailed out upon the horizon, and suddenly rounding the lighthouse, they were lost to view.

At last we, too, rounded the end of the Mole, and entered the harbour where the *Carlo Alberta* had moored three-quarters of an hour earlier. Fournier instantly invoked the aid of the dock police and, with them, we boarded the vessel, only, alas! to find that its owner and his English guest had landed and left, leaving orders to the captain to proceed to Southampton.

The vessel was, we found, spick and span, luxuriously appointed, and tremendously swift, though, on that run across the Mediterranean, one of the engines had been under repair when the Count and his friend had so unexpectedly come on board, and the other was working indifferently.

The captain, a dark-bearded, pleasant-faced Englishman from Portsmouth, believed that his master had dashed to catch the express for Rome. He had, he said, heard him speaking with Mr. Vernon as to whether they could catch it.

"Did they use the wireless apparatus on board?" I asked quickly.

"Once, sir," was the captain's reply. "The Comte was in the wireless cabin last night for nearly an hour. He's always experimenting."

"You don't know if he sent any messages—eh?"

"Oh, yes. He sent some, for I heard them, but I didn't trouble to try to read the sounds."

Therefore, having thanked Mr. Veale and his family, I set forth, accompanied by Fournier and the two Italian police officers, to the railway station up the hill, above the busy docks.

Eagerly I asked one of the ticket-collectors in Italian if the Rome express had gone, knowing well that in Italy long-distance trains are often an hour or more late.

"No, Signore," was his reply. "It is still here, fifty-five minutes late, from Turin." Then glancing down upon the lines, where several trains were standing in the huge, vaulted station, he added: "Platform number four. Hurry quickly, Signore, and you will catch it."

CHAPTER XXIX
THE HOUSE IN HAMPSTEAD

I dashed down to the platform, three steps at a time, followed by my three companions, but ere I gained it the train had begun to move out of the station.

One of the Italian police officers shouted to the scarlet-capped station-master to have the train stopped, but that stately official, his hands behind his back, only walked calmly in our direction to hear the voluble words which fell from the French officer's lips.

By that time the train had rounded the curve and was dropping from sight.

My heart sank within me. Once again Jeanjean had escaped!

We were making frantic inquiry regarding the two fugitives when a porter, who chanced to overhear my words, expressed a belief that they had not left by the Rome express, but for Turin by the train that had and started a quarter of an hour before.

I rushed to the booking office, and, after some inquiry of the lazy, cigar-smoking clerk, learned that two foreigners, answering the descriptions of the men I wanted, had taken tickets for London by way of the Mont Cenis Paris-Calais route. He gave me the ticket numbers.

Yes. The porter was correct. They had left by the express for Turin, and the frontier at Modane!

With Fournier and the two policemen, I went to the Questura, or Central Police Office, situated in a big, gloomy, old medieval palace — for Genoa is eminently a city of ancient palaces — and before the Chief of the Brigade Mobile, a dapper little man with bristling white hair and yellow boots, I laid information, requesting that the pair be detained at the frontier.

When I revealed the real name of the soi-disant Comte d'Esneux, the police official started, staring at me open-mouthed. Then, even as we sat in his bare, gloomy office with its heavily-barred windows — the original windows of the palace, in the days when it had also been a fortress — he spoke over the telephone with the Commissary of Police at Bardonnechia in the Alps, the last Italian station before the great Mont Cenis tunnel is entered.

After me he repeated over the wire a minute description of both men wanted, while the official at the other end wrote them down.

"They will probably travel by the train which arrives from Turin at 6.16," the Chief of the Brigade Mobile went on. "The numbers of their tickets are 4,176 B. and 4,177 B., issued to London. Search them, as they may have stolen jewels upon them. Understand?"

An affirmative reply was given, and the white-haired little man replaced the telephone receiver.

Thanking him I went outside into the Via Garibaldi, with a sigh of relief. At last the two men were running straight into the arms of the police. My chief thought now was of Lola. Where could she be, that she had not answered my urgent letters sent to the Poste Restante at Versailles?

The next train—the through sleeping-car express from Rome to Calais—left at a few minutes to six, and for this we were compelled to wait.

I recollected that Lola had told me how Jeanjean was in the habit of communicating with his confederate Hodrickx, who had also established a wireless station in Genoa. Thereupon I made inquiry, and found that aerial wires were placed high over the roof of a house close to the Acqua Sola Gardens at the end of the broad, handsome Via Roma.

The house, however, was tenantless, Hodrickx, apparently a Belgian, having sold his furniture and disappeared, no one knew where, a fortnight previously.

At six o'clock we entered the Calais express, and travelling by way of Alessandria and Turin, ascended, through the moon-lit Alps, that night a perfect fairyland, up the long steep incline, mounting ever higher and higher, until the two engines hauling the *train-de-luxe* at last, at midnight, pulled up at the little ill-lit station of Bardonnechia. There, we hastily alighted and sought the Commissary of Police.

To him Fournier presented his card of identity which every French detective carries, and at once the brown-bearded official told us that, although strict watch had been kept upon every train, the fugitives had not arrived!

"They may have left the train at Turin, and gone across to Milan, and thence by the Gotthard route to Basle and Paris," he suggested to me. "If they believe they were followed that is what they most certainly would do."

Then he swiftly turned over the leaves of a timetable upon the desk of his little office, and, after a minute examination, added in Italian—

"If they have gone by that route they will join the same Channel-boat at Calais as this train catches, whether they go from Basle, by way of Paris, or direct on to Calais."

The train we had travelled by was still waiting in the station, for one of the engines was being detached.

"Then you suggest that we had better go by this?" I said.

"I certainly should, Signore, if I were you," was his polite answer. "Besides they are wanted in England, you say, therefore it would be better to arrest them on the English steamer, or on their arrival in Dover, and thus avoid the long formalities of extradition. Our Government, as you know, never gives up criminals to England."

Instantly I realized the soundness of his argument, and, thanking him, we both climbed back into the *wagon-lit* we had occupied, and were soon slowly entering the black, stifling tunnel.

Need I further describe that eager, anxious journey, save to say that when next day we traversed the Ceinture in Paris, and arrived from the Gare de Lyon, at the Gare du Nord, we kept a vigilant and expectant watch, for it was there that the two men might join our train. Our watch, however, proved futile. They might have joined the ordinary express from Paris to Calais which had left half an hour before us—ours being a *train-de-luxe*. So we possessed ourselves in patience till at length, after a halt at Calais-Ville, we slowly drew up on the quay near where the big white Dover boat was lying.

The soft felt hat I had bought in Genoa, I pulled over my eyes, and then rushed along the gangway, and on board, with Fournier at my side, making a complete tour of the vessel, peeping into every cabin, and in every hole and corner, to discover the fugitives.

Already the gangway was up, and the three blasts sounded upon the siren announcing the departure of the boat. Therefore the pair, if on board, could not now escape.

Throughout the hour occupied in the crossing I was ever active, and when we were moored beside the pier in Dover Harbour, I stood at the gangway to watch every one leave.

Yet all my efforts were, alas! in vain.

They had evidently changed their route to London a second time, and had travelled from Bâle to Brussels and Ostend!

The thought occurred to me as I stood watching the last passengers leaving the steamer. If they had travelled direct by way of Ostend, then they would be seated in the train for Charing Cross, for the Ostend boat had been in half an hour, we were told.

The train, one of those gloomy, grimy, South-Eastern "expresses," was waiting close by. Therefore I ran frantically from end to end, peering into each carriage, but, to my dismay, the men I sought were not there!

So Fournier and I entered a first-class compartment and, full of bitter disappointment, travelled up to Charing Cross, where we arrived about seven o'clock.

I was alighting from the train into the usual crowd of arriving passengers, and their friends who were present to meet them, for there is always a quick bustle when the boat-train comes alongside the customs barrier, when of a sudden my quick eyes caught sight of two men in Homburg hats and overcoats.

My heart gave a bound.

Vernon and Jeanjean had alighted from the same train in which I and Fournier had travelled, and were hurrying out of the station.

Jeanjean carried a small brown leather handbag, while Vernon had only a walking-stick. Both men looked fagged, weary and travel-worn.

"Look!" I whispered to Fournier. "There they are!"

Then, holding back in the crowd, and keeping our eyes upon the hats of the fugitives, we followed them out into the station yard, where they hurriedly entered a taxi and drove away, all unconscious of our presence.

In another moment we were in a second taxi, following them up Regent Street, through Regent's Park, and along Finchley Road, until suddenly they turned into Arkwright Road.

Then I stopped our vehicle and descended, just in time to see them enter the house called Merton Lodge—the house which Rayner had described to me on the night of my long vigil at the corner of Hatton Garden.

For a few moments I stood, undecided how to act. Should I drive at once to Scotland Yard and lay the whole affair before them, or should I still keep my counsel until I rediscovered Lola?

I knew where they were hiding, and if I watched, I might learn something further. Both Rayner and Fournier were known to the two culprits. Therefore I decided to invoke the aid of an ex-detective-sergeant who, since his retirement from Scotland Yard, had more than once assisted me.

Truth to tell, I had a far higher opinion of the astuteness of the Paris police than that of Scotland Yard. The latter disregarded my theories, whereas Jonet was always ready to listen to me. For that reason I hesitated to go down to the "Yard," preferring to send word to Jonet, and allow him to act as he thought fit.

William Benham lived in the Camberwell New Road; so I went to the nearest telephone call-box and, ringing him up, asked him to meet me at Swiss Cottage Station and bring a trustworthy friend.

I knew that Merton Lodge had a convenient exit at the rear, hence, to be watched effectively, two men must be employed.

Towards half-past nine, leaving Fournier to watch at the end of the road, I met Benham, who came attired as one of the County Council employés engaged in watering the roads at night, accompanied by a burly-looking labourer who was introduced to me as an ex-detective from Vine Street. Without revealing the whole story, or who the two men were, I explained that I had followed them post-haste from Algiers, and that both were wanted for serious crimes. All I desired was that a strict surveillance should be placed upon them, and that they should be followed and all their movements watched.

"Very well, Mr. Vidal," Benham replied.

He was a pleasant-faced, grey-haired man, with a broad countenance, and a little grey moustache.

"I quite understand," he said. "We'll keep on them, and if I find it necessary, I'll get a third person. They won't get very far ahead of us, you bet," he laughed.

"They're extremely wary birds," I cautioned. "So you'll both of you be compelled to keep your eyes skinned."

"You merely want to know what's doing—eh?"

"Yes. I'm fagged out, and want a rest to-night. I'll come up and see you in the morning," I said.

Then we entered a bar, and having had a drink together, we went to Arkwright Road, where I rejoined Fournier, and with him returned to my rooms.

Next day nothing happened. The two men wanted, wearing different clothes, and Vernon in blue glasses, went out about eleven for a walk as far as Hampstead Heath, and returned to luncheon. That was all my watchers reported.

On the following evening, however, I met Benham by appointment in a bar in the Finchley Road, when he said—

"There's something in the wind, Mr. Vidal. But I can't make out what it is. This afternoon a well-dressed man, apparently an Italian, called, and about half an hour later a smart young French girl, with fair hair, and wearing a short dark blue dress and brown silk stockings and shoes, also paid the pair a visit. She's there now."

From the further description he gave of her, I found that it tallied exactly with the identity of Lola.

And she was there! with Vernon and his two confederates.

"There's also something else strange about that house, Mr. Vidal," added Benham. "I dare say you didn't notice it in the dark, but away, half-hidden by the trees in the garden, there's a long stretch of four wires, suspended from two high poles. A wireless telegraph, I take it to be."

"Wireless at Merton Lodge!" I cried.

"Yes. To-day I asked a man who was repairing an underground wire in the Finchley Road, and he says it's a very powerful station, and he wonders that the Post Office ever licensed it."

"It was probably licensed as a small station, and then its power was secretly increased," I suggested.

"But you say that the young French lady is still there?"

"Yes," replied Benham, "she was when I left ten minutes ago."

CHAPTER XXX
NARRATES A STARTLING AFFAIR

I lost no time, but quickly hurried round to Arkwright Road, strolling past the new, well-kept, red-brick house which, upon its gate, bore the words in neat white letters, "Merton Lodge."

In several of the windows were lights. What, I wondered, was the nature of the consultation going on within?

While I walked to the corner of Frognal, Benham remained at the Finchley Road end, within call.

I watched patiently, when, about half-past eight, the front door opened and Lola, descending the steps, left the house, walking alone in my direction.

Drawing back quickly, I resolved to follow her, and doing so, went after her straight up Arkwright Road, and up Fitzjohn's Avenue, till she came to the Hampstead Tube Station, where, in the entrance, I was astounded to see Edward Craig awaiting her.

He raised his hat and shook her hand warmly, while she, flushed with pleasure, strolled at his side up the steep hill towards the Heath.

The attitude of the man, who was once supposed to have been dead and buried, was now very different to what it had been when he had watched her in secret at Boscombe.

I stood watching the pair, puzzled and wondering. What could it mean?

They were both smart and handsome. She, with all the vivacious mannerisms of the chic Parisienne, was explaining something with much gesticulation, while he strode at her side, bending to listen.

Behind them, I came on unobserved, following them on the high road over the dark, windy Heath, past the well-known inn called *Jack Straw's Castle*—the Mecca of the East-End seeker after fresh air—and on across the long, straight road which led to the ancient Spaniards, one of the landmarks of suburban London.

Half-way along that wide, open road, at that hour deserted, they sat together upon a seat, talking earnestly, while I, leaving the road, lay hidden in a bush upon the Heath. Lola seemed to be making some long explanation, and then I distinctly saw him take her hand, and hold it sympathetically, as he looked her full in the face.

Presently they rose, and walked the whole length of the open road, which led across the top of the Heath, as far as the Spaniards. On either side, far below, lay the lights of London, while, above, the red night-glare was reflected from the lowering sky.

As they walked closely beside each other, with halting steps, as though the moments of their meeting were passing all too rapidly, the man from the grave was speaking, low and earnestly, into her ear.

She seemed to be listening to him in silence. And I watched on, half-inclined to the belief that they were lovers.

Nevertheless, such an idea seemed ridiculous after Craig's demeanour when he had watched her through the window on that night in Boscombe.

Yes. The friendship between Lola and the man whom every one believed to be in his grave, was a complete mystery.

I followed them back, past the infrequent street-lamps, to the seat whereon they had at first sat. Upon it they sank again, and until nearly ten o'clock they remained in deep, earnest conversation.

When they rose, at last, I thought he raised her hand reverently to his lips. But I was so far away that I could not be absolutely certain. As they sauntered slowly down the hill to the station, I lounged leisurely after them.

They were too occupied with each other to be conscious of my surveillance.

I saw them descend in the lift to the platform below, and I was compelled to take the next lift.

Fortunately, the train had not left ere I gained it, and I got in the rear carriage, keeping a wary eye upon each platform as we reached it.

At Oxford Street they alighted, and while they ascended by the lift, I tore up the stairs two steps at a time, reaching the street just as they entered the big, grey, closed motor-car, which was apparently there awaiting them, and moved off down the street.

In a moment I had hailed a taxi and was speeding after the grey car.

The red light showing the number-plate and the "G.B." plaque, went swiftly down to Piccadilly Circus, then turning to the right along Piccadilly, pulled up suddenly before the *Berkeley Hotel*, where both alighted.

Craig went as far as the door and stood speaking with her for a moment or two; then, raising his hat, re-entered the grey car and drove rapidly in the direction of Hyde Park Corner.

Having established the fact that Lola was staying at the *Berkeley*, I re-entered my taxi, and in about half an hour alighted once more at the junction of Arkwright Road with Finchley Road.

Benham quickly detected my arrival, and approaching me from the darkness, said —

"I wondered where you'd gone to, sir, all the evening. Nobody has come out. The three men are in there still."

I was very tired and hungry, therefore we both went into the neighbouring bar and swallowed some sandwiches. Then we went forth again, and though midnight chimed from a distant church clock, there was no sign of the interesting trio. Perhaps Vernon and Jeanjean were fatigued after their swift journey from the African coast.

The solution of the mystery at Cromer was still as far off as ever. The reappearance of the supposed dead man had increased the complications in the amazing problem which had, long ago, been given up by Frayne of the estimable Norfolk Constabulary as constituting an unsolvable "mystery." Both he and Treeton were, no doubt, busily engaged in trapping motorists who exceeded "the limit," for to secure a conviction is a far greater credit to the local police officer than the patient unravelling of a mystery of crime. Hence the persistent lack of intelligence amongst too many of the country police.

It was past one o'clock in the morning when, lurking together in a doorway, we saw the portals of Merton Lodge open, and Vernon with his two friends, all in evening dress, come out. They buttoned their black overcoats, pressed their crush-hats upon their heads against the wind, and all three sallied briskly forth in the direction of Fitzjohn's Avenue.

Bertini was, I noticed, carrying a small leather bag, very strong, like those used by bankers to convey their coin.

One thing, which struck me as curious, was that they made no noise whatever as they walked. They were seemingly wearing boots with rubber soles. Yet, being in evening clothes, they might all be wearing dancing-pumps.

We followed at a respectable distance, and, watching, saw some astounding manœuvres.

Passing down Fitzjohn's Avenue to Swiss Cottage Station, they separated, Vernon taking a taxi and the others crossing to the station, which still remained open.

I followed Vernon in another taxi while Benham, unknown to the other two, stood upon the kerb in the darkness and lit a cigarette.

Vernon's cab went direct to Tottenham Court Road, where, opposite the *Horse Shoe*, he alighted, and turning to the right, strolled along Oxford Street past the Oxford Music Hall, I dogging his steps all the time.

Half-way down Oxford Street he paused and, turning into Wells Street, lit a cigar. Then he glanced up and down in expectancy till, some ten minutes later, a taxi-cab pulled up some distance away, and his two friends alighted from it. Close on their heels came a second taxi, from which I saw Benham jump out.

The trio separated, and neither took any notice of the others.

Jeanjean came out into Oxford Street, where I was standing in the shadow, and walking a few doors down in the direction of Great Portland Street, halted suddenly before the door of a large jeweller's shop, swiftly unlocked it with a key he held ready in his hand, and, ere I could realize his intention, he was inside with the door closed behind him.

The key had, no doubt, been already prepared from a cast of the original, and the scene of action well prospected. Otherwise he would never have dared to act in that openly defiant manner almost under the very noses of the police.

I drew back and waited, watching the operations of the most notorious jewel-thief in Europe, Benham keeping a wary eye upon the other pair.

Vernon, after a few moments, crossed into Poland Street, a narrow thoroughfare nearly opposite, while Bertini, carrying the bag, slipped along to the jeweller's shop, and also entered by the unlocked door.

In the heavy iron revolving shutters were gratings, allowing the police on the beat to see within, but from where I stood I could see no light inside. All was quite quiet and unsuspicious. It was a marvel to me how silently and actively both men had slipped from view right under the noses of the police in Oxford Street, who are ever vigilant at night.

Vernon, watched by Benham, had hidden himself in a doorway with the evident intention of remaining until the *coup* was successfully effected, and to immediately take over the spoils and lock them away in his safes in Hatton Garden.

Five, ten, fifteen breathless minutes went by.

I saw the constable on the beat, walking with his sergeant, approaching me. Both were blissfully ignorant that within a few yards of them was the great Jules Jeanjean, for whose capture the French police had long ago offered a vast reward.

I was compelled to shift from my point of vantage, yet I remained in the vicinity unseen by either.

What if the constable were to try the jeweller's door as he passed?

I watched the pair strolling slowly, their shiny capes on their shoulders, for rain had begun to fall, watched them breathlessly.

Of a sudden the constable halted as he was passing the jeweller's shop door, and, stepping aside, tried it.

My heart stood still.

Next second, however, the truth was plain. The door had been re-fastened, and the constable, reassured, went on, resuming his night gossip with his sergeant at the point where he had broken off.

Yes. The two thieves were inside, no doubt sacking the place of all that was most valuable.

Their daring, swiftness, and expert methods were astounding. Truly Jules Jeanjean was a veritable prince among jewel-thieves. Not another man in the whole of Europe could approach him either for knowledge as to whether a gem were good or bad, for nerve and daring, for impudent effrontery, or for swift and decisive action. He was a king among jewel-thieves, and as such acknowledged by the dishonest fraternity whose special prey was precious stones.

I stood in blank wonder and amazement.

My first impulse was to turn and step along to Oxford Circus, where I knew another constable would be on point-duty. Indeed, I was about to raise the alarm without arousing old Vernon's suspicions, when I saw the jeweller's door open quickly and both men dashed out wildly and up Wells Street as fast as their legs could carry them.

In a moment I saw that they had been desperately alarmed and were fleeing without waiting to secure their booty, for next second a man—a watchman who had been sleeping on the premises—staggered out upon the pavement, shouting, "Murder! Help! Thieves!" and then fell on the ground senseless.

I rushed over to him, and by the light of the street-lamp saw that blood was flowing from a great wound in his skull. Then, in a moment, Benham was beside me, and the constable and sergeant came running back, being joined by a second constable.

Meanwhile Vernon, as well as the two thieves, had disappeared.

The man attacked was senseless. The wound in his head was a terrible one, apparently inflicted by a jemmy or life-preserver; so quickly an ambulance was sent for, and the poor fellow was swiftly conveyed, apparently in a dying condition, to the Middlesex Hospital.

At first the police regarded me with some suspicion, but when Benham explained who he was, and that our attention had been attracted by "something wrong," they were satisfied. We, however, went round to the police-station and there made a statement that, in passing we had seen two men—whom we described—enter the premises with a key, and as they did not emerge, we waited, until we saw them escape, followed by the injured watchman.

Then—it being about half-past three in the morning—we went back to the jeweller's, and there found the place in a state of great disorder. At the back of the window pieces of black linen had been suspended, in order to shut out the light from the small gratings in the shutters, and, in what they had believed to be perfect security, the thieves, wearing gloves, had forced open several show-cases and packed their most valuable contents in a cotton bag ready for removal. The big safe, one by a well-known maker, stood open, and the various valuable articles it contained had been pulled roughly out, examined, and placed aside ready to be packed up, together with a bag containing about one hundred sovereigns, and a small packet of banknotes.

On the floor lay a beautiful pearl collar, while everywhere empty cases were strewn about. Yet, as far as could be ascertained from the manager, who had come up hastily in a taxi, nothing had been taken.

Detectives came and began a thorough examination of the premises, and the damage done.

They were looking for finger-prints, but it was not likely that practised experts such as Jules Jeanjean and his companion would risk detection by leaving any.

I kept my knowledge to myself, and returned, weary and hungry, to my rooms, Benham accompanying me, and there we discussed our plans for the morrow.

CHAPTER XXXI
"SHEEP OF THY PASTURE"

The autumn sun shone brightly into the artistic little sitting-room at the *Berkeley Hotel*, overlooking Piccadilly and the Green Park, where, next morning, I was seated alone with Lola.

She was dressed in a pretty, neatly-made gown of a delicate brown shade, with silk stockings and smart little shoes to match, and as she leaned back in her cosy arm-chair, her pointed chin upon her white hand, her big blue eyes, so full of expression, were turned upon me, their brows slightly knit in her earnestness.

Upon the centre table stood a big silver bowl of dahlias and autumn foliage, while upon a sideboard was lying a fine bouquet of roses which a page-boy had brought in as we had been chatting.

I related my strange experience of the previous night, whereupon she had said, in a low, intense voice—

"Yes. I heard yesterday afternoon, when I was at Vernon's house in Hampstead, that an attempt was to be made somewhere. But I was not told where."

"Lola," I exclaimed, taking her hand tenderly, and looking into her eyes, "I am here this morning to save you from these people, and to save myself. If we remain inactive like this, they will deal us both a secret blow. They fear you, and in addition they know that I have discovered who they are, and the truth concerning some of their crimes."

She nodded, but no sound escaped her lips.

At last, however, by dint of long persuasion and argument, I succeeded in convincing her that I really was her friend, and that even if I exposed the gang, and caused them to be arrested, I could at the same time keep her out of the sensational affair which must inevitably result.

She rose, and for a long time stood at the window, gazing out upon the never-ceasing traffic in Piccadilly, her countenance very grave and thoughtful. By the quick rising and falling of her bosom, and by her pursed lips, I saw how deep was her agitation, how torn was her mind by conflicting emotions.

At last, as she leaned upon a chair, her eyes still fixed blankly out upon the long, rather monotonous façade of the *Ritz Hotel*, she began to tell me some of the facts she knew concerning her notorious uncle, Jules Jeanjean.

"He started life," she explained, "as an employé of the Nord Railway of France, and, being honest and hardworking, rose from an obscure situation in the goods-yard at Creil to become chief conductor on the express line between Calais and Paris. His sister, who was my mother, had married Felix Sorel, a leather-merchant in the Boulevard de Clichy, and they had one daughter, myself. Jules, however, remained unmarried. Apparently he held advanced Republican views, and soon entertained Anarchist ideas, yet no fault was ever found with the performance of his duties by the railway officials. He was, I have heard, a model servant, always punctual, sober, and so extremely polite that all the habitual passengers knew and liked him."

She paused, reflecting.

"It seems," she went on after a few moments, "it seems that as chief of the express which left Calais for Paris each day, after the arrival of the midday boat from Dover, his position was much coveted by the other employés. After about two and a half years of this, however, the Company one day offered him the post of Station-Inspector at Abbeville, where the boat expresses stop for water. But, to the surprise of his friends, he declined and, moreover, resigned from the service, pleading an internal trouble, and left France."

"Curious," I remarked. "He must have had some other motive than that for his sudden decision, I suppose."

Then, continuing her narrative, the pretty blue-eyed girl revealed to me a very remarkable story. From what she said it appeared that during his two and a half years' service between Calais and Dover, her uncle had been reaping a golden harvest and placing great sums of money in an English bank. The device by which the money had been gained was both ingenious and simple. Employed in the Customs House at the Maritime Station at Calais—through which all persons travelling from England by that route have to pass—was a *douanier* from Corsica who, though a French subject, bore an Italian name, Egisto Bertini. Between Bertini and the honest train-conductor a close friendship had arisen. Then Bertini, who had become acquainted with a London diamond-broker, Mr. Gregory Vernon, a constant traveller between the French and English capitals, one day introduced his friend. Before long Vernon's master-mind was at work, and at a meeting of the three men, held one evening on Dover cliffs, a very neat conspiracy was formed. It was simply this—

Bertini's duty was to examine passengers' baggage registered beyond Paris, and when it was placed upon the counter in the Customs House, he kept an open eye for any jewel-cases. Exercising his power, he would have them opened and inspect their contents, and then, being replaced, the box would be locked by the unsuspecting passenger. The Customs Officer would, however, chalk a peculiar mark upon the trunk containing the valuables, and during its transit between Calais and Paris Jeanjean would go to the baggage-wagon, and, with a big bunch of duplicate keys, unlock the marked trunks, abstract the jewellery, and relock it again. By the time the unfortunate passenger discovered the loss, the stolen property would probably be on its way into old Vernon's hands for disposal in Antwerp or Amsterdam.

Thus the two made some huge *coups*. In one instance, the pearls of the Duchess of Carcassonne, valued at forty-five thousand pounds, were secured, and never traced, for they were sold east of Suez. In another instance the celebrated diamond necklace belonging to Mademoiselle Montbard, the famous actress at the Ambigu in Paris, worth thirty thousand pounds, was abstracted from her baggage. Emeralds to the value of over twenty thousand pounds, the property of the wife of an American millionaire, and the whole of the famous jewels of the Princess Tchernowski were also among the articles stolen.

So constant, however, were these mysterious thefts, that at last the police established a strict surveillance upon all baggage, and hence the interesting little game was at an end.

Matters grew a trifle too warm, and though neither Jeanjean nor Bertini changed their mode of life with their rapidly-gained wealth, yet it was felt that to retire was best. So, within a month of each other, they left. Jeanjean crossed over to England, and Bertini accepted promotion to Boulogne, where he remained several months, fearing that if he resigned too quickly suspicions might be aroused.

Of course, after this, the organized thefts between Calais and Paris ceased suddenly, though the Company never entertained the slightest suspicion of the guilty persons, or of the mode in which each trunk containing jewellery was made known to the thief.

Vernon's craft and cunning were unequalled, for at his suggestion, Jeanjean, though he had over fifty thousand pounds in the Bank of England, now embarked upon the career of a jewel-thief, whose audacity, daring and elusiveness was astounding. His anarchist views prompted him to disregard human life wherever it interfered with his plans, and so clever and ingenious were his *coups*, that the police of Europe, whom he so often defied, stood dumbfounded.

About this time Lola's father, the honest leather-merchant of Paris, went bankrupt, and died a few weeks afterwards of phthisis, while Madame Sorel, brokenhearted, followed her husband to the grave two months later, leaving little Lola alone. She was then fifteen, and her uncle, seeing that she might be of use to him, adopted her as his daughter, and gradually initiated her into the arts and wiles of an expert-thief. His whole surroundings were criminal, she declared to me. She lived in an atmosphere of crime, for to the flat in the Boulevard Pereire, which her uncle made his headquarters when in Paris, came the men, Bertini, Vernon, Hodrickx, Hunzle, and others, great *coups* being discussed between them, and arranged, thefts carried out in various cities of Europe, often at great cost and frequently with the assistance of Lola, who was pressed into the service, and upon whom her uncle had bestowed the name of "The Nightingale," on account of her sweet voice.

Vernon was the brain of the organization. By his connection with the diamond trade he obtained information as to who had valuable gems in their possession, and by the exercise of his marvellous wit and subterfuge would devise deep and remarkable plots of which the assassination of the well-known Paris jeweller, M. Benoy, was one. In three years the daring gang, so perfectly organized, perpetrated no fewer than eighteen big jewel robberies as well as other smaller thefts and burglaries. In many, robbery was, alas! accompanied by brutal violence. The Paris *Sûreté*, Scotland Yard, and the Detective Departments of Berlin, Brussels, and Rome were ever on the alert endeavouring to trace, capture, and break up the gang, but with the large funds at their disposal they were able to bribe even responsible officials who became obnoxious, and by such means evade arrest. Of these bribings there had been many sinister whispers, as Henri Jonet told me months afterwards.

"Ah! Lola!" I exclaimed. "How strangely romantic your career has been!"

"Yes, M'sieur Vidal," she replied, turning her splendid eyes upon mine. "And were it not for your generosity towards me, I should have been arrested that night at Balmaclellan, and at this moment would have been in prison."

"I know that you have been associated with these men through no fault of your own—that you have been forced to become a confederate of thieves and assassins," I said. "Surely no other girl in all England, or, indeed, in Europe, has found herself in a similar position—the decoy of such a dangerous and unscrupulous gang."

"No," faltered the girl. "It was not my fault, I assure you. Ah! Heaven knows how, times without number, I have endeavoured to defy and break away from them. But they were always too artful, too strong for me. My uncle held me in his grip, and though he was never unkind, yet he was always determined, and constantly threatened me with exposure if I did not blindly do his bidding. Thus I was forced to remain his cat's paw, even till to-day," she added, in a voice full of sorrow and regret.

I recollected the scene I had witnessed on Hampstead Heath on the previous night—her meeting with the man who had so mysteriously died in Cromer, and as I gazed upon her fair face, I pondered.

What could it mean?

Apparently she was staying at the *Berkeley* alone, and I mentioned this fact.

"Oh, they know me well, here. When I'm alone, I often stay here," she explained, still speaking in French. "I like the place far better than the *Carlton* or the *Ritz*. I have had quite enough of the big hotels," she added with a meaning smile.

She referred to those hotels where she had lived in order to rub shoulders with women who possessed rich jewels.

At that moment a foreign waiter knocked at the door and interrupted our *tête-à-tête*, by announcing—

"Mr. Craig to see you, miss."

"Show him in," was her prompt reply in English, as she rose and glanced quickly at me. I saw that her cheeks were slightly flushed in her sudden excitement.

And a few seconds later I stood face to face with the man upon whose body a Coroner's verdict had been pronounced.

He was tall, good-looking, and smartly-dressed in a grey lounge-suit, carrying his plush Tyrolese hat in his hand.

On seeing me he drew back, and cast a quick, inquisitive glance at Lola.

"This is M'sieur Vidal," the girl exclaimed in her pretty broken English, introducing us. "My very good friend of whom I spoke yesterday—M'sieur Edouard Craig."

We bowed to each other, and I thought I saw upon his face a look of annoyance. He had evidently believed Lola to be alone.

In an instant, however, the shadow fled from the young man's face, and he exclaimed with frankness—

"I'm extremely pleased to know you, sir, more especially after what Lola has told me concerning you."

"What has she told you?" I asked, with a smile. "Nothing very terrible, I hope?"

For a second he did not reply. Then, looking over at her as she stood on the opposite side of the table, he replied—

"Well, she has told me of your long friendship and—and—may I be permitted to tell Mr. Vidal, Lola?" he suddenly asked, turning to her.

"Tell him what you wish," she answered.

"Then I will not conceal it," he went on, turning back to me. "Lola has explained to me her position, her connection with certain undesirable persons, whom we need not mention, and how you in your generosity allowed her her freedom."

"She has told you!" I gasped in surprise, not understanding in what position he stood towards the dainty little Parisienne. "Well, Mr. Craig, I thought you knew that long ago," I added after a pause.

"Until last night, I was in entire ignorance of the whole truth. I met Lola at Hampstead, and she explained many things that have astounded me."

"I have told Mr. Craig the truth," declared the girl, her cheeks flushed with excitement. "It was only right that he should know who and what I am—especially as——" she broke off suddenly.

"Especially as—what?" I asked.

"Especially as I love you, Lola, eh?" the young man chimed in, grasping her hand and raising it to his lips fondly.

This revelation staggered me. The pair were lovers! This man, whose attitude when he saw her in secret at Boscombe was so antagonistic, was now deeply in love with her! Surely I was living in a world of surprises!

How much, I wondered, had she revealed to this man who was believed to have been buried?

For some moments all three of us stood looking at each other, neither uttering a word.

Then I swiftly put to the young man several questions, and receiving answers, excused myself, and went below to the telephone.

I had three calls in various directions, and then returned to where Lola and her lover were standing together. Heedless of my presence, so deeply in love was he, that he was holding her hand and looking affectionately into the girl's eyes as he bent, whispering lovingly, to her.

Yes, they were indeed a well-matched pair standing there together. She sweet and innocent-looking, he tall and athletic, with all the appearance of a gentleman.

Yet it was Edward Craig, the man who had lived at Beacon House at Cromer, the man whom I had seen lying stark and dead, killed by some mysterious means which medical men could not discover. Edward Craig, the dead man in the flesh!

CHAPTER XXXII
THE TENTS OF UNGODLINESS

Frank Sommerville, Chief Inspector of the Criminal Investigation Department, a big, dark-moustached man, stretched his long legs from the easy chair in which he was sitting, some half an hour after my interview with Lola and Edward Craig, clasped his hands behind his head, and looking over at me, exclaimed—

"By Jove! Vidal. That's one of the most astounding stories I've ever heard! And the young lady is actually in the next room with the 'dead' man Craig?"

"Yes, they're ready to go up to Hampstead," I said. "If we are shrewd we shall catch all three. They did that burglary at Bennington's, in Oxford Street, last night."

"How do you know, my dear fellow?" he asked.

"For the simple reason that I was there," I laughed.

He looked astounded.

"I remember the report on the Cromer mystery, last June, perfectly well," he said. "But I never dreamed that you'd taken the matter up. We shall certainly do well if we can lay hands on Jeanjean, for we get constant reports from Paris about his wonderful exploits. I had one only this morning. He is suspected of having done a big job at a jeweller's in St. Petersburg, lately."

"Very well," I answered. "Let us take a taxi up to Arkwright Road at once. Benham, your ex-sergeant, is already there awaiting us, as well as my servant, Rayner."

Together we entered the next room, where Craig and Lola were sitting closely together, and I introduced them to the well-known Chief Detective-Inspector. Then, after Sommerville had telephoned to his office, and ordered up to Hampstead three of his men, we waited for another quarter of an hour to give them time to get to the appointed spot—the public-house in the Finchley Road.

At last we started, and on the way I explained many facts to my old friend Sommerville, who, with a hearty laugh, said—

"Well, Vidal, I know you're pretty painstaking over an inquiry, but I never thought you'd ferret out this great French jewel-thief when we had failed! Of course, we've looked upon this man Vernon with suspicion for some little time. He sold some stolen rubies in Antwerp two months ago, and it was reported to us, but we couldn't get sufficient evidence. I made some inquiry, and found that he's immensely wealthy, although he lives such a changeful life. The house in Arkwright Road is his, but he is never there more than two or three days at a time. He experiments in wireless telegraphy, judging from the masts and wires in his back garden."

I told him of Jeanjean's powerful station in Algiers, and we agreed that, by means of a code, the pair were in the habit of exchanging messages, just as Jeanjean did with his confederate in Genoa.

"Yes," Lola said. "At Merton Lodge there are big dynamos down in the cellars, and when I've been with my uncle at the Villa Beni Hassan, he has often come from the wireless room and told me he has been speaking with his friend Vernon in London. Wireless telegraphy is wonderful, is it not?"

Briefly I had described the murderous attack made upon the girl and myself at that untenanted house in Spring Grove, and, as I finished, the taxi drew up a few doors from the bar to which I had directed the man to drive.

Ere we could alight, Benham, in the guise of a loafer, had opened the door and touched his cap to me with a grin. .

In the bar we found the three sergeants from Scotland Yard, as well as Rayner, who was greatly excited, and, of course, unaware of the identity of the three men who had entered casually, and were chatting at his elbow.

"We're going to make three arrests in a house close by," Sommerville explained to the trio. "They may make a pretty tough fight, and they probably carry revolvers. So keep a sharp look-out."

"All right, sir," the men replied, and were quickly in readiness.

In order not to arouse the suspicion of the three men, we arranged that Lola should first go there alone. Then we would surround the house, back and front, while Sommerville went to the front door and made some pretext. With a man behind him, he would wait until the door opened, and then rush in, followed by myself and two detectives and the young man Craig.

The arrangements were made in the private room behind the bar, and presently Lola, bidding us a merry *au revoir*, tripped out.

We gave her about ten minutes, and then in pairs, and by different routes, we approached the quiet, highly-respectable-looking house, first having got a couple of constables off the beat.

While Benham, as a loafer, went round to the back entrance, under the pretext of asking for an odd job to clean up the garden, Sommerville and one of his men slipped in and up the front steps.

For a little time his ring remained unanswered, but suddenly the door was opened slightly by Bertini.

For a second there was a sharp tussle, the Italian raising the alarm, but in a few moments I found myself, with Craig and Sommerville, inside the house.

Those moments were indeed exciting ones. Craig's only thought was for Lola's safety, and I saw him rush down the prettily-furnished hall and take her in his arms.

Shouts were raised on all sides.

In the scurry old Vernon dashed out of the room on the left and, meeting Lola with her lover, raised the revolver he had drawn and fired point-blank at her.

Fortunately, he missed. One of the detectives instantly closed with him, and I sprang to the officer's assistance. The old fellow, his face livid, his eyes staring wildly from his head, fought like a tiger, trying to turn his weapon upon us. He had forced the barrel of his big revolver right against my jaw, and was in the act of firing, when I ducked my head, and seizing his wrist, twisted it.

At that moment there was a loud explosion, and before I knew the truth I found his grip relaxing.

The weapon had been turned upon him as he, in desperation, had fired, and the bullet, entering his brain, had struck him dead.

He collapsed in our arms and we laid him upon the tiled floor.

Within the room, whence the old man had come, a desperate struggle was in progress, and entering, I found it to be a small library, at one end of which, upon a large table, was arranged a quantity of electrical apparatus — the various instruments necessary for wireless telegraphy. Close to this table, as we entered, stood Jules Jeanjean in the hands of Benham and the two detectives, while Rayner was standing covering the culprit resolutely with the revolver which he had wrenched from the prisoner's grasp.

Jeanjean's face was changed, his eyes wild and full of evil. In his fierce dash for liberty his collar had been torn from its studs and the sleeve of his smart blue serge jacket torn out. His hair was awry, and from a long scratch on his left cheek blood was freely flowing.

Truly he presented a weird, unkempt appearance, held as he was in the grip of those three strong, burly officers.

"Be careful!" I urged. "He'll get away if you don't exercise every care. He's as slippery as an eel!"

At my words his captors forced him back against the wall, redoubling their grip upon him.

Sommerville and Craig were standing beside Lola, who looked on, nervous and pale-faced. She had been witness to the tragedy out in the hall, and realized what a narrow escape she had had from the vicious old scoundrel's bullet.

Bertini was in the hall, held in a merciless grip by the two constables who had been summoned from their beats, and was standing close to the fallen body of the man who had so long been his acknowledged master.

Jules Jeanjean, though forced against the wall by those four men, was still wildly defiant, his face distorted by anger. He ceased struggling in order to curse and abuse his captors, pouring out upon them torrents of voluble French, a language with which only one of the four men, Rayner, was acquainted, and he but slightly.

"Listen, Jules Jeanjean!" said Sommerville, in a hard, commanding voice. "I am a police officer, and I arrest you on charges of theft and murder."

"Fools!" snarled the prisoner in defiance. "You've made a mistake, a great mistake! Arrest that girl yonder. Make inquiries about her, and you will find lots that will interest you."

"It is sufficient for the present to arrest you, my friend," was the Chief Inspector's response. "One of your comrades is outside, dead, and the other is under arrest."

Then turning to Lola, he asked—

"Do you identify this man as Jules Jeanjean, Mademoiselle?"

"Yes," the girl replied. "He is my uncle."

"You infernal brat!" shrieked the prisoner, livid with fury. "So it is you who have given me away, after all! I should have taken the old man's advice, and have put you out of the way. *Dieu!* You and your friend, Vidal, over there, had a narrow escape at Spring Grove. Your grave was already dug for you!"

"And yours will also be dug for you before long—when the Judge has sentenced you to death!" I cried.

"Enough!" exclaimed Sommerville, holding up his hand to command silence. "We want no recriminations, only the truth. You, and your friend Bertini, will have plenty of opportunity for defending yourselves when before the court. I think, Mademoiselle," he added, turning to where Lola was standing beside the man once believed to be dead, "you will have a strange story to relate to the Judge."

"She'll lie, no doubt," declared Jeanjean with a sneer. "She always does."

"No," the girl cried in her pretty, broken English, "I shall the truth speak. All of the truth."

"Yes," I urged, eagerly. "Reveal to us now the truth concerning the mystery on Cromer Cliffs. How it is that Edward Craig, the man who died, is now standing beside you!"

The prisoner, with a frantic struggle to free his arms, and throw himself upon her, to silence her lips, made a sudden dash forward. But his captors closed with him, pinioned him, and held him fiercely by the throat.

Lola, standing by, drew a long breath, but remained silent.

Her frail little figure seemed unbalanced, she was unnerved and trembling, two bright spots showing in the centre of her pale cheeks, as she stood there. Upon her shoulder rested the tender hand of the man whose end had been so wrapped in mystery.

"Speak, Lola," I urged again. "Have no fear of these men now. Tell us the plain truth."

"Yes, Lola," Craig added earnestly, "tell them the strange story. There is nothing now to be afraid of. Speak the truth and let the law deal with that assassin."

Again Jeanjean went into a perfect paroxysm of rage. But all to no purpose, though he bit his lips till the blood came. The men held him so firmly that he could move neither hand nor foot.

The heavy hand of Justice had fallen upon him!

CHAPTER XXXIII
DISCLOSES A STRANGE TRUTH

"I think, Lola, I had better explain to them the circumstances in which we met," young Craig exclaimed with frankness. His hand was still upon her shoulder, his eyes gazing straight into hers with that intense love-light which, in this world of falsity and fraud, is one of the things which can never be feigned.

"Yes, do," she urged, clinging closely to him, her frail frame trembling, for she was still upset and unnerved.

"Well, last January, I was staying with my mother at the *Hôtel Adlon*, in Berlin, for though I have a place near Monmouth called Huttoft Hall, left to me by my father, Sir Alexander Craig, I am constantly on the Continent. As a bachelor I prefer life abroad, and indeed, at that time, I had not been in England since I came of age, four years before. At the hotel, I found Lola staying with her uncle—that man!" and he pointed to Jeanjean—held there prisoner. "He called himself Dr. Paul Arendt, and gave himself out to be a Belgian from Liège. He was very affable, and we became on friendly terms, while my mother took a great fancy to Lola. After about ten days or so an English friend of Arendt's, a young man named Richard Perceval, arrived, and we three men went about Berlin, and saw the sights and the night-life, a good deal together. This went on for nearly three weeks, Lola and I becoming very fast friends. At last, however, her uncle being suddenly recalled to Paris, we were compelled to part, though we constantly exchanged letters. From Berlin, my mother moved to Cannes, and I followed her. We spent February and March on the Riviera, and then went north to the Italian Lakes, the most lovely spot in Europe in the springtide." He paused and, turning to the girl, said, "Now, Lola, will you explain what happened?"

The man under arrest again fought violently for freedom. His face was flushed with exertion, his long teeth clenched, his black eyes starting wildly from his head. Now that the villainous old man he had obeyed as master was dead, he saw that he must, at all hazards, save himself.

From his grey lips there issued a torrent of abuse, and the most fearful maledictions, in the French tongue.

Lola, requested by her lover to speak, held her breath for a moment, and then, with an effort, calming the flood of emotion that arose within her, said in her pretty English—

"After we met in Berlin, I, at my uncle's orders, ingratiated myself with Lady Craig, for the purpose of ascertaining whether she had with her jewellery of any value. Meanwhile, finding that Edouard had become very friendly with me, he at once instituted inquiries and found that Lady Craig was widow of Sir Alexander Craig, Knight, who had died leaving his only son possessor of a great fortune and a large estate near Monmouth. He also, through inquiries made by Vernon, found that Edouard had not been in England since he came of age. Vernon and my uncle met secretly one day at Frankfort, whereupon the crafty old man elaborated an ingenious plan which, within a few days, was put into execution. Among Vernon's wily confederates was a very smart, gentlemanly young man named Richard Perceval, who had been an actor, and who was the same height and much the same build as Edouard. This man came to our hotel in Berlin, but with what object I was, then, entirely ignorant. I now know that the reason he joined us was in order to carefully watch Mr. Craig's manners, his gait, his style of dress, and all his idiosyncrasies. While Edouard was unaware of it, he took many snapshots of him in secret, and one day for a joke they both went to a photographer's and had their portraits taken, the object of my uncle and Perceval being to obtain a thoroughly good likeness of M'sieur Craig. After three weeks, however, their preparations being completed, though I, of course, had no suspicion as to what was intended, we left Berlin and returned to Paris."

"To Brussels," interrupted the notorious criminal. "Be correct, at least." And his face broadened in an evil grin.

"To Brussels first, and then next day to Paris," Lola went on. "For some weeks nothing was done, it seems. I had constant letters from Edouard, who was at Beau Site, at Cannes, and I frequently wrote to him there. Then I accompanied my uncle to Algiers, where we remained some time, our movements being always sudden and always uncertain. My uncle, at Algiers, was engaged with his wireless telegraphy, sending and receiving messages from nowhere. Meanwhile, old Vernon's wits were at work and he laid his plans for a great *coup*. He took Richard Perceval to Cromer, then dull, sleepy, and out-of-season, the young man arriving there as his nephew, Edward Craig. He possessed an exact counterpart of M'sieur Craig's wardrobe, his hair was cut in the style you see Edouard wearing it, and by means of certain small but expert touches to his countenance, so artistic as not to be discernible, he had become transformed into the exact counterpart of the owner of Huttoft. Early in June we returned from Algiers to Paris, and my uncle, leaving me, went to London. Then, when he returned to the Boulevard Pereire three days later, I noticed a great change in him. He seemed greatly incensed with the Master."

"Had they quarrelled?" I inquired eagerly.

"Yes, over the division of the profits arising from the theft, in the month of March, of four hundred thousand francs' worth of diamonds, and pearls from a Paris jeweller named Benoy, while he was in a motor-car in the Forest of Fontainebleau. Vernon, he told me, had sold the stones and had retained three-fourths of the plunder. My uncle was furious and vowed most terrible vengeance. Next day, he sent me from Paris direct to Norfolk with a letter to Vernon. On arrival in Cromer I was utterly astounded to meet Perceval in the street dressed as Edouard Craig and presenting an exact likeness to him! Perceval, however, did not see me, and I went to Beacon House, delivered the letter to the old man, obtained a reply, returned to London, and next day to Paris. From my uncle, who became more incensed than ever against Vernon on receipt of the reply to his letter, I managed to elicit what was intended. This was that Vernon, knowing that Edouard lived always on the Continent, and had not been home for four years, had devised a devilish plan by which Perceval, representing himself to be the owner of Huttoft, was to obtain from his late father's lawyers, a reputable firm whose address is in Lincoln's Inn Fields, the deeds relating to the great Huttoft estate, as well as a quantity of family jewels, and raise a large mortgage upon the property from a well-known firm of money-lenders. The preliminary negotiations with the latter had already been opened, and it was only a question of days when the bogus Edouard Craig, already practised in the art of forging the signature of the real M'sieur Craig, would present himself to his late father's solicitors. The deep cunning of the whole plot, and the fine and elaborate detail in which it had all been worked out, held me aghast. If carried out, it was expected that fully seventy thousand pounds would be neatly netted and the bogus Craig would disappear into thin air!"

"What did you do then?" I asked, amazed at her revelation.

"At once I wrote to M'sieur Craig, who was at Villa d'Este, on the Lake of Como, asking him to meet me in secret in Paris, at the earliest possible moment. He met me one afternoon in the tea-rooms in the corner of the Place Vendome, and there I told him what I had discovered. And—and—well, I was forced to confess to him, for the first time, that I was a thief." She added in a changed voice, "the cat's paw of my uncle. I know I——"

"That's enough, Lola!" exclaimed the young man. "We need not refer to that. With Mr. Vidal, I am fully aware that your connection with those terrible crimes has been a purely innocent one. You have been forced into assisting them—held to them and to silence on pain of death."

"Yes," I added, "that's true. Lola is innocent. I vouch for that."

"Yes. Put upon my guard by Lola," Craig exclaimed, "I crossed at once to London, and without revealing who it was who intended to personate me, I told old Jerningham, the solicitor, to be careful. I remained in London a week, and then, unable to further repress my curiosity, I went to Cromer. I——"

"Ah, perhaps I had better continue my narrative, so that we shall be rightly understood," Lola interrupted, with cheeks flushed in her excitement. "A couple of days after Edouard had gone to London, my uncle, stung to fury by a letter he had received from old Vernon, suddenly announced that we were both going to Cromer. Therefore, we left Paris, and duly landed at Charing Cross, just in time to catch the last train up to Cromer, where we arrived between ten and eleven o'clock at night. In order to spring a surprise upon Vernon, we evaded the hotel and went to some rooms in Overstrand Road for which he had already telegraphed, having seen an advertisement in a railway guide."

"To the house where he afterwards lodged?" I asked.

"Yes. He had taken the same name he had used in Berlin, Doctor Arendt," she replied. "Well, I had gone to my room, but was standing at the open window, without switching on the light, when I saw him leave the house. Wondering what might be in progress, I put on my knitted golf coat and cap, and went after him. He took a long night-ramble past the flashing lighthouse on the cliff, and away across the golf-links, towards Overstrand, apparently reflecting deeply, his anger rising more and more against Vernon, whom he had accused of robbing him. For a long time I watched as he sat upon a log on top of the cliffs about a mile and a half from the town, gazing out upon the sea, and smoking a cigar, I having hid myself behind a bush. I was rather sorry I had come out, yet in the circumstances, and in the interests of Edouard, I felt it my duty to watch in patience. At last my uncle rose and strolled back over the golf-course, along the cliff-path, towards the town. As he came along over the low hill from the lighthouse, strolling on the grass, and making no sound, he suddenly discerned upon a seat the figure of a man in wide-brimmed hat and cape seated with his back to him and looking out to sea. The night was warm and pleasant, a calm and perfect night on the North Sea——"

"Were you near him?" Sommerville interrupted.

"I was walking along under the shadow of the hedge, while he walked over the open, undulating ground," was the girl's reply. "On recognizing the Master seated there, he was apparently seized by a sudden impulse of revenge—perhaps cupidity as well—for I saw him creep up behind the seat, and taking something from his pocket, thrust it quick as a flash into the old man's face. The man attacked clawed the air frantically, rose to his feet, staggered a few steps, and reeling, fell to the ground without uttering a sound—dead. I saw, in my uncle's hand a strange-looking and most terrible instrument, which he sometimes carried when engaged on one of his desperate exploits, a specially-constructed pistol the barrel of which was of soft india-rubber and finishing in a bell-mouth about three inches across. This he had suddenly pressed over the old man's nose and mouth—as he had done, alas! I knew, in other cases where the victim had been found dead, and doctors had been unable to establish the mysterious cause—then, pulling the trigger, he had discharged a glass capsule containing a mixture of compressed amyl nitrate and hydrocyanic gas, which, when released, a single inhalation caused instant death. The discoverer of the compound killed himself accidentally by it. Aghast, I stood watching him. He bent and examined the dead man's face. Then he searched his pockets, took out something, and then, moving quickly, dashed away towards the town, evidently alarmed at his own action."

And the girl paused, the accused man before her shouting strenuous denials.

"The instant he had gone," she continued, "I crept over the grass, past the seat whereon the dead man had rested, and, bending to see if he was still breathing, I found to my horror and dismay that it was not the Master at all, but his supposed nephew, Richard Perceval! Back I hurried to the house where we had rooms, and entering noiselessly—for I had been taught to move without noise at night"—and she smiled grimly at me. "I found my uncle had, fortunately, not yet come in. Therefore I retired to bed. Next morning we left hurriedly for London, Jeanjean not daring to face Vernon after what had occurred, and moreover, ignorant of the fact that Vernon had left Cromer during the night, alarmed by the real Edouard Craig calling upon him, and hinting that he knew the truth concerning certain recent jewel robberies. Jeanjean, however, returned to Cromer a few days later, and I followed and helped to secure the jewels Vernon had left behind."

"Yes," Craig exclaimed. "True. I saw nothing of Perceval on that evening when I called upon old Vernon. My visit, however, completely upset him. Lola had telegraphed to me that she was coming to England, therefore I asked Vernon where she was. The old scoundrel replied that she was in Cromer, and that if I went at a certain hour at night to a seat upon the East Cliff, which he indicated, I should meet her there—that she had a tryst with a secret lover. This naturally upset me, and I went, only to discover Perceval, dressed in the old man's cape and hat, lying stark dead. Why was he wearing those clothes, I wonder?"

"I have only recently learnt the truth," Lola answered. "When you, saw the old man, he believed me to be still in Paris, but when you inquired for me he, keen and crafty as he was, instantly discerned a means by which to entrap you. Therefore, saying nothing of his fear and intended flight to Perceval, he arranged with that young impostor that the latter should go to the seat dressed as himself, face you on your arrival, Edouard, and close your mouth for ever by exactly the same dastardly, silent and instant method as that adopted by Jeanjean—the gas pistol. My uncle found the weapon upon the body and carried it off."

"You had a very narrow escape, Mr. Craig," I remarked. "I sincerely congratulate you."

"Ah! I know," the young man said hastily. "Had not that man yonder killed Perceval by mistake, I should most certainly by now have been a dead man. But when I quickly realized the tragedy that had happened, and feared lest I might be suspected, I went off, and making my way out of the town, I walked through the night for twenty miles to Norwich, whence I took train to London, and at once back to Italy."

"Did you afterwards read of the affair in the papers?" asked Sommerville, amazed, like ourselves at the startling revelations.

"Of course. I followed every detail. But I did not come forward, for two reasons. First I was—I frankly confess—deeply in love with Lola, and feared to implicate her; and, secondly, for my mother's sake. I had no desire to be mixed up in such an unsavoury and sensational affair, or with such a notorious gang of criminals."

"Did you see much of Lola after the affair at Cromer?" I queried.

"I saw her once in Petersburg, where I followed her, also in Paris, and again in London."

"And also once at Boscombe—eh?" I added, "when you were so very annoyed."

"How do you know," he asked, starting, and at the same time laughing.

"Because I met you, and believing you had arisen from the dead, I watched you."

"I was in entire ignorance of it," he declared. "Yes, I was annoyed that night, for, on looking inside the room, I saw a young man standing beside the piano, admiring Lola."

"Oh!" she cried. "How foolish of you, Edouard! That was Mr. Burton, who is engaged to Winifred Featherstone!"

While these revelations had been made, Jules Jeanjean, wanted by the police of nearly every country in Europe for a number of desperate crimes, remained silent, listening to the words of Lola and her lover, listening to the grim story of his own murderous treachery towards the man whom he had acknowledged as Master.

Suddenly, without warning, he burst from the men who held him, and with a spring bounded like some wild animal towards Lola, and would have thrown himself upon her, and strangled her, were it not that we all fell upon him with one accord, and threw him to the ground, while handcuffs were placed upon his wrists to prevent further violence.

"You infernal devils!" he cried in French. "I vowed you should never take me alive—and you shan't. You hear!" he yelled. "You shan't. I defy you!"

"Ah!" laughed Sommerville in triumph. "But thanks to Mr. Vidal, we have at last got you, my ingenious friend." Then turning to Rayner, he said: "Will you go and get two taxis? We'll take him to Bow Street, and the other fellow also."

Jeanjean cursed and shouted defiance, but his captors only laughed at him. In those gyves of steel he was their prisoner, and held for the justice he so richly deserved.

CHAPTER XXXIV
CONCERNS TO-DAY

The next day the London papers were full of the raid upon Merton Lodge, the tragic death of the well-known diamond-broker, Gregory Vernon, and the arrest of Jules Jeanjean and Egisto Bertini.

The police had given but the most meagre details to the Press, therefore the report was only vague, and no hint was forthcoming as to the actual charges against the three men, or that they had any connection with the cliff-mystery at Cromer.

The most sensational passage of the report, which was regarded as "the story," or principal feature by most of the papers, was the fact that Jules Jeanjean, having been charged at Bow Street with robbery and murder, was placed in the cells to be brought up next morning before the magistrate.

A warder, however, on going to the cell about half-past eight in the evening, found the prisoner standing before him in defiance.

"I refuse to be tried, after all!" he cried in English, in a loud voice, "I'll escape you yet!"

And before the man was aware of the prisoner's intention, he had placed his right hand to his mouth, and with his left held his nostrils tightly.

The warder sprung upon him, but beneath his teeth the prisoner crushed a small capsule of glass, while the fact that his nose was held caused him to inhale the gas compressed within the capsule, and next second he fell, inert, dead.

I read the report in breathless eagerness, and then I realized that Jules Jeanjean, alias Arendt, alias dozens of other names, had destroyed himself with that combination of nitrate of amyl and hydrocyanic gas, a single whiff of which was sufficient to cause instant death—the same lethal gas which the criminal had discharged in the face of young Perceval, and alas! into the faces of others of his victims who had been found mysteriously dead on the scenes of the bandit's daring and desperate exploits.

Truly he had been a veritable artist in crime, but as he sowed, so also had he reaped. The wages of sin are, indeed, death.

From Sommerville, a few weeks later, I gathered a few further interesting details.

The man Hodrickx, together with two other men named Kunzle and Lavelle, had been arrested while committing a clever burglary at a jeweller's in the Corso in Rome; while tests at the private wireless station in Arkwright Road and at the Villa Beni Hassan, near Algiers, had proved conclusively that messages could be exchanged, as no doubt they often were, but, being in a prearranged code, could not be read by the dozens of other receiving stations, commercial and amateur, which picked them up.

In due course Bertini, the ex-customs officer of Calais, was extradited to Paris, where he took his trial before the Assize Court of the Seine, and was sentenced to a long term of penal servitude, which he is at present serving at the penal island of New Caledonia, in the far Pacific.

As for myself, I still live in blessed singleness, and am a confirmed bachelor, and a constant investigator of problems of crime. With the ever-faithful Rayner, I still occupy my cosy rooms off Berkeley Square, and, I may add, am still an intimate friend of Lola.

But she is now Mrs. Edward Craig, mistress of Huttoft Hall, and wife of an immensely wealthy man. She is a prominent figure in the country, but none, save her husband, myself and Rayner, know that she was, not so long ago, the confederate of the cleverest gang of international thieves that has ever puzzled the police, or that she was then known to them as "The Nightingale."

Yes. The pair are both extremely happy, living solely for each other. Perhaps if I were not such a confirmed bachelor, an iron-grey-headed "uncle" to many a flapper niece, and jeered at by the schoolgirl reader of novels as an "old man," I might be just a little jealous.

But as things are, I am delighted to see my charming, delightful little friend so happy.

Often I am their guest at the fine, historic, sixteenth-century mansion standing in its broad park, a few miles out of Monmouth. Indeed, it is beneath their roof that, on this bright summer evening, while the crimson after-glow is shining over the tops of the distant belt of dark firs across the park, that I am setting down the concluding lines of this strange story of daring and ingenious crime, this drama which so nearly cost all three of us our lives at the hands of that unscrupulous gang of dastardly malefactors.

Edward Craig, and his wife, Lola, who returned from their honeymoon, spent first in Khartoum, and afterwards in India, six months ago, and have now quite settled, have just come in from tennis. As they stand together, upon the threshold of the big oak-panelled library, a handsome pair in white, hand-in-hand, hot and flushed from playing, Lola says, with a merry smile upon her bright, open countenance and a pretty accent in her voice—

"In your narrative of what has recently happened, M'sieur Vidal, please tell the reader, man and woman, that the long, grim night has at last passed, the dawn has broken, yet 'The Nightingale' still sings on more blithely than ever, for she is at last supremely happy. At last, Edouard!" she adds, throwing her white arms about her husband's neck. "At last!"

And the tall, handsome fellow in flannels bent until his lips met hers.

"Ah, yes, Lola, darling!" he whispered earnestly. "You are mine—mine—mine, for always. We have, as the Psalmist of old has put it, passed through the Place of Dragons, and been covered with the Shadow of Death. But God in His justice has smitten the transgressors, and we have been delivered from the hand of the ungodly, into a world of peace, of happiness, and of love."